A New Life

B. Kozer

ISBN: 979-8-8690-1047-6

*Dedicated to those whose lives were thrown off course, and
to those who found a new path in the ashes.*

Chapter 1

Lyla

PEOPLE SAY THAT time heals all wounds, and over that time, we start to realize things about ourselves that we hadn't before. Maybe it's something that we said during a conversation that we could have said better, or maybe it's how we carried ourselves in public that makes us cringe at the thought of our own personality. It's not unreasonable to think these things. Hindsight: it's what makes us human.

But what happens to us when we alter that perception, when everything we've ever done is thrown into question? Not by a third party, but ourselves. What happens when you can't turn back to the life that you used to lead? When you're forced to take matters into your own hands, move on from what you've accomplished, and start over?

These are questions that I didn't expect to be asking myself, especially during this vacation I was on. Thing is, I don't remember ever leaving. I do remember not feeling too well, and then walking into the woods outside of the cabin my friends and I were staying at. I remember the sounds of music playing from the speaker my friends had set up, just the worst of the worst new country. I remember drinking a lot with them. One of them lamenting they couldn't bring their boyfriend while the others promised that we'd all have fun without them, just us. I remember sitting by the fire, laughing about college classes as we all roasted marshmallows. I remember the sounds of the forest, the crickets, and the rustling of leaves coming from the critters that ran around in the darkness. I remember stumbling drunkenly into the bushes at the far end of the backyard. The only thing on my mind was that I didn't feel good. It makes sense, because I also remember vomiting heavily into the bushes before stumbling even farther into the woods.

I didn't feel any better after puking. Something felt off about the world, a sensation I can't describe clearly. As I stumbled into the forest to get some fresh air away from the party, that's where my memory becomes fuzzy. I remember passing out, and then waking up in the middle of the woods. I don't know how far I went. I remember stumbling onto a road and seeing what I thought was a pair of headlights. After that, nothing. Until now.

When I start to come to, I smell the sterile scent of what I can only assume are cleaning supplies. Lying on my back, I open my eyes for the first time since I saw those lights on the road. I feel a massive headache. I must be hungover. But, as my vision comes back and I start to force myself awake, I realize this… this isn't the cabin.

Terror fills every inch of my body. I have a pretty good memory, and I know where I was beforehand. Everything up to the party is crystal clear: pulling up with my friends, unpacking our things. One of them even brought an itinerary, describing everything we were going to do. I remember singing songs, making food, dancing, watching movies, and then, the fire.

But where I am now, it's not anything like the cabin. I wasn't there at all. Glancing around the small room, I can see the tiled floors checkered with an off blue and white, the walls painted with a heavy coat of beige, but it's clear that they're made from cinderblocks. This… This is a school. But it's not set up like any school I've ever seen. There are no desks, no chalkboard, the room isn't even big enough to fit more than a few desks, and on the wall next to the door are a sink, mirror, and trash can. If the tiled floors, cinderblock walls, and weird, popcorn-looking ceilings didn't scream *school* to me, there's a small window above where I'm lying, the early morning light shining through. But looking at the light for too long hurts.

I can barely move, as hard as I try. My body is rejecting whatever signals I'm sending from my brain. I feel nothing but fear, like if I move, something bad is going to happen. What doesn't make it any better is the sound of footsteps coming from the outside of the metal door. Heavy boots. I don't know if I want to know who's out there.

I attempt to open my mouth to say something, but nothing comes out... I can't be under the influence of any kind of drugs; I'm completely lucid. I know this can't be any kind of hangover because I've never seized up like this before. None of this makes sense. Why am I so terrified?

Slowly, I hear the footsteps of whoever's outside dissipate. With the sounds gone, almost like magic, I can finally get up. Rising out of bed, I get out of whatever I was sleeping on and look at where I was lying down. Sitting in front of me is a cheap frame and a single blue sheet on top of an extremely firm yet spongy mattress. Looking around the room, I'm now convinced that wherever I am is a prison, or at least some sort of prison.

But... why am I here? What's the point of being in here if I haven't done anything? I notice my reflection from my peripheral vision. I'm still wearing the black t-shirt I wore to the fire. So, whoever brought me here didn't change my clothes. But something seems off about my reflection. Turning towards the mirror, I feel uneasy, looking at the blob in front of me. I realize I can't see very well... I've never needed glasses, so why can't I see very far?

I start walking to the mirror, and slowly my reflection starts to become clearer. When I finally am able to get a good look at myself...

"...This isn't me."

Whatever I'm looking at, that's not me. It's wearing my clothes, it has my shirt on, it's wearing my jeans, it has my hair, but it's not me. It's not even human. This horrid monster in my reflection, beady eyes, a white face, black ears. This can't be me.

I try to back up and move before whatever this monster is jumps out of the mirror and attacks me, but I can't. I catch myself on the sink, holding myself up, and the monster does so as well. I'm forced into a staring contest with this monster in the mirror. It's not moving either; it's just staring back at me, sharing the same expression of perpetual shock I am. Except, this isn't the same feeling as when I was lying in bed. I feel bewildered, unable to process what I'm looking at. This has to be some dream. It can't be real. I'm sure that I'm still passed out in the woods, and I'll wake up eventually.

This is the lie I'm telling myself, hoping that if I believe it enough, it'll become true. But the more I gaze into the eyes of the monster in the mirror, the more I realize that this can't be a dream. I start regaining composure and pull my hands off the sink. As I back up, the monster does as well.

I know it's stupid to think that it's just some hallucination, but I still look down to see if whatever version of me is on this side of the mirror is the me from last night. It's not. My hands still look human, I have all five fingers, but now, my nails are replaced with claws. Grey hair coats my arms, like a sweater I'm constantly wearing. I step back to sit down on the bed, but something trips me, and I fall right onto my ass. A sickness sets in, as I start to process the appendage sitting on the floor next to me. It's a tail. That monster in the mirror....

Is me.

Instead of the feeling of pure terror I felt when I woke up, I feel sick instead. A horrid, gut-wrenching sickness emanating from my stomach and up to my throat. I know I'm going to throw up again, and the best thing for me to do is rush back to the sink. Picking myself up, I hurry to the metal bowl, trying not to look at my own reflection. I start heaving, but nothing is coming out. I can't throw up. Each dry heave isn't making me feel any better either. I feel nothing but disgust, like if I can throw up whatever is in my system, it'll make me normal again.

However, the fact that nothing is coming out is just a confirmation of my current situation. I didn't ask for this, I didn't want this. So why? Why out of all the people in the world did I turn into some horrible beast? What are my friends going to think? They should know by now that I'm gone. They should be searching for me! They could come through that door at any moment and come save me from this horrible nightmare. But if they see... this... are they even going to recognize me? If they do, are they going to want me back?

Now, I'm starting to cry, tears streaming down my now long face. Whatever I am is still capable of feeling emotion, so there's some solace in that. I pull myself together enough to sit back down on the bed, but I'm frozen once more, not in horror or bewilderment this time, but sorrow. Every muscle relaxes yet aches at the same time. I don't want to be like this, I don't want people to see me like this. I'm completely hideous.

Just then, I hear a voice whispering from somewhere in the room.

"Hello? Are... are you okay in there, miss?"

The voice sounds meek, like it's working up the courage to interact with me. I look around the room, but I don't see anything that the voice could be coming from. But the voice calls out again, whispering a little louder.

"Over here! In the wall!" The sound of his voice seems to be coming from the foot of the bed.

I get up again, wiping the tears from my face, and move towards the source of the voice cautiously. At the foot of the bed is a small crack in the wall. Not enough to see through, but enough to hear. I muster up enough courage to say something to the voice in the crack.

"...Hello?" My voice cracks slightly, like I just remembered how to form words. The sound, it's the same as I remember. I still have my voice.

The voice responds, "Are you okay… miss?"

I hesitate to respond. "No, I'm… I'm not."

The voice pauses, not responding for what seems longer than it probably was, but it responds once more, concern coating its words.

"Is… is there anything I can do?"

I feel insulted by this. What do you mean is there anything you can do? I'm a monster! But I don't think this person knows what happened to me. The anger in me subsides. I can't be upset at him for asking if I need help. I take a deep breath and talk once more.

"I don't think so. Something is wrong with me. I… I don't know how to explain it."

The voice's words are now more concise. "I might know what you're talking about."

Whoever this is, he must know something. I have to ask him more directly.

Raising my voice a little, I say "What do you know? You need to tell me!"

The voice whispers some words, but I can't understand them. They're whispering to themselves.

Taking a closer look at the wall, I notice now that the crack is larger than I originally thought. There's enough room for me to stick my nails… er, claws? … in. Quietly, I start to pry the piece of concrete out from the wall. It's right next to whatever's holding the blocks together, so it shouldn't be hard to remove. Surprisingly, it pops out like a piece of a puzzle.

"What are you doing?" the voice calls out in a whisper.

"Making it so I can hear you better, but I think it's big enough for me to see through," I reply.

I peer into the wall to see who this voice on the other side is. But I can't see anything. It's dark. I whisper back into the crack once more.

"Hello? You there?"

The voice does respond, but it's muffled slightly.

"I'm here, but I don't know if you're ready to see through the crack yet, miss, based on what I heard of you before."

The voice is right. Am I ready for whatever's on the other end? If we're here for the same thing, could he be a monster too? I'm still reeling from the shock of what I saw in the mirror myself. Whoever is on the other side, whatever they are, could it be worse than what I am? Although, this is the only other voice I've heard. If they're not a monster, they might be able to help me. If they are a monster like me, maybe I can find some solace in knowing I'm not alone.

So, here I am, sitting in front of a crack in the wall, with a voice on one side telling me I'm not ready to see, not ready to accept the truth of this absurd situation that I'm currently in, inside of some building I've never seen, stripped of my own identity, yet forced to remember every second of my past, of what I used to look like, turned into some creature like a warped version of a fairy tale I was told when I was a kid.

Am… am I ready to see?

"I'm ready."

CHAPTER 2

Lyla

I HOLD MY breath, waiting for the voice to answer once more and show me who's on the other side. The voice lets out a slight sigh and then says, "Okay." With the confirmation, I peer in.

On the other side of the wall is a room that's nearly identical to my own. However, the bed is sitting next to the door on the opposite side of the room from where I can see. And emerging from the outside of my field of view is the owner of the voice.

The owner of the other voice is a lanky creature, covered from head to toe in green scales. The only thing covering his body is a white shirt and torn shorts. He stands away from the hole in the wall, awkwardly holding his hands together as he averts his eyes from making contact with my gaze.

I jolt back, letting out an "Ahh!"

Without thinking, I hurry to put the piece I took out back in place.

I move back as quickly as possible before whatever creature is on the other side attempts to make more contact with me. I thought I could handle this; I knew this was a possibility, but it's too much now.

I may not be alone, but I wasn't ready to see... that.

Still pushing myself back, I hear a door click open. My door. Oh no, someone's in here. I turn around slowly, as the door creaks open. The feeling of fear from when I woke up returns to me, and with every inch the door opens, I can feel myself becoming frozen in fear.

The door opens completely, but I'm not met with another monster; instead, I'm met with a human woman, in a sky-blue polo.

She smiles warmly at me, as if my appearance isn't an issue to her. "Great to see you moving around!"

The feeling of fear dissipates. Now, the only thought on my mind is getting help and getting answers. I pull myself up, approaching the woman, trying my best not to scare her. "Lady, you have to help me," I say. "I've been turned into some kind of monster!"

The lady chuckles, looking at her clipboard. "Being scared about your new appearance is normal. You're perfectly fine. If anything, I think you look great!"

This lady's confusing me. What does she mean, I look great? Are we not looking at the same thing? I saw what I look like; I'm far from great. But my new appearance? What does she mean? Did *these people* do this to me?

I approach the lady. Now confused, I ask, "What did you people do to me?"

The lady, still fiddling with her clipboard, responds, "We didn't do anything to you! From all we know, this is some kind of freak accident. Follow me if you will." The woman walks out of the room, stopping in the doorway before turning to me and gesturing for me to follow her.

Reluctantly, I decide to follow. I may not know what's going on, but sitting in this room isn't going to get me any answers. The woman in the polo seems unbothered by what's happening. There's a chance she might not be a bad person.

We walk into a hallway composed of the same stuff as the room I was in. My theory that this building has to be some kind of school is now confirmed. Lockers line the walls as the lady and I walk down the hallway. She turns to me and starts speaking again.

"This building you find yourself in is one of the RCC Rehabilitation facilities."

Confounded, I ask, "R…C….C?"

She grins, continuing down the hallway. "Yes, RCC, it's short for Reform Corporation for the Changed. We're an organization that specializes in rehabilitation efforts for *changed* individuals like yourself!"

"Changed… individuals?"

The lady stops in front of a door labeled "Physician." She hands me a slip of paper, some kind of medical record. "Yep!" the woman says with a bright smile. "Changed! Humans who were affected by the astronomical event that happened three weeks ago. Hundreds of thousands of people from around the world all experienced a massive metamorphic event, which changed their physical appearance into hybrids of both human and animal. You're one of those few people who changed!"

Wait.…. Three weeks? Have I been missing for three weeks? I start to raise my voice to the lady. "Ma'am, have I been out for three weeks? I need to get out of here! My friends know that I'm missing! I have to go find them! You gotta let me leave!"

The lady nods and gives me a warm smile. "We will! Don't you worry, but we need to make sure you're in good shape before letting you out. First step is the physician's office. Please, go inside."

The woman opens the door to the physician's office, gesturing me with her clipboard. "You have nothing to worry about; it's just a physical." She shakes the clipboard, ushering me in. I slowly walk into the room, which is set up like a doctor's office. The bench, the wall of medical supplies, even the jar of cotton balls. As soon as I enter, the door closes behind me, and I watch through the window as the woman with the clipboard walks away down the hallway.

Just as she disappears, the sound of another door catches my attention. A man, dressed in doctor's clothing, enters the room. He doesn't look much older than forty, and he's also carrying a clipboard.

"Ah, good to see you're up and about. I'll take that paper from you. Please, sit on the bench." With nowhere else to go, I go to take a seat on the bench; however, I end up sitting on the tail I forgot I had. Readjusting my sitting position, I wait for whatever is going to happen next.

The man in the lab coat sits down on one of those swivel chairs doctors have, as he takes a pen to his clipboard. "Okay, miss, do you remember your name and your age?"

"Lyla, I'm twenty-four," I reply.

The doctor scribbles some notes onto the paper I gave him. "Okay, Miss Lyla, do you have a last name?"

"It's Hagen."

The doctor scribbles onto the page again, mumbling to himself, "Patient remembers her name." He looks up. "Thank you, Miss Hagen. Now, how much did the representative tell you?"

I start to recount the conversation I had with the woman in the polo. I mention how I'm not human anymore, and how I've supposedly been out for three weeks.

The man writes down more notes onto his page. It's hard for me to not think he's just writing for the sake of doing it. "Okay, thank you. Let me explain this a little better for you. About three weeks ago, a massive astronomical event caused a lot of people to experience a synchronous fainting spell. Somehow, this fainting spell also coincided with everyone affected going through a biological metamorphosis into what our company has been calling *changed*. Somehow, everyone affected has had their biological makeup mixed with currently existing species of animal."

"I'm one of those people."

The doctor nods. "Yes, that's correct."

"But you can change me back, right?" I ask hopefully.

"I'm sorry to say, Miss Hagen, there's no cure for what's happened to you, but we're here to help," the man responds.

This was the final straw for me, hearing it from someone official and knowing now that I can't be changed back. This is it. I'm ruined. How am I ever going to go back to the way things were, looking like this? It seems unfair. Like some cruel joke played by the universe on me.

My heart sinks, and I look down at the floor, contemplating the situation I'm in.

The man in the coat starts talking again. "But there is a way to try to go back to the way things were." I sigh and look up at him. The doctor gestures to a poster on the wall of two people dressed in the same polo shirt as the woman, guiding someone who looks like a dog to a building, featuring a logo of a human hand, except it's cut in half, the other replaced with a stereotypical animal paw.

"The company I'm being contracted by, the RCC, is looking to help you guys get back into society as fast as possible. Soon, you'll be able to go back to your normal lives. Sure, you'll look different, but it's what's on the inside that counts, right?" The man in the coat chuckles, trying to make light of the situation.

The man then slides over to a desk and grabs some tools from the wall. "But first things first, we need to make sure you're in good health, so we don't have to keep you longer than you need to be. Don't worry, the procedure is completely non-intrusive, just a simple checkup."

He puts the tools onto a dish, scoots back over to where I'm at, and points at the clipboard once again. "I almost forgot; I have to ask you what your subspecies is."

I tilt my head in confusion. "Subspecies? Like, what kind of monst— I mean, what kind of animal I turned into?" I look down at my hands, observing the grey fur on my arms. "I don't know what I'm supposed to be. I've been unconscious for three weeks."

The doctor gives a sympathetic smile and writes on his clipboard. "I already know, don't worry. It's standard procedure; however, to say that you've been out for a few weeks is a bit of a fabrication. What's actually happened is that you and a lot of other changed have suffered from a special type of amnesia. The public calls it *altered amnesia*, but we've dubbed it *changed confusion* here. We try to be more tactful towards those being affected. Depending on the person, those who have experienced a change but aren't mentally ready to accept their new appearance will go into an amnesiac state. Of course, we've been taking care of you during the three weeks you've been here; however, with most cases of changed confusion, the person affected will spend their time only sleeping and eating when given food. Talking isn't something a lot of people do. The working theory is that it comes from a mental battle in the mind, a mix of animalistic instinct and human thoughts clashing for dominance. Once someone makes it through the amnesia, they normally don't remember what's happened during their mental battle."

The doctor points to his clipboard. "Another interesting fact about changed confusion is that people who have been changed will forget the species they are as well. It's a side effect of coming out of the amnesiac state."

"So, that's why I don't know what I am? This… changed confusion is the reason?" I reply.

"Yep, but since it's been such a short time since everyone has been affected, this is all a working theory. A way to explain why some people are responding to the change in different ways. Some people will wake up and not go through what you did."

Okay, this seems to be making a little more sense, but I still have questions about all of this. I take a deep breath and respond to the doctor. "Okay, so I don't know what I'm supposed to be. What am I then? How much of the old me is still here?"

The doctor sets the clipboard down and takes one of those rubber hammer things out of the dish he put them in. He holds the hammer to my knee. "From what we've gathered during your amnesiac state, you're a Didelphis Virginiana, also known as the Virginia Opossum. While you do look like one and have a lot of similar traits like eyesight, possible animal instincts, and other abilities, certain identifiable human traits remain as well, such as walking upright, your hair, and torso structure. Like everyone else here, you're half animal, half person. So there's some of you still there." He then taps the hammer onto my knee, causing my leg to kick forward slightly. "We've done X-rays as well. Aside from your skeletal structure changing slightly to accommodate your tail, legs, and your new head shape, it's still pretty much human."

Listening intently to the doctor, the words he's saying crash into me. I sit there silent, as he walks around and performs more exams on me. He shines the light in my ears, passes a flashlight across my face, checks my blood pressure, and uses the stethoscope to check my breathing. I'm not paying attention as he tries to make small talk. The only thing on my mind is what he told me. There's still parts of me on the inside, and still parts of me on the outside. But to anyone who's never met me, I look like a freakin' possum. The animal that always plays dead and eats trash. The more I process this, the more absurd it sounds. I could've been turned into something cool, but I got stuck with a possum. I don't even know if I'm scared anymore. I just feel numb now. Like, really? A possum? Out of all the animals ever, I get one of the most BS animals on the planet? Just my luck.

The doctor's voice calls me out of my trance. "And we're done. You seem to be in perfect health. I don't see a single problem with you."

"You're kidding, right?" I respond. "I'm a possum."

The doctor shrugs, "Health wise, you're fine, Miss Hagen. I don't know what to tell you. Between you and me, this is all new to me too. Before this, I was a veterinarian. Your physical appearance may be that of an animal, but if you were to break a bone or something, I wouldn't be able to do as good of a job as a human doctor. But I can tell you that even though you're a possum, you could've had it worse. You got pretty lucky being turned into an animal local to the region."

I sigh. A slight anger fills my body, not enough to lash out, but to say the least, I'm upset. "I just want to get out of here now. Thanks for the help, doc."

The doctor responds, "Call me Vince, and it's no problem. I know I can't fix things, but everyone that's working here are good people. We do genuinely want to help; someone should be here to get you soon."

I stand up from the bench and walk to the door. I nod and open the door to leave. The anger inside starts swelling. I want to punch something, but I don't think making a scene is going to be in my best interest. Starting to walk down the hallway, I hear a voice call out to me, "Hey, miss! Over here!" Turning around, I jump back a little. It's the guy from the crack in the wall. Now that I can actually get a good look at him, I can see this guy is a chameleon. He's walking up to me with another person. It's a human, about the same height as me, and he's dressed in the same polo as the woman who walked me to the physician's office.

"Oh, it's you. You spooked me walking up like that," I say, trying to keep my anger to myself. I don't want to start pissing people off, especially the guy who tried to help me this morning.

The guy in the polo shirt turns to the chameleon. "She a friend of yours?" he asks.

The chameleon looks at me, then back at the guy in the polo. "Yeah, she's a friend," he says, looking at me. I don't know if he's trying to wink, but whatever he's doing with his eyes kind of looks like it.

"You know that you're not supposed to be wandering the halls alone until after lunch, right?" The guy in the polo turns to me.

"Oh, sorry, I just got done at the physician's. Someone's supposed to come get me. Apparently, I don't remember the past few weeks," I say, trying not to start something.

The man in the polo smiles. "Ah, gotcha, you must've been suffering from changed confusion. Sorry, I didn't mean to come off as cross. My name is Carter. Nice to meet you, miss." He extends his hand out.

Reluctantly, I shake his hand. "Nice to meet you, I'm Lyla," I say.

"It's good to have you here, Lyla. James and I are about to go to lunch. You should come with us now that you're up and around. I'm sure that's where they were taking you anyways," Carter says, giving a genuine smile I haven't seen on any of these blue-polo guys before.

James nods. "Apparently Carter says that another food truck has come in, so they've brought in more options today."

I look both people in front of me up and down. Something about this Carter guy seems off, but to be honest, anyone in a polo here is giving me the creeps. James, on the other hand: It's my fault I left him hanging like that back in my room, and I should try to at least be his friend.

"Sure, I'll tag along," I reply.

Carter nods, giving both of us a smile. "Sounds good. Let's go then."

CHAPTER 3

Lyla

BOTH CARTER AND James start walking down the hall, and I follow behind. The two seem like they know one another. They're talking normally, as if nothing is wrong about this whole situation. It's infuriating. How can these guys be so calm about this?

Carter turns to me. "So, how long have you been up? Few days?"

I shake my head. "No, I only woke up this morning."

Carter nods. "Ah, so you must still be a little weirded out by all of this, huh?"

"Yeah, it's… it's all a little much to be fair. I don't know if I'll ever get used to it," I reply.

James chimes in now, looking at both of us, literally. "Oh, I know what you mean. When I woke up like this a few weeks ago, I freaked out. Could you imagine waking up and then seeing in two different directions at all times? I was horrified!" He chuckles. "I brought myself here. I couldn't bear to let my family see me this way." His smile sinks a little. "But I'm sure once more people get accustomed to this massive influx of changed, I'll go home, and my family won't mind one bit."

Carter jabs him on the shoulder lightly. "Now that's the spirit! You'll be outta here in no time. Your subspecies isn't a violent one, so you should get your pass soon enough."

I take this opportunity to ask a vital question. "Pass? What're you two talking about?"

Carter turns to me fully, walking backwards now. "Ah, you probably don't know! Anyhow, the short of it is, if you don't cause problems, we'll give ya a pass, saying that you're ready to get back into society. It's like a diploma, or a doctor's note." Carter points to the badge he's wearing, with the same human hand and paw logo on it. "When I wear this badge, the one thing on my mind is making sure you guys are safe and comfortable. Based on the changed's subspecies, they might become overwhelmed with instinct from their animal counterpart. So could you imagine if someone with giant claws thought you looked like dinner? We wouldn't want that!" He laughs and continues, "However, if we can prove that you guys still got humanity inside ya, we'll send you back home, and you can live your life like it was."

I suppose he makes sense; it lines up with what that vet guy, uh… Vince was telling me earlier. I still have questions. It's my turn to speak. "You said you wanna keep us safe and comfortable, but this place seems more like a prison than somewhere where we can be safe."

Carter turns back around and nods. "Yeah, I'll be honest with you, Lyla, this place ain't in the best shape. Actually, and I'm sure you already noticed, this place used to be a school. Turns out after the whole metamorphosis thing, the school shut down and the RCC started borrowing the place. Some of the staff are still here, changed like you guys. I heard from the higher ups that parents wanted to keep their kids regardless of changed status. Some whole families were changed. We try to be respectful to those affected. We don't force people to come in here."

"That's a little eye opening. If they don't force people to come here, how did I end up here?" I ask. Carter stops, pondering my question. His face turns to genuine confusion. "Hmm, that's… a good question. Do you remember coming here?"

I shake my head. Now things aren't making sense again. "No, I don't remember coming here at all."

Carter gives me an expression, the same confusion I have. "That's odd…" he says. "It could be your changed confusion. But once I drop you guys off, I'll grab your file from the office and take a look at it for you. Maybe you came to us while you were amnesiac? Someone did that a few days after their change."

I shake my head. "I have a vague memory of what happened. Just promise me once you get the information, you'll let me know," I tell him. Carter nods and gives me a grin. "Of course, I wouldn't be helpful to you guys if I didn't. Should be easy."

Carter starts walking again. "Anyways, we gotta get you guys to the cafeteria. It may be a school, but they actually seem to make some decent food here." Raising an eyebrow, I ask, "What're they gonna feed us? Some kinda dog food?" Carter laughs. "Nah, that wouldn't fit James's diet, would it?"

James responds, "They actually feed us real food. We're still people, ya know."

"I know, I know, just seems with the shitty building and the prison-like rooms, we'd be eating like animals too," I say sarcastically.

"You make a fair point, Ms. Possum, would you like me to give you something from the trash?" Carter snaps back. I give Carter a glare. "Really?" Carter responds. "You started it!" He laughs. Despite this situation, Carter's been the most *human* human I've met so far. I can't help but brush off his comment; he's just being an ass.

Carter stops us in front of a double door leading into the cafeteria. "Looks like this is where we part ways, guys," he says. "It's been nice talking to you, Lyla. I'll be sure to take a look at the file for ya." He gestures to James. "He'll be your guide from now on. I'll come find you two when I get a good look at the file. James'll show ya the ropes."

James nods. "I'm sure everything'll be fine." Carter pats James on the shoulder. "Nice. Stay outta trouble, you two." Carter then grabs the door and opens it, letting us walk into the cafeteria.

Entering the cafeteria, I come face to face with fifty other people who have met the same fate as me, people who've been turned into animals. Groups of people: bears, wolves, cats, dogs, sheep, goats, raccoons, squirrels, you name it. There's not a single type of changed I don't see. Honestly, it's a lot, maybe a little too much. That same freezing feeling is starting to creep up my legs again, working its way through my body, causing me to stop moving altogether. Just before I can't move anymore, James grabs my arm and pulls me out of it. "Come on," he says, "let's go get in line."

We start working our way into the line, moving slowly, as people are served food from the same setup used in school. Now, instead of feeling like a prison, I feel like I'm back in high school. Now I feel embarrassed. While I'm standing in line, I feel a sharp pain come from behind me, I jolt and realize that someone stepped onto my tail. This is the third time I've gotten hurt from this stupid thing. I think it's the one part of me that's pissing me off the most.

Looking back to see who's behind me, I notice a small rodent creature in a sweater about waist height standing behind me, looking around. They're looking up at me, their beady eyes obscured by the fur on their face.

They speak to me in a stammering voice. "I...I'm sorry, I didn't mean to hurt you."

I rotate to face them, moving my stupid tail out of the way. "It's all right," I respond.

"I've... I've been such a clutz lately. I used to be able to get around okay, but now I can barely see anything. The doctors say that I've become a mole," the rodent stutters out, clearly embarrassed by the situation it's in.

I sigh. This person's got it worse than me. "I'm sorry to hear that. I... I don't know what to say."

"You don't have to say any…anything," the mole responds. "I'm just lucky I didn't wander into traffic. This is probably the safest place for me. I'll be more careful, miss…"

I respond once more, "All right… Take care then." The mole gives a happy nod, as if our small conversation was the best thing that happened to them today.

I turn around, again following James. I don't even know what to say to that person. Jeez, imagine being them. I'm glad I can still see.

James and I continue through the line, and finally, we make it to where the food's being served. It's real people food, and not the crap they sell at schools. However, the dry erase board says that they're doing subs today. So, I guess I'm getting a sandwich.

Once we grab our sandwich, they give us an option between a water bottle and one of those little milk cartons that they normally give out at schools. I'd rather take the water; too many spoiled milks in school ruined my appetite for anything in a small carton.

I absent-mindedly follow James to the table, and on the way, I can spot some more changed at the tables. Now, I'm noticing there's people who've been turned into foxes, deer, rabbits, and even someone who's been turned into a mountain lion. I didn't think this would be the first time I saw a mountain lion in person, but I guess this is it.

Sitting down at a relatively empty table, I sit across from James. He still kind of weirds me out, being that he's, ya know, a chameleon. But since I've seen an Ark's worth of changed, it's not as bad as it was when I saw him through the crack in the wall.

As we unwrap our sandwiches, James decides to break the silence. "What'd you pick out?" he asks.

"I got roast beef," I respond.

"That's an odd choice. I don't think I've met someone who actually enjoys roast beef," he says.

"Yeah, well, I used to make 'em all the time in college," I reply. "It's a comfort food, I suppose."

We sit in silence for a bit more before I chime in, "What'd you decide on?"

James responds, "I got a vegetarian option."

"Why's that?" I ask. "Something to do with you being a lizard?"

"Nah," he says, "I just don't like lunch meat."

"Gotcha," I reply. I move the sandwich to my mouth to take a bite, before I realize that... I... I don't know how to fit this in my mouth. I'm so used to doing things how I normally would, I didn't account for the fact that my face is different. Sighing, I move the sandwich around and finally find a way to eat it comfortably. It still tastes like I remember, so on the bright side, some things about me didn't change.

Sitting in silence with James, it's hard to find something to talk about with him. I don't really know him all that well, but the fact we're in this weird situation, I don't know if I should ask him about what he used to do before this.

But I guess James had the same thought, since he starts the conversation again. "What'd you do before all this?" he asks.

I shrug. "I used to work at a supermarket," I reply. "It wasn't anything special. I just stocked shelves and worked to pay off my student loans."

James nods. "Sounds like you were living the real college kid life, huh?"

I glance up from my sandwich. "College kid life? I've been done with college for a few years now. How old are you anyways?" I ask.

"I'm twenty-six. I just never finished college. My dad used to be a house painter. I took up the business a while back," James replies.

I nod. "Gotcha, the family business was more important then, huh?" I say.

James shakes his head. "I didn't want to. My dad passed away six years ago. I had to drop out of college." James looks away. "I ended up taking the family business over, and I've been painting homes since then. I've been the man of the house up until now."

Jeez, this isn't how I thought it was going to go. "I'm… I'm sorry for prying," I say.

"Oh, it's fine, I asked first." James pauses before continuing. "It's just me and my sister now. My mom didn't handle the loss of our dad very well. She's out of the picture now, said I'm old enough to take care of us both."

Concerned, I ask, "Is your sister going to be fine while you're here?"

James nods. "She's twenty. I'd be gone for hours at a time. However, when I woke up like… this, she was at school. I left her a voicemail back home telling her I'd be back sometime soon, and I also left a note. I wanted to call her once I got here. But I never got the chance."

"Why not?" I ask.

"I left my phone at home, and when I got there, I asked to call, and they said they'd do it for me," he responds.

"That's odd," I say. "Why wouldn't they let you call?" I ask.

"Beats me," James says. "I asked again, and they said that I'd be able to go home soon, so not to worry."

I set my sandwich down and shake my head. "That doesn't sound right. We should find a way to get you a phone," I say.

"We could always ask Carter," James says. "He's been the guy who always gets me every morning, so I've gotten pretty chummy with him."

James reaches for his bottle of water. "But enough about me, what about you?" he asks. "You got family?"

"Kinda," I say. "I lived with some friends of mine, away from where I grew up, but I didn't talk to my parents much."

"Why? You guys estranged or something?" James asks, going back to his sandwich.

"No," I say. "My parents were always very busy. They had me at a young age, called me their 'happy little accident.' They both worked a lot, and I grew up with my aunt until I was old enough to start taking care of myself." I go back to my sandwich, trying not to think about my parents. I just realized now that the first thought when I woke up here wasn't what my parents would think, but what my friends would think. God, I'm selfish. I start talking again. "I know my parents cared about me. My aunt Jessie always said so. She used to tell me about all their plans while my mom was still pregnant with me. She said my parents were so hell-bent on making sure I grew up with nice things that my dad and her decided to quit their dream of starting a restaurant."

"Sounds like your parents really loved you," James replies.

I sigh. "Maybe as a kid. I stopped taking their calls when I moved out. Once I was gone, they just kinda… forgot about me. Started following their dreams again. Even tried dragging me into the family business too. Pretty messed up, huh?" I look up at James, who's now done with his lunch.

He takes a drink from his water bottle and says, "There's always time to reconcile. Once we get outta here, you can go see them."

I take the last bite of my sandwich and reply, "Looking like this? You kidding me? What a way to come back into your parents' lives. Hey, Mom and Dad, I'm a possum now. How's things?"

James chuckles. "Better to come back a possum than to never come back at all."

I let out a defeated sigh. "Maybe. Once we get out of here, I'll think about going to see them. I'll be in the area," I say. Looking up from our conversation, a good amount of people have vanished from the cafeteria. "Where'd everyone go?" I ask.

"Probably outside or wandering around the building," James says. "It's that time of day where we can just wander around. They have workshops and stuff for us to do."

"So… free time?" I ask.

James nods. "Yeah, everything is scheduled, but they're laid back about doing it. The only thing we really have to do is go talk to the psychologist every week."

I raise an eyebrow. "They have a shrink here?" I ask.

James stands up, grabbing both his plate and mine. "Yeah, they usually ask about instinct and stuff. It's not that big of a deal. If you're not acting like your subspecies, you'll be out really fast."

I shake my head. I guess it makes sense, a shrink. But I'm not really one to talk to some doctor about my problems. Just doesn't seem right; that's what my friends are for.

James walks away, dropping the plates at a little stand next to the trash. "Come on," he says, "let me show you around."

I stand up, grabbing my water bottle. "Sure, let's go," I say. We both turn to the door leading out from the cafeteria and start walking the facility.

James walks me down the hallway and into a massive room. Inside is a massive pool, and a group of changed people lounging in the water and swimming. Some people are sitting on reclining beach chairs outside of the pool, reading books.

"This is the pool room," James says. "I don't come in here very often. It's sometimes crowded."

"Dang. They've got a whole ass pool here, huh?" I ask. "That's impressive."

"It used to be a school. Some things don't change," James says. "Come on, there's still more to see." James walks me out of the pool room and back into the hallway. We keep walking down the hall and turn into another room. This one is filled to the brim with books of all kinds. "This is the library. It's still completely intact from before all this happened. Reading a good book is a nice way to unwind, at least, that's what some of the people in here say," James says, smiling.

"Nice, I dunno if I'm much of a reader, though," I say. The room looks nice, however. It seems like a good place to relax if I need some peace and quiet.

"You don't really strike me as the reading type." James chuckles. "I'm not much of a reader myself. I used to read a lot of comics when I was younger."

"Sounds like my childhood," I reply. I walk around the library, looking at the books. All manner of genres, mystery, fiction, nonfiction, even some textbooks, line the walls. Some of the horror books are mixed in with the mystery ones. I recognize one of them from when I was in high school. *'Penelope Radiant and the Aztec Fortune'* I poke inside and thumb around the book for a moment. "Man, this one brings back memories," I say.

I turn around, and James is already outside the door. I set the book back on the shelf and rush a little to catch up to him as he takes me around the facility more.

After a few minutes, we both reach a set of double doors. Opening the doors, we enter into a massive gymnasium. The room is currently occupied by some changed playing a game of basketball. There's some people sitting on the bleachers, talking to one another.

"This is the gym. But I'm sure you already knew that." James grins.

"Yes, I've seen a gym before." I laugh.

The gym seems spacy, pretty big for what used to be a normal school. I don't think I'll be seeing myself in there anytime soon.

"You play anything? Before all this?" James asks.

"I used to play tennis," I say. "Something my parents wanted me to do, said it'd be fun, and it wasn't like any of the other sports."

"Gotcha, you still play?" James's expression shows interest.

"No, I haven't played since high school," I reply.

It's true, I haven't touched a tennis racket since I was in high school. I lost interest when I got older. Never really had a reason to play.

"That's a shame. I didn't play anything," James says, putting his hands on his hips. "I used to be really good at cards, though, played that with my family all the time. Everyone thought I was cheating!" James laughs.

"Come on," he says. "There's still some other places we need to go." James walks out of the gym and back down the hall. I start following again. Soon enough, we make our way into a room at the far end of the school, filled with an astounding amount of art supplies, as well as more changed, painting, sculpting clay, and even taking pictures.

One of them, a person who's been turned into a cat, snaps a photo of us. The flash blinds me for a short moment. Rubbing my eyes, I look up, and the cat is handing me a polaroid, with James and me on it. James is smiling, but I look like a deer caught in the headlights, despite looking identical to a possum.

"Here you go!" the cat says. "Something to brighten up your day!"

"Thanks," I say, taking the polaroid from the cat's paw.

James grins. "This is the art room. It's where they hold workshops for most of us here. They're optional, of course. But sometimes I'll come in to draw."

"Do you paint?" I ask.

"Only houses. My artistic talent is relegated to flat colors on a wall, rather than anything else." James laughs. "Only one more place to go." James leads me out of the room and back into the hall.

We walk for a while, until reaching another set of double doors, farther into the secluded part of the school. "What's this place?" I ask.

"You'll see," James says, opening the door. We both walk into a large auditorium, with a projection screen playing a movie on it. Some old fantasy film I can't remember the name of.

"I'm sure I don't have to explain this place." James laughs.

I grin. "It's an auditorium. Turned into a makeshift movie theater, I suppose?"

"You got it. We can watch some movies whenever we want. They're always playing something different every time I come in," James says. "You like movies, Lyla?"

"Are you hitting on me?" I ask.

"What? No, no! I'm just making conversation," James says, taken aback.

"I know, I'm messing with you. I used to watch a lot of movies with my friends, but we never went to the theater very much," I say.

"Oh, I see. Well, maybe we can make some new friends and try to rectify that," James says with a grin.

"Maybe," I say.

We both leave the auditorium. I spend the next few hours wandering the rest of the school with James, and for a moment, things seem normal. Like this whole ordeal never happened. Sure, I'm wandering a school with a relative stranger, but as we roam the halls and James points out some of the people we pass, it feels like things went back to the way they were. But, as we walk back to where my room is, the realization of my current situation falls on me once more. I can't help but get a sinking feeling when we stop in front of my room.

"It's getting late. They're probably going to start asking us to hunker down for the night. I hope you had some fun on your first day, Lyla," James says.

I force a smile. "Thanks, I'm glad you showed me around."

"You okay?" James asks.

"Yeah, I'm... I'm fine," I respond, lying through my teeth.

"Okay, well... if you need anything, you can just talk through the wall," James says.

"Yeah, I know, I might take you up on that," I respond.

Suddenly, the PA system activates. A man's voice comes through the speakers lining the halls. "Attention residents. It is 9 p.m. If you're not in your rooms currently, please make your way to your rooms. Lights will shut off in fifteen minutes. Thank you and have a good night!"

"I guess we'd better go to our rooms," I say.

"Sounds like it," James responds.

I open the door, and I walk in. Closing the door behind me, I can see James wave me goodbye as the door closes. Now, I'm back in my room again. Where this whole debacle started. The light coming through the window is dimming. With the sun setting and the doors closed. I'm left with my thoughts once more.

What a surreal experience this all is. I still can't get over it. Walking around, sitting in the cafeteria, doing normal things. For those few moments throughout the day, it felt like things were normal. I was spending time with my friends, walking around. All familiar feelings. But everything surrounding it felt off. Like some kind of fever dream I can't escape. Even now, looking at myself in the mirror once more, I see… me. But a different me. Spending all day like this, I'm not as taken aback by the inhuman form I've taken. But still, it feels like a part of me is… well… lost. Something about me that I can't get back, something about me that I know isn't going to come back.

I walk back to my bed and sit on it, staring into my hands. They're mine, but they're new. I look down to my side, and I see a tail, something I've never had before. Another reminder that I'm not who I used to be on the outside. Thing is, I know I'm still me on the inside. I know what's inside my head hasn't changed. I know that despite my outward appearance, I'm still me. I don't know if I'm ever really going to get used to this. I look down to the foot of my bed, and I can see the piece of wall I pulled out this morning, protruding out of the concrete.

Slowly, I move to the end of my bed and lean my arm over the front of the bed, pulling the piece of wall out. I hear the sound of footsteps coming to the hole in the wall.

"You… need something, Lyla?" James's voice calls from the hole in the wall.

"I guess," I say. "Have you… gotten used to this whole ordeal? Ya know, not being human anymore?"

"I mean… not really," James responds. "I still sometimes see my-self and get taken aback. But it wasn't like… the first time I woke up like this."

"What was it like?" I ask. "How did you deal with it?"

"Well… I guess it was like any other day. I didn't really realize what had happened until I looked in the mirror when I went to shower," James responds. "It was mostly silent, just freaking out inside my head. I wandered around the house to make sure that my sister wasn't like me. But she was gone by then. When I looked at the note on the fridge to see where she went, from the writing, I don't think anything happened to her like what happened to me. I panicked after that. I threw my clothes on and opened the door. I saw someone walking down the sidewalk. I called out to them since… they were in a similar situation."

"What was that like?" I ask. "Meeting someone else like you for the first time?"

"It was both a bit of relief and a bit of a shock," James replies. "They were… a dog, I think. Some kind of dog. I asked them what was going on, and they told me they knew as much as I did. Said that someone told them about a place where people like us could go, to find answers and understand what was going on. Work through it, you know? I ended up following them, but they got cold feet when the buses showed up. The bus took us here. That's when I met Carter. He was one of the first people to greet us off the bus. Think he knew I was a little more freaked out than everyone else. So I guess we became friends, and turns out he was the guy assigned to waking me up every morning too. One could call it a coincidence, but I think it's something more."

"What, like divine intervention?" I ask.

"Maybe," James says with a chuckle. "Who knows. All I know is that as long as I give you the same kindness Carter gave me, we'll all make it through."

"You think… this happened for a reason?" I ask. "Since I brought up divine intervention. It's strange how some people changed, and some didn't. Why did it happen to us?"

"Maybe it's because we're special?" James replies.

"Maybe, but I don't think I'm very special," I say.

"It could be something to do with our personalities. Maybe we're so much like our subspecies in personality, the world made some kind of 'correction'? That could be a possibility," James replies.

I lie on my back. "It could be. I dunno, this whole thing is just surreal. It's scary," I say.

"You've got every right to be scared," James responds. "It's not every day something like this happens."

"I know… I guess I'm just having trouble processing it all," I reply. "I froze up when I first saw myself this morning, like it wasn't me, but it still was at the same time. Like a… uh…"

James pauses for a moment and then finishes my thought for me. "Like a caricature?"

"That."

"I know how you feel. Heck, all of us here know how you feel. You're not alone," James says.

"Yeah, but it's still weird to see people who… aren't people. It's like strangers, but worse," I say.

"You have a problem with strangers?" James asks.

"No, I guess it's the same feeling like when you're a kid, and people who are older than you that you don't know look scary and menacing. That's what weird about it, that's what's scary. Now, I'm older, but that feeling is back, because I'm staring down someone who used to be a human, but they're now some massive animal I've only seen on TV," I reply.

"They're still that same person on the inside, though," James responds.

"Yeah, I know. I had that thought about myself," I say. "Still, though, what happens if I'm not? Like, this isn't over?"

"What, you think we're going to change again? Lose our humanity?" James asks.

"I mean, it's not out of the question, is it?" I say. "We've changed once. What if we change again?"

I turn to my side, bringing my legs up to my chest. For a moment, I feel comforted. But the unease of my situation still keeps me lucid enough from falling asleep.

"I think you're thinking too hard about it," James replies. "It's only been a couple weeks, and people haven't changed again. Personally, I don't think we're going to change again, Lyla," James says.

"Well, I hope not..." I pause for a moment, chewing on James's words. "Thanks for talking to me," I say into the hole in the wall.

"Of course. We're friends, aren't we?" James replies. I can feel his optimism radiating through the wall.

"Yeah, we are," I say, smiling.

"Good, you turning in?" James asks.

"Yep, talk to you tomorrow," I reply.

"Talk to you tomorrow!"

I pick up the piece of wall from the floor and slot it back into its home on the wall. Spinning myself so my head hits the pillow, I grab the starchy blanket from the bed and then pull the covers over me. It's less coverage than I'm used to, but because of the fact I'm covered head to toe in hair, it does its job just fine.

Lying in bed, I replay the day through my brain. Waking up, freaking out, meeting Carter and James, exploring the facility. It doesn't feel like I did a lot. But I can't help but get tired at the thought of everything I've done today. Maybe it's just the fact that my brain is fried from this whole ordeal. Whatever the reason for my extreme tiredness, I find myself drifting off into sleep quickly, as my vision dissipates, and the soft sound of my breathing is all that remains.

CHAPTER 4

Lyla

THE SOUND OF knocking on the door wakes me up. I sit up in bed as I hear the beep of the electric lock twist, and the door swings open.

"Helloooooo! Good morning!" says the voice coming from the door. Rubbing my eyes, I notice it's the woman who came to my door the previous day to take me to their "doctor."

"Mornin'…" I say, slowly clambering out of bed and walking to the sink.

Looking in the mirror, it's still me. Same as I was yesterday. Looking at my reflection, I can't help but feel a wave of disappointment.

"Someone wake up on the wrong side of the bed?" the woman asks me, her grin sincere, yet somehow irritating.

"I suppose, who are you again?" I respond, still half-awake. I turn on the sink and try to run some water through my hair to fix whatever cowlicks remain. She's holding a toothbrush and some toothpaste and a Ziploc bag.

"You don't remember? I took you to the doctor yesterday morning. I'm Ada." She hands me the assorted items. "Here, once you're done, please put them in the bag and give them back to me. After that, we can take you to the cafeteria. They're serving breakfast," Ada says, still retaining her cheery disposition.

"Sorry, Ada, it's been a weird day." I groan, taking the toothbrush from her and making my way to the sink. Brushing is also surprisingly difficult, but I manage to get used to changing up the way I do regular things. Once I'm done, I put the toothpaste and brush back in the bag and hand it to the woman. When I go to give it to her, I notice she has some hair ties on her wrist.

"Hey," I say. "Are those hair ties?"

"Yes, they are. I keep them on my wrist so I don't lose them," Ada replies.

"…You mind if I have one?" I ask.

She pauses. Looks at me up and down. Like she's talking to an addict asking for another hit.

"I just want to tie my hair back," I say.

"Oh, well, I suppose it wouldn't hurt," Ada responds, handing me a black hair tie.

"Thank you," I say, turning back to the mirror and tying my unkempt hair into a slightly kempt ponytail. Though, my bangs still get in my face.

I walk out into the hallway with the woman, and she guides me down the hall to the cafeteria. She opens the door for me as I walk in.

"Have a good morning!" She says as the door shuts behind me. I'm still groggy from being woken up, and the sunlight coming through the glass makes everything feel extra bright. Like the sun is constantly in my eyes. Walking into the line, I make my way through to where they're handing out food. I see a tin filled to the brim with actual pancakes. Wow, I can't remember the last time I had real pancakes. They look decent, and they're all not perfectly round compared to something you'd find at a fast food restaurant.

Looking behind the glass pane and into the kitchen area, I see something that I didn't think I would have seen before. There's a guy cooking the pancakes, but next to him is a changed. A deer. They're working together to make more pancakes, both of them laughing and working the stove. It's not something I'd expect to see here, but the thought of everyone getting along is a comforting one.

I move farther down the line, picking a couple of decent-sized pancakes, and one of those little syrup cups you'd get at school. Grabbing an apple from the fruit tray, I turn around to the tables. Scanning the room, I faintly notice a shape in the back that's waving at me. It's James.

I shuffle my way over to the table he's sitting at and sit down across from him.

"Hey, Lyla, you sleep okay?" he asks.

"Yeah, I suppose. I slept, but I woke up kinda awkward. I'm still super tired," I reply, working my way into the food.

"I remember having to get used to the beds here, but you'll get used to it soon enough," James says.

"Here's to hoping," I say.

We both sit in silence, waking up and chowing down on the food. It's good, but I don't know if it's because I'm tired or that I haven't eaten since yesterday. Regardless, next thing I know, I'm back in the hallway with James.

"So, what's on the docket for today?" he asks.

"I'm not sure," I reply, finally becoming fully lucid. "What're you planning on doing?"

"Don't know yet. I think I might go to the art room and doodle or something. I'm feeling creative today," James says, grinning.

"Gotcha, well, I might wander around, see if something catches my eye," I reply.

"All righty! If you need me, I'll be in the art room!" James beams, walking down the hallway.

Now, all alone again, I decide to walk down the hall to see if I can find something to do. While I'm walking down the hallway, I manage to pass Carter, who stops in his tracks and approaches me.

"Hey, Lyla! Ready to take on the new day?" he asks.

"Sorta, finally just woke up. Now I'm walking around," I say.

"Sounds like fun! Where you going?" he asks.

"Not sure," I say. "Just looking for something to do."

"Gotcha, well, there's plenty to do. I'm sure James showed you all of it yesterday?" Carter smiles.

"Yeah, he did a good job," I say with a grin.

"Good to know! Glad he was able to show you the ropes. They're showing *Mystery of Marshall Manor* after lunch! I requested that one. That'd be something to do," Carter says.

"I'm not really in the mood for a movie," I say. "But thanks for the offer."

"No worries! Hope you find something to do! I gotta grab some pancakes before they run out! They're letting staff get in line now that you guys are finishing up." Carter smiles, walking away.

But before Carter can get too far from me, I stop him.

"Hey, Carter," I call out.

"Yeah? What's up?" he asks.

"You take a look at my file yet?" I question.

"Not yet. They're in the office, and I got caught up with some work yesterday, but I'll be sure to take a look and come find you as soon as I do," Carter says. "But now, I gotta grab some food before it's gone."

Carter's walk now turns into a racewalk as he hurries down the hall to the cafeteria. Answerless, I continue my stroll down the hallway. Attempting to remember the places that James told me about the first time, I start passing small cliques of changed. It's strange; now that I've been here for a bit longer, there's something I've noticed. Changed of the same subspecies will actually hang out in groups. While I was walking down the hallway, I noticed groups of deer, cats, and dogs, all walking with one another. Funnily enough, I haven't seen any other possums around here. I'm surprised that there's a lot of animals that people would find in suburban aeras. Realizing I've spent all of my time people watching, I now don't know where I am. I think I rounded a corner or two? I'm not sure. I should look for a landmark and reorient myself. Looking around the hall where I'm in, I notice a place I have been before, the library. I guess since I have nothing better to do, and now that I know where I am, I could go in and see if there's something worthwhile in there.

Walking into the library, I find myself browsing the bookshelves, looking for something to read. There's a lot of books, but they're more teen drama novels, and the idea of reliving my high school years of love triangles and supernatural boyfriends is not in the forefront of my mind. I'm looking for something else.

Then, a book catches my eye. The gold embossed spine and the green hardcover are completely unmistakable. It can't be....

I walk over to the fantasy section and grab the thin yet large book from the short bookshelf. *Tales from Across the Troll's Bridge*... no way. My mom used to read this to me all the time when I was a kid. She said she lost it when I got older... I didn't think I'd ever see this book again!

I have to check and see if this is the same one... It is.

Overwhelmed with a sense of nostalgia for children's fairy tales, I find a beanbag on the floor and take a seat, opening the book on my lap. Looking inside, I start flipping through the pages. These illustrations bring me back. To warmer memories. Picking a random story from the table of contents, I turn to a page and start reading one of the stories from my childhood.

The Damsel in Blue
Once upon a time in a closed off town,
there lived a woman who wore a blue gown.
She was fair and bright, and a wonderful sight,
Although, she never left her house.

Many thought she was a witch,
Perhaps hiding a lich?
Something was seriously wrong.
She never came to the market,
never talked, never bargained,
this mystery made her quite the target.

The truth did arise on a dark and stormy night,
Someone decided to pay her a visit.
They knocked on the door and heard a mighty roar,
They knew there was someone else in it!

So the peasants rallied and cried
"There's a monster inside!"
And torches and pitchforks they grabbed!
The townsfolk raced to the house,
"Hit the door, knock it down!"
With a crash, the door was smashed.

Yet what they saw that night was a terrible sight,
The woman they knew, what a horrible fright!
No dame, no witch, not hiding a lich!
The woman was a dragon! All the townsfolk flinched!

The dragon snarled and sneered,
As the townsfolk feared, would their fate be sewn tonight?
The dragon bellowed and roared as it spoke to the horde,
"Hear me, humans! For you've discovered my plight!"

"I wanted to be one of you, live happy and free,
Now with curtains drawn, you crumble and scream!"
The townsfolk cried, "Wyvern be gone!
Or we will slay you here, every one of us!"

They pointed their weapons at their former fair maiden,
The woman they all once adored.

While they all loved her before,
she now faced the sword,
The only way out was a bargain.

"Hear my plea, your outburst is not needed,
For if you kill me, a curse will be seeded."
The weapons drawn fell to their feet,
The townsfolk listened, for what did she mean?

"If I die, it will be something you rue,
as nature takes over every one of you.
"Let me live, and return to my home,
I'll take the curse with me and leave you alone."

The townsfolk pondered if it was a bluff,
Would this dragon come back? Would they all become dust?
However, they decided that it would be best,
that they took their chances, as the dragon got up, and left.

Nothing had happened in the town after that night,
With the dragon gone, the town was set right.
Perhaps one day the Dragon might return,
With a new colored gown, and a lesson, well learned.

Man, that story… brings me back. I remember my mom telling me that the moral of the story was not to keep secrets or something. I think she was just mad at me for lying about stealing a cookie or something that day.

I set the book down and put it back on the shelf. I wonder what's next? What will I read myself? Great, now I'm rhyming. Shaking the rhyming structure of the book out of my head, I notice another book nearby. It looks near identical to the one that I just read; however, the green hardcover has been replaced with a white one. Curiously, I pick the book up and take a look at it. *Tales from Mount Olympus?* Looking at the publisher, it's the same as the previous book. It looks like the book is a collection of Greek myths from a while ago. I wonder why we never had this one.

I open the book and flip to a page at the end of one of the stories.

"You've been kind and treated me well,"
said the Phoenix to the woman.
"You took me in when I was a man and treated me with com-
passion. For your honesty, I grant you an everlasting flame.
As a reminder that I will protect you whenever you need me."
The Phoenix then disappeared; the woman smiled. Knowing her
kindness granted her a guardian as she did the people of her town.

Bit of a strange story, something about kindness? From the looks of it I think it's more in line with not judging a book by its cover. Seems apt for a book like this. I can see why my mom only bought the fairy tale one, though.

Putting the book back on the shelf once more, I wander around the library, looking for something to do. I'm kind of bored. Checking the clock, I've still got about an hour to kill before lunch. I guess I could go find James and see what's up.

Leaving the library, I try to remember the day before, where James and I walked to get to the art room. Racking my brain, I eventually find my way back into the art room. Once I open the door again, the same cat from the previous day appears with the camera.

"Welcome back! Want another picture?" they ask.

"Sure!" I say, flashing the peace sign.

With a click from the camera, the cat hands me another polaroid. This time, I actually look good.

"Thank you." I smile.

I walk farther into the room and see James, sitting in the back by himself. I walk up to him and take a seat across the table.

"What're ya drawing?" I ask.

"Oh, just some doodles, nothing too special," James says, focusing on the picture he's making.

I look down at the picture. It's a house, but not like a drawing of a house; it's like... an actual picture of a house, perfect perspective and everything.

"Is that a house?" I say. "It looks really good."

"You think so?" James replies. "I wanted to be an architect. Guess working on buildings runs in the family." James chuckles. "I've been handy at drawing houses and other buildings. Unfortunately, anything else is harder."

James draws a small man next to the house. It looks decent for the general shape of a man. "That's about the best I can do." James laughs.

"Better than me," I say.

"You sure?" James questions.

"I mean, I'm not much of an artist," I say.

"Have you tried?" James slides me a piece of paper and a pen. "I'm assuming you're bored anyways."

"I mean, I guess I could doodle," I respond, picking up the pen.

I take the pen to the paper, but I stop. What the hell do I even draw?

I'm not good at this. I just scribble, not actually make art. Compared to James, he's kind of out of my league in the artistic sense.

"What do I even draw?" I say.

"What do you feel like drawing?" James questions.

"I don't know. That's why I'm asking you," I respond, shooting him a playful glare.

"Hmmm…" James ponders for a moment, before responding with an idea.

"Draw a picture of a tree," James says.

"A tree? Okay." I take the pen to the paper and draw out my best tree. It's not bad. I put some actual detail into it. The trunk of the tree isn't perfect, nor are the leaves. I just kind of detailed a basic tree shape. It's amateur, but it's mine. I turn the picture around to show to James.

"There you go, a tree."

"That's not half bad," James says. "It's pretty good for someone who claims they can't draw."

"You asked for a tree, not much else," I respond.

"You want something harder?" James says, cracking a smile.

"Sure, hit me," I say.

"All right, draw…." James leans over to the side, looking behind me. "Draw Gus."

"Who?" I ask.

"Gus, that guy." He points to the cat with the polaroid camera. "Hey, Gus!" James calls out.

The cat's ears perk up and rotate slightly over to our direction at the mention of his name. Gus then walks over to the table. "What's up, James?" Gus asks.

"I asked Lyla to draw you. Sit down and be her model." James laughs.

"Whoa, wait, I'm not that good!" I exclaim.

"Ah, it's no biggie, just do your best!" Gus says, sitting down next to me.

"It'll be a fun test of your real skills!" James laughs.

Cornered in this, I guess my only way out is to draw. So, I look up at Gus and put my pen to another piece of paper. First, I draw the general shape of Gus's head. Then I move on to…. What do I even do next? I glance up at both of them. James is now stopping his drawing to watch me work. The pressure is on. This is intense.

Scanning Gus for any defining features, I start drawing again. I draw his ears, then his eyes, then the rest of his face. The more I draw, the more I can see them watching me. Judging me. I don't know why I feel like this, but I'm starting to get that feeling again from yesterday morning. I can feel my legs freeze up, and I can't move my lower half. I keep going. What else does this guy have on? A shirt? What color? I've only got the pen; it doesn't matter. What about the color of his face? The one part of it that's all black, covering his eye like an eye patch. I draw that next.

Now I can't move my head. My eyes are glued to the page… The stares from James and Gus feel like massive weights on my shoulders. I feel something wet running down my cheek. Am I… crying? Why can't I move anymore? I hear a muffled voice calling to me. "Lyla, Lyla!"

I snap out of it, looking up from the drawing; it's seemingly done. It's not good, not as good as the tree. But it's serviceable. James is waving his hand in front of my face.

"Lyla, you okay?" he asks.

"Yeah, I'm fine," I say. "Just was a little intense with you guys staring at me like that."

"Sorry," James says. "I didn't mean to put the pressure on."

"Oh no, it's fine. It's kinda my fault. I should've said something," I reply.

"You done with the picture?" James asks.

"Yeah, here you go," I say, wiping my face. Why was I crying? That doesn't make any sense.

"Oh, wow! Look at this!" Gus says, grabbing the picture. "This is wonderful!"

"It's not that good, dude," I say.

"And? You still took the time to draw me. You could've said no," Gus says, folding the picture up and putting it into his pocket. "I appreciate it, thank you."

"You're welcome," I respond.

The sound of the PA turning on emanates through the room. "Hello! It's five minutes until we'll start serving lunch, so please make your way to the cafeteria! Thank you!"

I get up from my chair and start making my way out to the hallway once more. James gets up, pockets his drawing, and starts following me. We both walk down the hall to the cafeteria, where a line has formed. With us waiting outside of the cafeteria, there's not much else for us to do. James speaks up.

"What do you think they're making today?" he asks.

"Beats me," I say. "It's like, what? My second day here?"

"Fair, they did sandwiches yesterday." James pauses. "Say, if you could eat anything right now, what would it be?"

I stop and ponder James's question. "Anything, huh?" I say. "Oh, I know. There was this one Japanese place nearby my house, they cooked on these massive griddles in the middle of the table. It was like a performance or something. They'd grill up shrimp and put it on a plate with noodles and vegetables. That was good. I would want that."

"I don't think I've ever heard of some place like that," James responds. "Sounds neat, though. You gonna go there after you get out?"

"Who knows, maybe," I say. "I haven't been to that place in a while, and I don't even know if I have any money."

"I'm sure they're accounting for that," James says. "At least, that's what Carter told me."

"Speaking of, I ran into him earlier," I say.

"Yeah? What'd they say?" James responds.

"They said they were lookin' into my file. Something about not having the time yesterday."

"Maybe we'll hear more today." James smiles.

"Hopefully," I reply.

We both follow the line into the cafeteria. They're giving out those flat cardboard pizza things that the school did. I assume that since not a lot of people eat breakfast anymore but everyone eats lunch, they can't spend a lot of time cooking. I don't mind the school grade pizza, but now I'm thinking about the question that James asked me. My stomach grumbles at the thought of cooked shrimp on a grill.

We eat lunch in silence, picking away at the pizza, thinking about all the food I'm missing out on. After that, we end up walking the food off in the hallways for a bit. We both find ourselves in the auditorium and watch that movie that Carter requested. I was hoping that we'd run into him. But even though the film plays in its entirety, I don't see Carter.

Walking out of the auditorium, James turns to me. "Well, that was pretty good. I liked the part where they put together all the clues and found out that it was the estranged brother who killed the mom," he says with a grin.

"Yeah, it was okay," I respond. "I'm not much for mystery flicks, but it was good enough to kill some time."

"So, what do you want to do now?" James asks.

"I'm not sure," I respond.

"We could always go outside," James says.

"We haven't been outside, have we?" I respond.

"No, we haven't," James replies. "There's always room for fresh air."

"Sure, that sounds fine," I say.

We both walk down the hallway back towards where the cafeteria is. In front of us are two metal doors, leading to the rec yard outside.

The doors open, and I'm blinded by the late afternoon light coming in. It takes a second, but I eventually get my eyes to adjust enough to the outside. It's bright, and I can't see a lot, but I can see enough. How long has it been since I've gone outside? The warm breeze of late summer hits me, and it feels refreshing compared to the inside.

Looking around, I see that we're in a recess yard. A large chain-link fence outlines the area we're in. It seems newly installed, with the chain-link fence going up a solid fifteen feet into the air. Barbed wire lines the top of the fence. "What's the point of the fence?" I ask James.

"It's to keep us from going off somewhere." James starts walking to the grassy section just past the basketball court. "Not like any of us can climb it; they've electrified it."

"Electrified it?" I ask. "Why would they need to electrify the fence?"

James turns around, facing me now. "They say it's to keep us safe. I can see where they're coming from, some people might not be as well off as we are, but still, I don't think it does much for morale. We're still people, ya know?"

I nod. "I guess. You're right on the morale thing, though, it's not really doing much to make me comfortable."

James gestures to the grass ahead of us. "Yeah, but on the bright side, we can stretch our legs for a bit before going back in." James starts sauntering over the grass. I guess I can see where he's coming from, but looking at the electrified fence, it doesn't make me feel like I'm in a rehab.

Walking behind James, I spot people playing on the basketball court. They're all just like me. But unlike me, they're still trying to have some fun. Despite everything, people seem to be enjoying themselves. Looking over to the grassy area that we're heading towards, I notice some other people, deer again. They're running laps around the perimeter of the fence. Looks like they're excited to be outside. Can't tell if it's because we're all cooped up inside, or if it's their "instinct." James and I make it to the grass, and James sits down.

"Oh yeah..." he says, stretching out his legs on the grass. "I needed that. I've been standing and sitting most of today, haven't had an opportunity to really stretch out."

I sit down next to him. "It's definitely been a weird day. Sitting outside feels like I'm back in middle school again." I lie on my back. "The feeling is nostalgic, keeps you grounded, I guess."

"Nostalgic?" James asks. "Wanna elaborate on that?"

I shrug. "Sure, why not." I rest my head on my hands, looking up into the sky. "Everyone hates middle school, but it's the last time we really had anything resembling recess. I remember when I was younger, me and some of my friends would spend our time playing foursquare, or just doing this. The school didn't have a big rec yard like this. But I do know that there was a hill we spent a lot of time on. Tuning out the rest of the world. Making up stories. Ya know, normal little kid stuff."

I sigh before continuing. "I wasn't the most popular kid, even into high school. To be honest, I was kind of a punk. I got into trouble, did stupid shit. Never went to jail, just normal rebellious teenager stuff. But sometimes, I'd go to this field when I was down in the dumps. And I'd sit on the hill, look into the sky, and tune out the outside world, just like this. It's peaceful."

"That was a lot deeper than I expected!" James chuckles.

I sit up, shooting him a look. "You asked to elaborate on it!"

James waves me away. "I know, I know. I just didn't think you'd go so deep into it! Hey, I get it, though, we've all got things that keep us sane."

"Oh yeah? Well, what's yours?" I ask.

James sighs. "My sister, but I won't bore you with stories of my family right now."

I nod. "Gotcha, I won't pry."

Just then, a voice sounds behind us. "Hey, guys, looks like you two are getting along!"

Both James and I turn around and see Carter standing above us, grinning.

We both stand up and turn to him. "Oh, hey, Carter!" James replies. "What's up?"

Carter turns to me. "So I just got back from the office. I looked into your file, Lyla."

"Oh? Well, what's it say?" I ask excitedly. Finally, some answers!

"I can't tell you here. Something about both of your files is strange… You're going to have to come with me so we can talk privately."

I tilt my head in confusion. "I'm… not in trouble…am I?" I ask.

"No… No. This concerns the both of you," Carter says, his face turning concerned. "I just noticed something's up with the files. I don't know if being outside is the best option to talk about it." Carter's stance shifts. His eyes look past me, and his hand rests on a long stick hanging from his belt.

"What is that?" I ask, glancing down at the metal rod attached to a holster in his belt.

"Something I won't have to use, if you come along quickly."

"What? You're… not threatening me? Are you?" I ask.

Carter's glance shifts to me, his face becoming confused. "What? No! I'm trying to get out of here before—"

Suddenly, I hear another voice from behind me, one I've never heard before.

"You shouldn't be talking to this guy, miss."

I turn around, and in front of me, almost towering over me, is a giant guy. Covered from head to toe in brown fur. Wearing only a slightly torn flannel shirt and jeans. This guy is a bear, in the literal sense. "Hello… Paul," says Carter.

"Like I said, miss. You shouldn't be talking to these guys," Paul says calmly.

"Why not?" I ask. Carter seems to be a nice guy.

James starts backing up slowly, standing next to me. "C-carter's my friend, he wouldn't do anything to us."

"He may be a nice guy on the outside. But just like the other people in those blue polos, he's got one goal. Keeping us in here," Paul says, still retaining the same calm demeanor despite his gruff, slightly southern voice. "I've been here since this started. Haven't tried anything once, been a model citizen."

Carter pipes up now. "I understand you're tired of waiting, Paul. But the only reason you're still here is 'cause of the slip-up a week ago." His hand now grips the metal rod in his holster, waiting for when things go south.

"All of you know me by now. That wasn't a slip-up at all. I had a nightmare that night. That's why I slashed the wall. That's not a sign of instinct. You stood up for me and then told the psychiatrist that it *could* have been." Paul steps closer to Carter, now towering over him.

Carter, starting to sweat, pulls out the metal rod, holding it in front of him, then pressing a button, the end sparks up.

Carter pulled out a cattle prod.

Paul doesn't pay any attention to the sound, retaining his tough demeanor. "You stood up for me when I was there, and then rolled over like a dog behind my back. You still have it good, being human, Carter. That's what irritates me, and I'm not going to let you do the same to these new people. They don't know you'll turn on them, just like you did on me."

Carter, sweat pouring down his face, says, "Paul, buddy, I'm sorry. They asked me if that would count as instinct. I said, I guess… But I didn't know it would be taken like that!"

Paul sighs once more. "I get it, you got caught in a bind. I'm not happy about it, and I don't trust you as much. But it cost me an early leave." Paul raises his hand. "But I know deep down, there's some good in you." Paul starts to put his hand on Carter's shoulder. "So you better fix thi—"

Just then, the sound of the prod going off causes everyone to turn their attention to the three of us. I look in shock, as Carter pushes the cattle prod into Paul's stomach. Paul falls back on his behind, dazed. James slinks behind me.

Carter starts stammering over his words. "O-oh no… Paul. I-I'm so sorry! I didn't think—"

Paul stands up again with a defeated look on his face. "You didn't think… that's apt. I thought you were a good guy, Carter." Paul starts walking towards Carter once more. "I'm about to kick your ass. The old-fashioned way, no claws, no teeth, so you know this isn't an instinct thing. Tell 'em all you went behind my back, Carter. But I'm gonna give you a beating the same way I did before all this animal nonsense."

I start walking towards them. I put myself in between Paul and Carter. If Carter gets his ass kicked… I'm not going to figure out what was wrong about my file, about how I got here. But… I don't remember much about this. Next thing I know, Paul's talking to me.

"Listen, Possum. This ain't your fight. You should get out of here before things get ugly," Paul says, still remaining calm throughout all this. How does this guy do it?

"I… I can't," I say. "I need this guy for something, and it has to be with him not beat up."

Paul scoffs. "So what, you're gonna fight in his place? That's cute. I'm not dealing with it."

Paul starts walking around me, but I push him back. It doesn't do much. But he gives me a glare and steps back to say something to me, before falling back again. Paul, now lying on his back, reveals what really knocked him over. James. Completely invisible aside from his clothes.

James reappears, crawling on all fours, staring at me. I just accidentally table topped Paul.

Looking down at James, I yell at him, "What are you doing?"

"Trying to get out of here. You see that guy? He's too big for you to handle!" James replies.

"Now you've dragged us both into it!" I yell.

Suddenly, Paul sits up again, staring at both of us.

"You pissed me off. That's it, both of you are a part of this now." Paul stands up and starts walking towards us, readying his fists.

James, now standing up, starts to back away. Paul reels back and throws a punch at both of us. Not knowing what to do, I duck and hope for the best. The air from Paul's fist narrowly caving in my skull whooshes over me, as somehow, my stupid idea worked.

I start trying to slink away, but Paul throws another punch directly above me. I dive out of the way, feeling his fist nick the end of my tail. The sharp pain of Paul's narrow miss shoots up my tail, into my spine. That... didn't feel good at all...

Paul growls, looking at me. "Listen, missy, I can do this all day. Either you're going to get tired, or I'm going to get lucky."

Carter, now standing next to me, says to Paul, "She's got nothing to do with this. Just leave her out of this."

Paul shakes his head. "Nope, she started your fight, Carter. You're both in it now." Carter and I ready ourselves as Paul starts walking towards us. James, now materializing behind us, trembles and readies himself. It's three on one. This should be easy... Right?

Paul starts swinging, aiming for both of us. Carter dodges and weaves through Paul's flurry of fists. Apparently, he's done this before. Me on the other hand? I'm just backing up. I don't know what's going on, but he's too slow for me to get hit if I'm moving backwards. That's what's working, and I'm doing it. James, now standing by the fence, is watching the whole thing go down, not doing anything.

Carter hits Paul with another stun from the cattle prod. This shock doesn't faze Paul, as he decks Carter in the shoulder, knocking him on his ass. Carter struggles to get back onto his feet but gets right back up.

Paul starts stomping, yelling at Carter. "You're just like the rest! You two-faced, lying, scheming, little piece of—" Paul is now fuming, as he continues his tirade, the calm demeanor now completely vanished, leaving nothing but a terrifying beast of what once was a man. "I just want to go home! See my kid! Hug my wife! Do you know how scared they were when I woke up like this?" Paul's anger continues to swell, as it feels like the ground is shaking with every word that comes out of his mouth. "I used to be happy! I know that nothing will be the same, but I came here so my family would know I'm safe! Instead, you evil bastards keep me here to what? Rot? Until I eventually die? Never to go back to my loved ones again? It's been weeks! I'm not going to deal with your bullshit anymore!"

Paul throws his fist into the ground, but instead of his fist stopping when it hits the pavement, it makes a shockwave of earth and concrete ripple towards us. Like… an actual shockwave. The concrete breaking and rising, like a wave coming directly towards us. Carter and I both stumble as the ripple dissipates, throwing us around with the moving earth beneath us.

Paul looks at the damage he's caused. "What… What is this?" He focuses on the ground, raises his foot, and lays all his weight into the ground. The force of his foot hitting the concrete causes the immediate area where he's standing to sink a little into the ground, breaking the concrete beneath his feet. Raising his hands up slowly, the ground beneath him begins to rise, slowly at first, but then shooting him upwards. Through… something, Paul is standing on top of a pillar about the same height as the fence.

"I don't know what's going on, but I'm leaving," Paul says, jumping the fence, causing more earth to rise up in pillars like before, catching him, and then setting him down on the outside of the fence.

Carter, James, and I are completely surprised. How did Paul do what he just did? He controlled the earth, bending it to his will.

"See you, Carter, Miss." Paul starts running into the wilderness lining the outside of the school.

Carter, now in a robotic state, pulls out his walkie talkie. "We've got a code black! One of the changed has jumped the fence!" Suddenly, people in tactical gear start emerging from every door in the building. Groups of people with rifles run into the woods. More people emerge from the doors and starts taking people inside. Two guards, both wearing balaclavas, approach James and me.

Carter stops them and says, "They're with me. They helped in my scuffle with Paul." One of them responds with, "You mean 012." Carter sighs. "Yes, 012."

The other man speaks. "You still let him get away. We're going to escort 019 and 028 to their rooms. Think about what you've done, and make sure there's a full report at the end of the night." Both of the men turn to James and me. "We're taking you to your rooms, come on. Mandatory curfew while the situation is assessed." They start pushing us into the doors. Soon enough, we're both in our rooms once again.

Once I get to my room, the guard ushers me in. "All right, 028, stay in here. Someone will come get you tomorrow." The guard then slams the door in my face. Now, I'm back where it all started. It's my third day here and I'm already causing trouble.

I turn around and walk back to the crack in the wall. Pulling out the piece I replaced and crouching down, I peer inside of James's room. "Psst... James, you there?" I call out. I hear the shuffling of feet, and his head comes into view.

"Yeah, I'm here," he says, still looking shook up from our encounter with Paul.

"What the hell happened out there? You froze up and didn't help!" I ask. After I knocked Paul over by accident with James, he disappeared, figuratively and literally.

"I don't like conflict; I'm used to just painting houses and going home.

Getting into fights isn't my idea of rehabilitation! I didn't know you were going to push that Paul guy over me. Let alone get into a fight!" James responds. "On top of that, now we find out that one of the biggest guys here is able to literally move the earth? He jumped the fence, and now the whole place is going crazy!" James sighs, sitting down in front of the crack in the wall. "I don't know what's going to happen next," James says. "This isn't good. I've never seen those guys in the SWAT uniforms before."

"Yeah, you heard what they called us, right? Some numbers. I think mine was 28…" I say.

"This is starting to seem less and less like a rehabilitation center," James replies. "The only time I've seen my number, 19, is because I was the nineteenth person to show up here. But, hearing it in this context, I'm certain that something is up now." James has a defeated look on his face. "You heard what Paul was yelling to Carter about, right?"

I nod. "Yeah, it doesn't look like this place is meant to help us at all. He seemed like he was at his limit."

"And now, on top of that, what the heck was that thing with Paul moving the ground like that? It's like some shit out of a comic book," James says.

"I don't know, it certainly wasn't natural. I don't know what to think," I say.

"As much as I would like to contemplate what happened outside… I'll be honest, I'm more focused on what Carter said, and those men in the SWAT suits," James replies.

"You're right," I respond. "We should try to look for a way to get out of here. I know how much you want to go home, and how you've been a model citizen, just like Paul," I say.

"That's what scares me: some kind of sign that I'm not completely human, and my stay here becomes just a little longer. Edging on the possibility of never ending. I'm not going to wait until I freak out like that. But we can't leave now. They've got this whole place on lockdown."

"I know," I respond. "They're going to be on high alert, but that doesn't mean we can't find a way. We can bide our time a bit longer, don't you think?" I ask.

"I mean, we could. I've been here long enough to know what we could use, but it… it could be risky. If we get caught…" James is about to continue, but I cut him off.

"We don't have to worry about getting caught. We're just considering the option of—"

Just then, I hear a knock at my door, and the sound of the handle opening. I scramble to put the piece of the wall back in its place, and just in time as the door finishes opening. When I turn around, it's Carter, looking defeated, wearing a sling on his arm.

"Carter, what're you doing in here? Are you okay?" I ask.

Carter nods. "I told you I had to talk to you in private." Carter winces before continuing. "Jesus, Paul got me good. The onsite medic told me if I was hit any harder, I could've broke something. Luckily, it was only dislocated, but I can't use it as much for the time being. Regardless, I told you we needed to talk in private. Seems to be a good time anyhow."

Carter walks over to my bed and sits down. I stand across from him against the wall. "Well, you did poke him with an electrified stick. It's par for the course that you'd get some damage dealt back."

"I expected as much. I wanted to thank you and James for helping out. If you two didn't push him over, I probably would've got my ass kicked more than I did."

"We didn't really do anything," I said. "You were the one that started that whole fight."

Carter nods. "I'm just being polite. Part of the job, I guess."

"Were the numbers part of the job, Carter?" I ask. "Or are you going to write in that report of yours that there's a possibility that James and I used some instinct to assist you?"

"I'm not going to even mention the two of you helping, you were just in the wrong place, at the wrong time," Carter responds, the look of remorse on his face. "What happened with Paul was a fluke. You really think I did that on purpose? I know you have every reason to be skeptical, but I have a feeling you'd know better." Carter sighs. "Anyways, there's two things that you should know. I did go look at your file."

Carter stands up and peers out the window for my door, before stepping away and turning to face me. "What I found isn't good, Lyla. When I checked the office looking for records of you, it says you were picked up on a highway in Iowa."

"I…Iowa… We're not in Iowa?" I ask. "That's where I was with my friends before all this happened…"

Carter continues. "No, Lyla, we're in Indiana. They moved you across two states, said that some of the personnel transferring here found you."

"Wait…" I say. "I'm two states away? Why?"

"Since they were coming here, they brought you with them, said you only woke up once, but you were in a daze. You mentioned a party, and something about close family. They said that you started trying to use your phone, but they confiscated it. After that, you passed out," Carter says. He pauses for a moment, before continuing.

"That's not all… They found you in the middle of the road. They drove up, and you collapsed. They thought you were someone trying to… take the easy way out. But when they investigated to see if you were okay, they said that's when they found you as a changed. You were… playing dead."

"Are you saying that's in my file too… One of these signs of instinct that Paul mentioned?" I ask.

"From the looks of it, yes." Carter stops, peers through the window once more, and continues talking. "Here's the biggest thing about this… your file, aside from your age, height, and all that crap. Your personal information is completely redacted. In fact, everyone's files are like this. No driver's licenses, no emergency contacts, nothing." Carter continues, "To be honest, none of us look at the files. That's for the psychologist and the higher-ups to do. We handle interpersonal matters. I've seen all the normal questions asked. Information that should be in there isn't there. So, looking at your file, James's file, I can't find anything about you regarding what your life once was."

Carter stops and walks to the corner of the room next to the door. The sound of boots trampling down the hallway can be heard, followed by muffled voices and the sound of a cattle prod. Then, the noise subsides. Carter slowly steps out from the corner.

"Here's the thing: they're only keeping track of two things here, your physical appearance and your 'outbursts.' That's what they're calling these moments of instinct, like they did with Paul. Anything else you had on you, like your phone, it's here, somewhere. Since they found you during one of these outbursts, they're keeping you for much longer than you think, even with the fact that you've been unconscious for the past three weeks." Carter pauses, as if he's listening for someone walking down the hallway. "I hate to say it, but I think Paul's right, and they're finding every reason to keep you here. I'm sorry that I have to be the one to tell you. I really thought this place was going to help you guys, but I'm concerned that you guys are in some serious trouble. You have lives to get to."

"Are you... telling me to escape?" I ask.

"No," Carter says. "I can't tell you to escape. That'd be breaking my oath as being a beacon of rehabilitation, and with this new information, I should be keeping that promise. But, if I was in your situation, I wouldn't be surprised if an opening appears and you took it." Carter pauses once more, then continues, "Anyhow, the second thing I wanted to tell you is that they're going to be holding an assembly tomorrow morning. They're keeping you all inside for the night. Tomorrow, they're going to talk about Paul's escape. I don't know what's going to happen, but stick with James. You two can make it through this."

Carter steps to the door. "I'll try to meet up with you guys after the assembly, just… be careful. Everyone out there's on edge. Don't try to start anything like you did with Paul. I won't be there to help." Carter then opens the door and walks away.

With all of these new revelations in my mind, I sit down on my bed. My file is empty? Everything about my previous life… gone… This doesn't make sense at all. What're they trying to do to people like me? What's their end game? What's their plan for me? I know now more than ever I have to get out of here… If I do… What's the next step? After I escape, where do I go? I know that my friends are back in Iowa, probably worried sick about me. But, then again, I talked to James about my family. I haven't seen my parents in years… Now that I think about it… they're probably back home. That's in Wisconsin. I've got to go back and find them first. I told James I would, and I have a feeling I should make it back there. Just to let them know I'm okay. But for now, I've got to get out of here, and fast…

Chapter 5

James

THE HOLE IN the wall closes in front of me. For a brief moment I can still see through the hole, it looks like the door is opening in Lyla's room. I hope she's okay. With the thoughts of our previous encounter with Paul, I stand up and walk to the other side of the room back to my bed. Sitting down, I stare at the wall. I can't believe what happened. One second, Lyla and I were sitting in the grass talking about memories from before all this, and the next, I'm slinking away from a fight trying to not get into trouble. But… I ended up causing more trouble than I intended to. It's just another stroke of bad luck for me, I suppose.

Now… This whole place is on lockdown. I still hear those guys in the SWAT outfits patrolling the halls… It's not good. Each footstep echoing through the halls, this lockdown, it's my fault it happened. I look over to the mirror on the other end of the wall. My face is just partly visible from where I'm sitting. It's weird, seeing something else in the mirror when I look into it. It's actually kind of ironic now that I think about it.

A painter, turned into a chameleon. I chuckle to myself. None of this feels real, yet it is all the same.

I can't help but feel like I should've done something in the fight. Lyla's words saying "You froze up!" keep replaying in my mind like one of those old CD players that skips when you hold it wrong. I knew

I could've done more, and I didn't. But with our new plan to get out of here, this is going to be another chance to actually do something. I know I'm capable of it. It's not like I'm not. It just seems so daunting when you can't trust anyone. Is it that? Or is it the small piece inside me that still believes I could get out of this place without risking staying any longer…

I honestly don't know.

It's been a wild evening. To top it all, the PA goes off and a voice comes through the speakers. "Attention, residents, we are holding a practice lockdown for the remainder of the night. You will be escorted to your rooms, in which the lockdown will end tomorrow morning. Thank you for your cooperation."

Jeez, now they're keeping us inside for the rest of the night? Sitting on my bed, I wonder what's going on in Lyla's room. Who's the person in there? Is it Carter? Should I try to intervene and see what's going on? No, I shouldn't. Thinking about it, I know that if it's not him, it's going to put a larger target on our backs. Lyla pulled out a chunk of the wall for god's sake, and if they find out, not only will they seal it, but they could prevent us from talking like we have been the past two days.

But if something else is going on, there's a chance that Lyla could be in danger.

I have to do something.

Right?

I get up and walk to the crack in the wall, I lean in to see if I hear anything, but I can only make out some muffled voices.

"…make it through this…"

Who's on the other side? Is it Carter? I need to know.

"…don't…start… anything…"

Who is that? I can faintly hear the door closing from Lyla's room. Waiting a few minutes, I tap on the piece of the wall Lyla pulled out.

"Lyla? Hello?"

Tapping more on the piece of the wall, the piece falls out, leaving the hole between Lyla's room and mine wide open. I can tell Lyla hears the piece fall onto the floor, as the sound of her clawed feet hitting the tile comes closer to the whole in the wall.

"James? What're you doing?"

"Who was that?" I ask. "It sounded super bad. I waited until they were gone so I didn't get you caught."

"It was Carter. He told me about the file. Something messed up is going on, James. We need to think really hard about getting out of here."

"What was it?" I ask.

"It's not good, he said that the files removed—"

The sound of my door opening catches Lyla's attention, and she makes a quiet shrieking sound before putting the piece back in the wall. Seeing her do this, I simultaneously dart upwards and move to the sink right next to the hole in the wall. Splashing my face with water as fast as possible, I turn around.

Looking at the door, a blonde woman enters, wearing the same blue polo that every other person, Carter included, is wearing. She's looking down at a clipboard, seemingly oblivious to what happened as she was opening the door.

"James?" the woman asks.

"That's me," I respond.

"Hey, I'm sure you heard the PA, but I'm going to be picking you up tomorrow morning for an assembly before they start serving breakfast. I know it's not the normal schedule, so I'm making the rounds to let you guys know."

"All right, thanks," I say.

The woman goes to leave but stops, looking up at me in front of the sink.

"You… you good?" the woman asks.

"Yeah, I'm fine, just cleaning up before going to bed," I reply.

"…All right," the woman says, closing the door.

Wait… hold on, who is this woman?

"Actually…" I say.

The woman stops closing the door, opening it enough to see me. "What's up?"

"What happened to Carter? Normally, he takes me to breakfast," I ask.

"Oh. Carter," the woman says. "I'm taking over for him for tomorrow, since it's a mass wakeup, rather than individuals."

"Gotcha," I reply. "Thank you."

The woman gives me a nod before closing the door, the electric lock clicking into place as she walks away.

Waiting another few moments to make sure the woman is gone, I return to the crack in the wall.

"Lyla, you there?" I say.

Silence.

"Hello?" I call out.

"…I'm here," Lyla says. "Nobody in there?"

"Yeah, some woman showed up to tell me about an assembly," I respond. "So, what did Carter say?" I ask.

"I want to tell you, but with these two close calls already, I think we should wait until tomorrow," Lyla says. "I don't want to take any chances. Can you wait until after the assembly tomorrow?"

"Yeah, I can wait. Good idea," I respond. "Good night, Lyla."

Silence.

"Good night, James."

I get up from the crack in the wall and lie down in my bed. It's been a wild day. Still, there's thoughts inside of my head that are preventing me from sleeping. I could've done more, I could have gone out of my way to defend my friends. Instead, I accidentally instigated the fight.

Instead of helping, I cowered behind Lyla and fled when they needed me. I don't know why. Is it because of my nature? I know I'm not one to do things like this. I know that I would stand up for my sister when she needed me. Has this place gotten to my head? Am I starting to become more animal than man? It doesn't make sense, and yet, I'm sitting here, dwelling on it. I don't mean to beat myself up about it, but I do know that I could have done something.

The more I think about what could have been, the more I suffocate myself as I lie awake. These conflicting thoughts intrude themselves into my head until I can't think about anything else, and somehow, as I'm drowning in my thoughts, I fall asleep.

Still within my dreams, while I don't remember much, I do remember running. I don't know from what, but the feeling of being caught is something that I can't fathom, not that I want to. I'm sprinting, but I keep falling over myself. Running isn't something I'm capable of doing as I stumble over my new feet. The feeling keeps getting closer, and I know that if I look back, I'm done for. However, I do. I don't remember what I saw, as right when I turned around to face whatever was chasing me, the sound of the door opening wakes me up.

"James? Rise and shine," the familiar voice says.

I sit up in bed and look to the door at the foot of my bed. It's the same woman who entered my room last night. She tosses me a Ziploc bag with the number nineteen written in marker.

"Clean up and come on, you need to get to the assembly," the woman says, closing the door.

I quickly get around, using the Ziploc bag and the toiletries inside to clean up, then head to the door, where the woman is waiting outside with a group.

"Lead the way," I respond.

The woman gestures for me and the rest of the people to follow her. We all start moving, as I slink back to the back of the line. We walk about a couple steps before someone pipes up, a mountain lion.

"'Scuse me, miss," the lion says. "What's this assembly for again?"

The woman looks at her clipboard for a short moment before responding. "Something about the incident that happened outside yesterday."

The lion shakes his head as the caravan of people keeps moving.

While we're walking, I hear someone from behind me. "Yo, lizard." I look to my side as another smaller person catches up from the back of the line. It's a raccoon. Wearing a bright red hoodie and shorts. "You know what's going on?" it asks.

"You weren't paying attention? It's supposed to be some assembly," I reply.

"Well, yeah… I know that," the raccoon says, rolling its eyes. "I'm asking if you know what it's about."

"So… you weren't listening. It's about what happened outside yesterday," I say.

The raccoon responds, "I wasn't outside. What happened? A bunch of SWAT guys were telling us to head back to our rooms last night." The raccoon looks at me for an answer. I don't know how much this person knows, and tying myself to the incident doesn't seem like a good idea, especially with everyone being so on edge.

"Someone hopped the fence," I say. "Dunno how, but they made a break for it. I only saw them on the other side, booking it."

"Seriously?" The raccoon's eyes light up. "You're kidding, someone actually made a break for it?"

"As far as I know, yes," I respond.

"That's freakin' awesome," the raccoon says before her expression changes to one of surprise, like she forgot her keys at home. "Oh shit, I'm sorry. What's your name, dude?"

"Uh… James," I respond.

"Nice to meet you, James. I'm Kellie." Kellie extends their hand for a handshake. I shake their hand as we continue walking.

"So, what else did you see?" Kellie asks.

"Not much," I respond. "Just some guys chasing after the person who escaped."

"Damn," Kellie says. "I was hoping for some action here." She frowns. "How long you been here?"

"Uh… About a few weeks, I think?" I say.

"Really? Longer than me," she responds. We walk in awkward silence before she pipes up again. "How you handling the whole, um… being an animal thing?"

"I, uh… I don't know how to respond to that. I guess I'm handling it fine? I was kind of freaked out at first," I say. "I'm used to it now."

"Really?" she says. "When I woke up like this, I was freakin' stoked, dude," she says, beaming. "Like, of course I didn't want it at first, but how freakin' cool is this?" She spins around while walking, gesturing to herself. "I'm, like, not a human anymore. My life was pretty freakin' boring before this happened. Now, I guess, I'm special."

"I mean, I guess?" I say. "Not really anything special about being an animal, though. We just look different."

"Look different?" Kellie says. "Dude, I have a freakin' tail now. I can see in the dark, and I'm never freezing. This is probably the coolest thing that's happened to me… like… ever." Kellie does a little dance, before she catches back up to me. "I don't like being so small, though. It's annoying to have to run so fast to catch up to everyone."

"There's cons to everything, I suppose," I say. We all stop. The blonde woman opens two doors, and we enter a gymnasium. Sports equipment is strewn across the floor, as all of the people from the cafeteria and outside are in here. Two people pull out bleachers from the wall. A small platform is at the other end, with a microphone on it. I look through the crowd to see if I can find Lyla, but she's nowhere to be seen.

"Looking for someone?" Kellie asks, poking me in the leg.

"Yeah," I say. "A friend."

"Were they outside with you?" Kellie asks.

"She was. She didn't see much either if that's what you're asking."

"Oh, a girl?" Kellie says. "She cute?"

I glance down at her, confused. She looks up at me with the same expression. "Dude, if you're trying to give me some look, it ain't working. I can't tell if you're making a face with those weird freakin' eyes of yours."

I sigh.

Finally, people start moving, and I get close to the bleachers, this Kellie girl following me. I feel someone tug at my shirt. Looking to the side, I see Lyla. Finally, someone I know.

"There you are," she says. "How you holding up?"

"I'm fine," I respond. "Still a little shaken up."

"Oh! So this is your friend," Kellie says, butting into the conversation. "Hello! Oooh! You're a possum! That's so freakin' cute! I'm gonna die!"

"Th… Thanks?" Lyla says. She turns to me. "Who's this?"

"This is Kellie," I respond. "She was in the group I was with walking here."

"Gotcha. Well, hello, Kellie," Lyla says. "Nice to uh... meet you?"

"Oh yeah, definitely nice to meet you! What's it like… bein' a possum?" Kellie says, smiling big.

Lyla stops, her facial features changing from confusion to a blank stare. The three of us stand in silence for a moment, as Lyla freezes in place.

"Lyla… you… you okay?" I ask, waving a hand in front of her.

She starts moving again, turning to me. "I'm fine, sorry, zoned out there for a second."

A single tear runs down Lyla's cheek. Something's up with her. This happened in the art room yesterday too. Kellie's excited expression turns to one of remorse, like she went too far on a joke that didn't land. I grab her arm. "Let's go find a place to sit," I say.

Kellie, now not saying anything, follows us as we walk up the stairs to one of the spots near the middle of the bleachers. I put myself between both Kellie and Lyla. Kellie's abrasive, but whatever she said to Lyla about her not being human must've done something to her. I don't want to risk that again, have the people here think she's having some kind of episode.

Now that we're sitting down here, I never realized how small this place was. I'm only seeing about three hundred people here. It's not a lot, but I thought it was going to be bigger, that's for sure.

Once everyone's sat down, the people in blue polos start coming out. All lined up, all with cattle prods at their sides. A feeling of nervousness rushes over me, looking at both Lyla and Kellie. From their expressions, I'm not the only one.

Now, I see the main person walk through. It's the psychologist for this place. Dr. Thorn. He's a tall, lanky guy. He always has on a white lab coat, but aside from that, the only defining features of this guy are his round glasses and longish hair. He's been here since the beginning; I've only talked to him a few times in my three weeks of being here. It's clear he's important. I think I remember Carter saying something about him being the backbone of the RCC, travelling from facility to facility. Guess he's here for now.

Dr. Thorn steps up to the platform and taps on the mic. "Hello, everyone. It's good to see all of you again." Thorn pauses and looks around at the group. "I understand yesterday was very eventful. I know that a lot of you, mostly those who weren't outside yesterday afternoon, are confused as to why we're holding this meeting."

Thorn's voice rings through the gymnasium, but voices can be heard whispering underneath the speech. "This morning, one of our esteemed citizens, Paul Miller, has decided to 'check out early.'" Thorn pauses, and for a moment, it appears that he locks eyes with both Lyla and me. I'm not sure if I'm seeing things, but it sure felt like it.

Thorn continues. "Paul Miller has escaped. He's most likely not going to be coming back, and on top of this, there's been murmurs among all of you saying Miller possesses some... special abilities. However, I've brought everyone together to assure everyone that this is false. Please bear in mind..." He chuckles to himself. "Pun not intended... that there's an explanation for almost everything. While we don't know the cause of your physical changes, what we do know is that yesterday afternoon... one of our teams looking into expanding the basement has tunneled underneath the outside yard. Combining this with the cave in underground..."

Thorn uses his hands to demonstrate a wedge shape pushing something upwards.

"This caused a pillar of earth to be pushed up into the air, which is just where Miller happened to be standing. This is what gave him the necessary height to allow him to clear the fence. There wasn't any special abilities involved. Miller doesn't have control of rocks or the ground. It was merely a strange coincidence."

Murmurs from the crowd pick up. Thorn raises his hand, as people's voices start to calm down again. "If you don't believe me, that's fine. However, I hope you all remember that what we do here is to keep you safe until we know that you can return to your normal lives. We don't really have the need to lie to all of you. That would most definitely put us in a situation where this wouldn't be a relaxing and human experience for you," Thorn says. "Remember, here at the RCC, we're all in this together, and if you're still concerned about the situation, you're more than welcome to come and talk to me. I'm always going to be here for each and every one of you."

People shift in their seats, and a small moment of silence from all parties fills the room. Thorn then speaks up. "From here on, until the ground is repaired and the work underground is complete, we will be closing off the recreational area. Anyone caught outside in the rec aera will be escorted back to their room. This gymnasium will serve as the place for all outdoor sports and exercise to be done. I know you all don't like being cooped up in here, and it hurts me to have to do this, but we can't risk having someone get a bright idea and try to climb the pillar that Miller jumped from." Thorn pauses once more. I feel like he's been picking his words very carefully since he started talking. "Until we can find a way to remove the pillar and replace the broken concrete from our mistake, we'll be looking for a way to get you all fresh air. I promise, this whole debacle will be over before you all know it." Thorn smiles.

"That's all I have for you. After breakfast, you can all go back to your current activities. Remember, if you have a scheduled appointment today, please come in at the right time. I know some people have been missing appointments. If we don't talk to you, we can't help you! Have a great rest of your day, everyone!" The people in blue polos start dispersing. People start walking down from the bleachers and spread out around the gym.

Lyla, Kellie, and I all get up and start walking down the stairs. "That was boring," Kellie says. She turns to both of us. "You guys doing anything? I don't really got anything going on right now, if you're interested in eating breakfast with me."

"Not this time, sorry," Lyla says. Lyla looks at me. "I gotta talk to you about something."

"Sorry, Kellie," I say. Kellie's pointed ears flatten as she tries to fake her smile.

"All right. I'm sorry if I said anything to upset you guys. I'll be around if you two change your mind."

"It's fine, Kellie," Lyla says. "Actually, go first and grab us a table. We'll be there."

Kellie manages to perk up a little, probably at the thought of hanging out with us. "Okie dokie, I'll talk to you guys later then." Kellie starts walking out of the gym, leaving only me and Lyla. Lyla starts looking around the gym, then turns to me.

"Have you seen Carter?" she asks.

"No," I say. "I haven't seen him since outside."

"He said he'd link up with us after the assembly. Follow me." She starts walking out of the gym and into the hallway.

Walking out into the hallway, the halls are lined with some of the people we saw outside, and some of the people I recognized from our group. I can overhear some conversations about the assembly. People talking about how boring it was, comments about Thorn, and the cattle prods the people in the polos brandished into the gym.

I overhear a person who's been turned into a goat talking to the mountain lion from my group. "I understand where this guy is coming from, but something doesn't sit right with me. Why were they working underground?" the goat says.

"Beats me," the mountain lion responds. "I don't think we should be complaining. I heard from someone outside before the whole assembly thing that the guard involved was shocking Miller before he hopped the fence. We should probably keep our heads down for now."

Lyla and I continue walking, then stop at the back of the line for breakfast. She starts letting people go in front of us, putting us at the back. She checks around to see if someone's nearby before talking. "So, about the file, I told you we'd talk about it after the assembly," she says.

"Yeah, we're doing it now?" I reply.

"Only time I can tell you, too many people in the cafeteria," Lyla says, looking around, checking to see if anyone is coming closer. "There's… nothing about us in there."

"What're you talking about?" I ask. "That doesn't make any sense."

"That's what I said too," Lyla replies. "But I'm not talking about us right now, I'm talking about us before. Like, our previous lives."

"You mean, what we were when we were... human?" I ask.

"Exactly. It's either blank or blacked out," Lyla says. "At least, that's what Carter told me." Lyla pauses. Her ears perk up, as if she's checking to hear for someone. "Carter also said a report mentioned that the people who picked me up found me..." She sighs. "Playing dead."

"What?" I say. "You gotta be joking."

"No, that's what's written down. Have they caught you doing something like that?" she asks.

I think back to my time here. "The only thing I do is blend in, but they know that," I respond. "The guy running this place, Thorn, says it's not an issue at the moment."

Lyla's face turns into a frown. "Well, you might've gotten off lucky, but I don't think I will. So we need to start thinking about checking out soon."

"So you're saying..." I respond.

"We gotta find a way out, James," Lyla says. "I don't know how, and I don't know when. But it's gotta be soon. I've already got a lead."

"What is it?" I ask.

"Carter mentioned something important. My phone," Lyla says. "Apparently, they confiscated it when they picked me up. It's gotta be here somewhere."

"Where do you think it is?" I ask.

"I don't know," Lyla responds. "But Carter might. We should find him." Lyla stops, and her ears perk up once more. "Someone's coming," she says.

I look down the hall to see another person in a blue polo coming down to us. "It's not Carter," I say. Lyla turns around to face the person in the blue polo.

The person in the polo speaks up while walking towards us. "Oh, I remember you! You're the girl I gave one of my hair ties to. Hello again," the woman says.

"Hello, Ada, uh… need me for something else?" Lyla asks.

"Yeah, since it's been a few days, you haven't spoken to the psychologist yet. I'm sure you saw him, Dr. Thorn," Ada replies.

"The guy on stage earlier? Yeah, I saw him," Lyla responds.

"Well, he's asking anyone who finds you to take you to his office, since you've suffered from changed confusion. He's asking to see you first while he has some time before the rest of his appointments for the day. I'm sure it's no problem if you spared a little bit of time, right?" Ada says, smiling.

"I don't really think I have a choice, do I?" Lyla says.

"Yes and no," She responds. "Technically, since it's your first visit, it's mandatory. If it were further along in your rehabilitation, you'd be able to reschedule. Thorn wants to make sure you're all right up there with you not coming in since you've woken up. Don't worry, we'll make sure you have something to eat after the appointment." The woman smiles.

Lyla pauses, processing what the woman says, before speaking again. "…All right, let's go." She turns to me. "I'll see you in a bit then, James." I can tell from the look in her eyes she's not on board for what's about to happen. The woman gestures for her to follow, and she starts walking away. Now, I'm left with my own thoughts. I know something's up. Lyla mentioned that Carter might know something about her phone. I should go find him first. However, I can't just… skip out on eating breakfast, and if I go now, I'll probably run into Kellie again. I can't help but feel bad about blowing her off in the gym, so if anything, I can at least eat breakfast with her.

Walking into the line, I see that they've opted to do scrambled eggs and toast today, same two guys making breakfast, since so many people are skipping out. I know I should be going to find out where Carter is, but I also know that I shouldn't be making enemies here either. Who knows what this Kellie girl is capable of. On top of that, Lyla should be with me to talk to Carter, so killing time might be the best course of action. Grabbing my food from the line, I finally step out into the open area of the cafeteria. A voice calls out to me.

"James! Over here!" I see Kellie again, sitting at a secluded table, with a book and her food. She waves her hand, gesturing me to come over. Lyla and I told her we weren't going to sit with her, but now with Lyla gone, I guess I'm going back on that. I walk up to the table and sit down.

"Changed your mind, huh? She looks around. "Where's that Lyla girl?" Kellie says, setting her book down.

"She's being taken to the office of that Thorn guy from the assembly, he's the current psychologist, remember?" I respond.

"Oh yeah, I think I've only talked to him once or twice," Kellie says. "He seems like a decent guy, a little strange, though, don't you think?"

I nod. "Yeah, he's kinda weird, but I guess I haven't really talked to many psychologists."

"What'd he wanna see Lyla for?" Kellie asks, leaning forward on the table. It's obvious she's being nosy.

"Mandatory evaluation. One of the people in the polos said that since she dodged it for two days, he's asking for her," I respond.

"Oh yeah, I remember having to do that. Feels like so long ago, but it's only been a few weeks, hasn't it?" Kellie says. "Strange how time has gone by so slowly since this all happened."

"It's definitely strange," I respond. "I guess we've all lost track of time. What're you reading?" I ask, shifting the conversation.

"Oh, this?" Kellie says, gesturing to her book. "It's called…" She peers at the cover, seemingly trying to decipher the title on the front page. "*Alfonso Rivières: The Man Who Stole My Heart.* It's a book about a Spanish noblewoman who falls in love with a vigilante thief who takes from the rich and gives to the poor, and how the woman starts to hate her rich upbringing. Instead, she wants to go on daring adventures with

Alfonso. Sounds neat, but I'm more in it for the parts where Alfonso swings his sword around and cuts up the bad guys. It's just more my style, you know what I mean?" Kellie exclaims, swinging her arm around like a sword, certainly energetic.

"Sounds neat. Maybe I'll—" I go to finish my sentence, but Kellie interrupts.

"I really hope I didn't make Lyla angry. She's not mad at me, is she? I would hate myself if I said something that made her upset."

"I think you just caught her off guard. She's only been awake for a couple days. She's still getting used to this whole situation," I respond.

"Oh, so she was like, what? In a coma?" Kellie asks, tilting her head.

"I mean, I guess you could say that. One of the guards, Carter, said something about her having changed confusion."

"Oh! I know Carter! He's that kinda tall guy who wakes you up, right? I think we are in the same hall. It was weird seeing someone else get us today. Is he okay? Do you know?" Kellie says.

"Slow down. Yeah, I think we are in the same hall. He used to wake me up too," I respond.

"You think he was a part of that whole escape thing Dr. Thorn was talking about this morning?" she asks.

"I don't know about that," I respond. "I was only there for a short bit."

"We should find him and ask him. He's always been nice," Kellie says. "Maybe he'll give us some insider info!" Kellie mimics the sound of a spy movie soundtrack.

"I don't know if he'd be willing to tell us something about the escape. Everyone's still kinda on edge about it," I respond. "I should go look for him after I'm done here, though. Lyla said something about talking to him after she got out of the office."

"We should go find him together then. I wanna know what happened outside!" Kellie replies with a big grin on her face.

"I don't know…" I respond.

"Well, I'm not one for secrets, we gotta find out all the juicy details! I'm itching for some excitement," Kellie says. "I'm coming."

"I was just going to go when Lyla gets back," I respond.

"We can tell her all about it after she's done. What if we miss Carter?" Kellie says, starting to dig into her plate of food.

"I don't know about that," I say. This girl is pushy.

"You'll be fine!" Kellie responds, finishing her food in record time. "Let's go!"

"I'm not done yet," I say.

"Well, I'm going to look for him, with or without you!" Kellie flashes a sly grin, grabbing her book and heading out the door.

She's leaving without me? Crap! I try to each as much food as I can while walking out the door, throwing my leftovers in the trash. I didn't eat a lot, but I did manage to eat enough. By the time I get out of the door, Kellie is already walking down the hallway a good thirty feet ahead of me.

"Wait up!" I call out, trying to catch up to her.

CHAPTER 6

James

KELLIE CONTINUES TO run through the halls. Once I catch up to her, we're in front of the doctor's office. Right as I stop to catch my breath, we both spot Carter almost to the end of the hallway, about to turn a corner. Kellie calls out for us, "Yo! Carter! Perfect timing!"

Carter stops and turns around. His arm is now in a sling. He stops walking and starts coming towards us. "Oh, hey, James!" Carter walks up, looking at Kellie and me. Carter turns to Kellie and says, "It's Kellie, right?"

Kellie smiles. "Yeah! You remembered huh?"

Carter grins. "I've just got a knack for remembering names." Carter looks at me. "Where's Lyla? I'm sorry I didn't link up with you guys after the assembly. The doctor wanted to take another look at my arm. I hope my absence didn't upset you guys."

"Ouch, that looks like it hurts," I say.

"Eh, it looks worse than it is," Carter says. "It's not that bad." Carter stops and pulls me to the side. "Give us just a moment, Kellie." Carter walks me away from Kellie, and we form a pseudo huddle. Carter starts talking to me. "I dunno how much Lyla told you, but things aren't looking so good right now."

"She told me enough, but things are getting worse. Lyla's suggesting we find an opening," I reply in a hushed voice.

Carter pauses. "I don't blame you for wanting to, but I dunno how much help I'm going to be."

"I'm aware," I respond. "What's more is that I met... Kellie on the way to the assembly, and she's trying to find out what happened outside yesterday. She... kind of weaseled her way in..."

Carter pauses and looks back at Kellie, who waves at him.

"Can you get rid of her?" Carter asks.

"I... I don't think that's a choice. It'll only give her a reason to snoop. She's the really, *really* nosy type," I say.

"Jesus, James," Carter says. "You don't know how to say no, do you?"

I look down to the floor. "Apparently not," I reply.

"Well, I guess now that she's here, we can turn this into an opportunity. I can help more people, and you guys might have a new ally," Carter says.

"Can we trust her?" I ask.

"She's energetic, but she might have a good heart. Let's find out." Carter turns around and walks up to Kellie.

"Can I trust you?" he asks.

Kellie smirks. "Depends, you asking me as a friend? Or as someone with a blue polo on?"

Carter's expression becomes more serious than it already was. "I'm not here to play coy with you, Kellie. I'm asking you, again, as a friend of James. Can I trust you?"

Kellie's demeanor sinks, she puts a paw on the back of her neck, and sighs. "Y-yeah, you can trust me."

Carter, still remaining stone-faced, says, "I hope so. Both of you, come on." Carter then rounds the corner of the hallway where Kellie and I found him. The three of us walk down the hallway until we make it down to a secluded section away from prying eyes. Carter looks around and turns to us. "Okay, James, what did Lyla tell you after the assembly?"

"Lyla said that the files you found don't contain anything about who we were before we changed," I respond.

"Wait, are you serious?" Kellie asks.

Carter nods. "Yeah, that's true. As far as anyone in my position is concerned, you're a chameleon, and you're a raccoon. Nothing more."

"So, what's the goal then?" Kellie asks. "If they don't know anything about who we previously are, then how're they supposed to help us?"

Carter shrugs. "I'm not sure. As much as I want to believe they're doing good work, this whole ordeal with Paul and the content I found in the files is making me think that you're only here to have an eye kept on you." Carter pauses. "I'm not even sure we're helping anyone."

"Are you the only one that knows this?" I ask.

"Possibly?" Carter says, "My co-workers seem to have the same goal as me, but I don't think they're clued in on what's exactly happening, and with Paul's escape, the office is now barred to those guys in the SWAT uniforms, so if anyone knows, it's most likely just me."

"So, what else did Lyla tell you then?" Kellie asks, turning to me.

"She said that while Carter mentioned that there's nothing in the files, they're only tracking a few things about us. One of which is if we have any signs of instinct," I respond.

"So if we're acting like the animals we look like, they're keeping a record of that?" Kellie asks.

Carter nods again. "I know you weren't outside, but Paul mentioned that he was about to leave before they kept him in here, because he damaged a wall during a nightmare. The fact that in his sleep, he managed to lash out, they ruled it as him not being fully human anymore. Which kept him for longer."

"So, they're just looking for reasons to keep us here then?" Kellie asks.

"That's what it seems like," Carter responds. "I want to help you guys, genuinely. But it seems like this place isn't going to do that."

"You could help us break out of here!" Kellie exclaims.

Carter shakes his head. "It's not that simple. Right now, I'm tied to

Lyla and James for being a part of the fight with Paul. If I spend too much time around you guys, people are going to get suspicious, especially since Paul managed to escape."

"Wait, wait… So you were involved?" Kellie says, turning to me. "I had a hunch you knew something!"

"I just met you. How am I supposed to know that you're not going to talk to someone else and tell them how I was involved?" I reply.

"Still, it doesn't make sense, you guys are planning an escape. You should be telling other people anyways," Kellie says.

"You're not going to be able to help everyone," Carter replies. "Paul didn't come back for you guys, did he?"

"No, I guess he didn't," Kellie responds.

"You guys are still people, and people are selfish. That's kind of how the world works. You put the people you care about first over strangers," Carter responds. "I've known James since I started here. He's a friend, and I want to help him and his friends. But I know I can't help everyone. It's selfish, I know. But that's life."

Kellie sighs. I use the small moment of silence to continue the conversation. "Carter, Lyla mentioned that her phone was taken. Do you think that could be of any use to us?"

Carter pauses. "It could. I have an idea of where they keep the phones, but we're not allowed in there. But maybe there's a way in."

"Elaborate, please," I ask.

"Okay," Carter responds. "There's a back room down the west hall. The door's labeled *band room*. It's the biggest room in the facility. It's where those guys in the SWAT uniforms stash their stuff. The door's always locked, and they use regular keys compared to the swipe cards we normally use for your doors. There's a chance that you could find a way in and grab the phones. I remember handing someone's phone off to one of the guys in the uniforms at the end of their first night."

"Okay, so we might know where the phones are," Kellie says. "I can always get my phone from where they keep it."

"You should try to grab everyone's phones. You brought your phone here, right, James?" Carter asks me.

"I didn't, I left it at home before I came here," I respond. "But Lyla's phone should be there, so Kellie should grab them both."

"Okay, so what do we do when we get the phones?" Kellie asks. "Do we call someone?"

"That's not a good idea. With Paul's escape, they'll expect someone to attempt contact with the outside. Any attention to the facility isn't going to help. They're going to go back into lockdown and find the person who called. At least, that's what I think is going to happen. I wouldn't risk it."

"So once we get outside and away from the facility, it'll be a lot easier to contact someone," I say. "It makes sense. There's really no cars around either."

"Yeah, they brought us in on buses when we got to the pick-up spot. You think our cars are still there?" Kellie says.

"I walked, but if your car is there, we might be able to use it to go somewhere," I reply.

"I've got a spare set of keys on my car. I used to lock myself out all the time, so I have a hiding spot on the outside of the car where I keep my keys. We should be able to use it," Kellie says.

"Now, one step at a time," Carter says. "First things first, the phones. You're going to want to get into contact with your families and friends first. Once you're outside."

"So that just means the only phones we need to get are Lyla's and yours," I say to Kellie.

"We just have to find Lyla now," Kellie responds.

"You guys know where she is?" Carter asks.

I reply, "One of your colleagues has her with Dr. Thorn. They're doing a mandatory session."

CHAPTER 7

Lyla

I'M ON MY own now. I'm walking with Ada, leaving James behind me. It's up to him to figure out where Carter is. Apparently, I have an appointment with the facility's psychologist.

She walks me down the hall, and after a few twists and turns, I find myself in a secluded hallway where not a lot of people are. On the side of a hall is the office for the building, and taking the spot of the principal's office is a sign that says "Dr. Bartholomew Thorn" taped over where the original sign is.

"He's already waiting for you," Ada says. "Just go in, it shouldn't take too long." The woman smiles and then steps out of the office, leaving me alone. Standing in front of the door is one thing, but thinking about what's going to happen when I go inside is another.

A lot has happened. Not only have I woken up like this, but I also got into a fight. Based on what Paul said to Carter, they're going to be looking for ways to keep us in here, so trusting this guy would be a bad choice. What's going to happen when I go inside? Is this going to be a conversation? Or an interrogation? What does this guy actually know? Looking behind me, I can still see the woman, watching me from outside the door. She may have left me alone, but I don't think she's going to let me skip out on this one. I have no choice. I have to enter.

I place my hand on the handle and slowly twist to open it. The door makes a noticeable creak as I push the door open and peer inside. Right across from the entrance is a desk, ladened with stacks of paper, and a computer. Dr. Thorn, the guy I'm supposed to be here to see, is sitting at the desk, typing on the computer. The room's well kept, and the guy's really made it his home away from home. It's adorned with awards and other pictures of him shaking hands. Across from his desk is a couch, the classic therapist furnishing.

Thorn looks up from his desk and sees me poking my head in.

"You must be Lyla. Please, come in," he says before looking back to his computer. "I've just got to send this report, and we should be all good to go. Please, take a seat on the couch. I'll be right with you."

I slink into the room and take a seat on the couch, waiting for this guy to finish whatever he's supposed to be doing. Thorn stops typing on the computer and rolls his chair from behind his desk and in front of the couch. He grabs a clipboard from the desk, and a pen from his lab coat. He clicks the pen and then starts talking.

"I don't think we've properly met. My name is Dr. Thorn, pleasure to meet you."

Thorn extends a hand. I reach out and shake it. His grip is firm, a tough squeeze, but not enough to feel like my hand is being crushed. "It's, uhh… a pleasure to meet you as well," I say.

Thorn gives off a slight smile and then leans back in his chair, readying his pen to write. "You seem nervous. Something going on?" he asks.

"Been a while since I've spoken to a shrink, that's for sure. But I'm fine, it's just been a long day," I reply.

Thorn nods. "Understandable. Today's the third day you've been lucid, correct?" he asks.

"According to your, uh… doctor, yeah," I reply.

"I see, well, the doctor and some of the people who have been taking care of you while you were out said that you're in good shape physically. However, when you're unresponsive vocally, we can't see if you're doing okay up here." Thorn taps the pen to his head.

"Please, feel free to be open with me, by the way. I am a licensed psychologist after all. Making sure you're sound of mind is kind of my job." Thorn chuckles.

"Gotcha, what do you want to talk about with me then?" I ask.

"A lot of things, but let's start out small. How're you feeling?" he asks.

"I suppose I'm feeling fine. I'm not particularly thrilled about my... new look, so to speak. I'm still getting used to it," I respond.

"I see, I see," Thorn says. "I may not know how you're feeling, but I can assure you that's something I've been told a lot. Getting used to your new 'look,' as you call it, is very normal. Have you been struggling with that?"

I pause. "Well, it's only the third day, so of course. I still remember what I used to look like, but when I looked in the mirror for the first time, I felt, scared? Is that the right word?"

"Is that an accurate way to describe what you were feeling? You sound unsure," Thorn asks.

"I don't know. I know I felt scared. It's not every day you wake up in another body. It's weird. It still looks like me. I can recognize myself in the mirror. Not just because I'm the one looking at me, but because I know it's me. So, seeing something that's both me and not me in the mirror, I guess could qualify as scared."

Thorn starts writing down on his clipboard. "Hmm, interesting way to put it." He scribbles onto the clipboard. "Now, on the topic of being scared, do you feel yourself tensing up and losing focus of things?"

I pause. He's right; I do. But this question is one that's not geared towards people like me. It's directly towards me. Carter's mention of what they found me like is probably something that Thorn knows about, so now I'm going to have to answer my questions very carefully.

"Not all the time. I used to do it before all this. So it's been something I've dealt with for a while," I reply.

"That's good and all, but this is more of a now kind of thing," Thorn replies. "Since you mentioned it, however, that makes things more interesting. Let me rephrase the question for you. Compared to before your change, do you find yourself seizing up in situations where you're uncomfortable?"

I breathe in and reply, "It's about the same, yes."

Thorn scribbles down on their clipboard once more. "Interesting, interesting. Okay, so let's move on to another one. Do you still feel human?"

"Yes," I reply.

"Good, good," Thorn says. "How about your eating habits? Have you found yourself craving anything that you normally wouldn't eat?"

"No," I reply.

"All right," Thorn mutters under his breath. "Good to know. Now, let's discuss something else."

Thorn writes more on his clipboard. "What's your first thing you're planning on doing once we let you go?"

"Go home," I reply. "I didn't ask to come here, so I'm hoping to get out soon."

"You didn't ask to come here?" Thorn asks, quizzically.

"Yes, I don't know how I got here," I lie through my teeth. "I woke up here."

"Ah, that's what you mean," he says, setting his clipboard aside. "You were brought in by someone on their way here. Two of my colleagues. In fact, you asked to come with!" Thorn replies, a smile on his face.

"I… I did?" I reply. This doesn't add up. Carter said differently. "I wouldn't have asked to come to some place I don't know about."

"Well, you said that during your amnesiac state. It's no surprise you don't remember," Thorn says. "You were brought in, and you mostly sat in your room since the beginning of this whole debacle. Until yesterday, that is."

Thorn leans forward in his chair. "You've been making some interesting friends, Miss Hagen. That chameleon, James. Carter, Paul. Quite a way to start your stay here. It was only a matter of time before you came in my office anyhow." Thorn's expression turns from jovial to smug.

"However, your little stunt, standing up for Carter, it caused quite a stir in the rec area. We've got good medical staff here. Should've backed off when you had the chance."

"That… Paul guy was picking on Carter. I'm not gonna let him do that." I pick my words carefully; it's clear he knows more than he's letting on.

"His fight was with Carter, not you. Or your friend," Thorn says. "It's very unlike… you to do something like that anyhow. Not in your nature… I suppose?"

Thorn stands up and starts pacing. "You see, throughout the first three weeks of this whole ordeal, we've learned a lot of things. One of them is that this change isn't just a physical one, Miss Hagen. It's more than that. It changes you from the inside. It worms its way into your brain, and you start to develop… tics of sort."

Thorn taps on his clipboard. "Sometimes, people don't have those tics for a while, but they do happen. Now, we don't know how severe it is. But the working theory is that every person's subspecies is tied to a tinge of their personality. Some more introverted people, like your friend, James. They'll literally blend into the background when they're threatened. Like during that fight of yours."

It's like he enjoys this; he's practically showboating his knowledge of the fight in front of me.

He turns around and stares me down. "You see, word spreads fast here. I know a lot of things. It's my job, after all. To take care of you guys. However, for that to happen, we must make sure that we don't get into trouble. Someone like Paul running away, that's bad for the facility, but we can recover from it."

Thorn walks up to me. "Did Paul say anything? Before he ran off?"

I go to open my mouth to answer, but Thorn cuts me off. "I know what he said. Carter spoke to me about it. Said that I used his words out of context, said that Paul wasn't having an episode during the night he tore off part of his wall. That's right, isn't it?"

I nod. This guy is starting to weird me out… But I can't leave, not now. If I try anything, he'll use it against me.

Thorn laughs. "Carter's not right. Perhaps he's losing sight of the mission. To make sure you guys are rehabilitated, so he's making sure that we go easy on you. Thing is, anything happening, Paul's nightmare, your friend's invisibility. Those are the tics we're looking for. We assess them, and we make sure that you guys can overcome them and function without relying on inhuman instinct."

Thorn walks up to me and stares me down. "I've always been really good at figuring people out. So, what's your tic, Lyla?"

Is… is he testing me? He must know about what's in the files, but he doesn't know Carter told me about it. So, I can't ask him directly if he knows. Worst part about this, I can feel that freezing sensation again. I'm starting to lose my ability to move. Chills run up my spine. With every second he stares at me, I feel like he's peering right into my head, like he's reading my thoughts.

The silence is deafening. It's just me and Thorn. Him staring me down. Me, sweating, frozen in place, trying to not make eye contact with this guy. He's intimidating for such a lanky guy. What he lacks in strength, he makes up for in smarts. A single tear runs down my face.

Thorn chuckles to himself. "I figured it out." He sits back down on his chair and starts scribbling onto his clipboard once more.

With him preoccupied once again, I finally have some room to breathe. I let out an exhale and manage to speak again. "You... do this to everyone who comes in here?"

"Only the squirmy ones," he says, not looking up from his clipboard. "Sometimes, people have a façade of being strong, and with you being quite the troublemaker lately, I had to see if you were all talk and no tango. Sorry 'bout that."

Thorn looks up from his clipboard. "It may be a little intense, but you guys are just as much of a threat to the public as someone like Paul. We had a guy come in a couple weeks ago, hit by a car on the first day. You know what animal he was?"

"Uh... a deer?" I respond jokingly.

Thorn snaps his fingers, giving me a clever nod. "Exactly. Poor sap was crossing the street and froze up when a car came. Luckily, he wasn't injured too bad, just a busted leg. We fixed him right up, and he's here. Works in the kitchen. I'm sure you've seen him. I talk to him 'bout every week since I got here." Thorn sets his clipboard down. "Sorry again to spook you like that, but it's a necessary evil, especially with something as strange as what's happened to you." Thorn stands up and looks at me once more. "Just don't go causing any more trouble from now on, okay?"

I stand up and head to the door. "Sure thing," I reply. I go to open the door and leave, but Thorn's voice makes me turn around.

"Oh, I almost forgot."

I turn around. "What is it?" I ask.

"How's your sight?" Thorn says.

"It's fine?" I say.

"No, I mean actually, I know your subspecies has constant dilation in their eyes. I assume it's not pleasant. Things are a lot brighter than expected, right?" Thorn says with a warm smile.

"I mean, I've noticed that, yes," I respond.

"Here." Thorn tosses me a pair of round sunglasses. "I've had these extras sitting around in my office for a while now, and one of my employees brought me a new pair today; they're a little bent. Consider it a token of good will, something to show you I'm not your enemy."

"Thanks…" I say, putting the glasses on top of my head like I normally would.

"Of course. I wouldn't be doing my job if I wasn't looking out for you," Thorn says, flashing a smile, the most genuine thing I've seen him do so far.

I go to leave again, but Thorn stops me one more time.

"Oh, one more thing."

"Okay?" I respond.

"Just… Don't let the door hit your tail on the way out. Several other people here have had it happen to them. Said it wasn't pleasant," Thorn says with a cheeky grin.

"Gotcha… Thanks," I say, making sure that I'm all the way out of the door when it closes.

Walking out into the hallway, I have a sigh of relief. That guy, I don't know what to say about him. He's scary sometimes. I don't want to talk to him again. Walking back out into the hallway, I work my way back to where my room is. As I'm walking down the door, I hear a familiar voice. "Lyla!"

I turn around, and it's James, followed by that girl Kellie, and Carter.

"Oh, hey, guys," I say.

"You don't look so good," Kellie says.

"That psychologist guy… He knows a lot about all of us. It's… scary," I say.

"All the more reason to find a way home," Kellie responds.

"What're you talking about?" I ask.

Carter puts a hand on my shoulder. "It's okay, we can trust her," he says.

I scan Kellie up and down. While I'm doing so, she smiles at me and says, "I want the same thing you guys do. I'm… I want to apologize again about getting so excited while meeting you. I didn't know you were that new."

I sigh. "It's fine, Kellie. I appreciate your apology."

"That's a relief. I thought you were going to be super upset with me," Kellie says, mimicking wiping sweat from her brow. "Cool glasses," she says, pointing to the glasses on my head. "Where'd you get 'em?"

"That Thorn guy gave them to me," I reply. "I guess he trying to get on my good side."

"Well, it also means he's watching you," Carter says. "He doesn't give out many gifts, not that I know of."

"Never gave me anything," James says.

"Anyhow," Carter proclaims, getting the conversation back on track, "we need to talk about the phones."

Chapter 8

Kellie

Lyla opens the door to her room and invites us all inside. Walking inside of Lyla's room, we see there's not a lot going on. The room is plain and barren, much like the rest of our rooms, but they never really gave us anything to spice it up. I remember asking someone about it when I got here, and they said that it was a funding issue.

"So, we know where the phones are, but how do we get to them?" Carter asks.

"There's a couple things we could try," James says. "There's always trying to get you in there, Carter."

"I would, but with me being involved in the fight with Paul, they'll be expecting me to do something, especially since I spoke with Thorn about the incident."

"We could try to get the keys from one of the SWAT guys," Lyla says. "With those, we could just sneak in there."

"Possibly," James responds. "However, if we get caught in either of those situations, they'll definitely either keep an eye on us or keep us in lockdown."

"What else could we do?" Carter asks.

Everyone sits in silence, thinking about a possibility of how to get the phones from the band room. Luckily, an idea comes to my head. "What about the vents?" I say.

"The vents?" Carter inquires. "What about them?"

This is my chance; I speak up again. "Well, the vents, this place has a ventilation system, right? And if spy movies have taught me anything, every room is connected to the vents. Me being as small as I am, I could climb through and get into the band room, take the phones, and get out without having to use the keys or put any of you guys in trouble."

I pause but then start talking again.

"Even more, I haven't started anything, unlike you guys." I point to the three of them. "I'm the perfect candidate for this."

Everyone looks at me, puzzled expressions across their faces. I mean, it's a good idea. I don't think there's any better idea. But I also know that they all just met me, so it's like… they might not be on board for this kind of thing.

"I could see it working," James says.

"If it's done right, it could," Carter adds.

"If you guys think it's a good idea, we can do it," Lyla replies.

Carter turns to me. "You seriously think you could be able to do this without messing up?"

I respond. "Oh yeah, dude, you know me. I'm small, nimble, and I'm able to sneak around. It's like I was made for this." I gesture to myself. "I mean, look at me. Does this not say 'small creature that steals things'? Like come on, you know I'm perfect for this."

Carter shakes his head. "You're… very enthusiastic about this… aren't you?"

"Yes, yes, I am, and I finally get to do something cool with this new body. Instead of sitting around and doing the same shit I've always done. It's exciting."

"You do realize that we're not playing pretend, right?" Lyla says. "You mess this up and we'll all never be able to go home."

"I know, I know, I'm just having a little bit of fun. There's nothing wrong with that, right?" I reply.

"I guess not, but we should be serious about this," Lyla replies. "I just want to ensure that I get out of here… with you guys, of course."

"The most important thing right now is finding out how we're going to pull this off, where the vents go, and when we need to do this," Carter says. "We can go looking, but when we do it is paramount."

I chime in, "Let's do it tonight."

"Tonight?" James says. "Why tonight?"

"Well, there's still time left in the day. I can go case the place, since I'm not in any kind of trouble. Me wandering around isn't going to get attention. We find a way in, and Carter lets me out of my room tonight. I get the phones and give them to you tomorrow."

"Don't you think that's a little early?" James says. "We literally had the assembly today."

"True, but they're not going to expect someone to pull something right now. They're going to think anyone trying anything is going to be waiting for a moment. In a sense, it could be their most vulnerable point," I reply.

Carter ponders before responding once more. "So, all I have to do is let you out?" he asks.

"Yeah," I say. "Once I know how to get in, I can sneak around on my own, grab the phones, and come back to my room. You'll just have to lock it once I get back. We set like a time or something."

"And I'm not involved?" Carter asks.

"It'll be a me thing, going by myself. No one will expect me, and you two don't have to do anything." I point at Lyla and James. "I'll get your phones by tomorrow."

"And what if you get caught?" Lyla questions. "What then?"

"I won't say anything about it," I respond. "I can make something up. I'm good at that."

Lyla pauses, looking at me again, scanning me. I know she probably doesn't trust me, and to be honest, I don't even know if the plan is going to work. But I have a craving to do something, anything. I want to feel the rush of breaking the rules, and I know I want to be able to show them that I'm perfectly capable of helping out. So, despite my better judgement, I'm sticking to this plan.

"All right," Lyla says. "Since it's mostly you doing all the work, I guess it's not a bad idea. Keeps our heads low, and if you're willing to take one for the team if you get caught, it should be fine."

"Kind of a weird way to put it, but awesome!" I reply, grinning. Finally, my chance. "Now, I just need to figure out how to get in."

"I could probably help with that," Carter says. "I can walk around and check out the band room. I'd suggest that you guys try to find some tools in the event you need to use them."

"Sounds like a plan," Lyla says. "After we find the tools, what then?"

Silence fills the room, as we all ponder what to do with the tools. James then speaks up.

"What if he hid them nearby?" he says.

"Where?" Carter replies.

"One of the lockers could be a good spot," James claims.

"Wouldn't that be a little loud?" I ask.

"Sure, but what if it's in a secluded hallway, somewhere where nobody really goes. We know the band room is where the SWAT guys go, and in the event some of them are still there, we could always find a hallway that's out of the way. Where that noise wouldn't matter. That or you're quiet," James says.

"I can look when I scout," Carter says. "I've got one of those master keys. Something that can open all the lockers. They gave them to us to check for contraband."

"Okay, so we have a plan. Now we just have to execute it," Lyla says. "James and I will split up and find those tools. Carter and Kellie can scout ahead, look into the room where the phones are, and find a locker to put the tools in."

With our plan now set, Carter looks at his watch. "We've got a few hours before you guys are supposed to go to bed for the night, so that will give us enough time to get this done. We sure we want to do this so early?"

I nod. "Yes, I think this is the perfect time to do it."

"Then we'll try our hardest," James says. "Let's get it done now, so that we can send Kellie to the room tonight."

I put my hand in front of me. "Let's do this, team."

"Team?" Lyla says. "We're a team now?"

"Well, there's four of us, isn't there? That would qualify as a team," I reply.

James puts his hand on top of mine. "We'll get out of here. If we work together."

Lyla pauses and then puts her hand in. "All right, yeah, we're a team."

Everyone looks at Carter, who's hesitant. After a moment of silence, he nods and puts his hand in as well.

"I'm doing this for you guys. Let's go."

"Awesome," I say. "Let's do this!"

Chapter 9

Carter

STEPPING OUT INTO the hallway from Lyla's room, we all start splitting off into our teams of two.

"We're going to check out the art room and see if someone's got stuff there," James says.

"Sounds good, catch you guys later," I say, watching them walk down the hallway. Now, it's time for Kellie and me to start working.

"This way," I say, heading off into the depths of the school.

"So, where exactly is this band room thing? I don't think I've seen it while I was here," Kellie asks.

"Well, it's kinda closed off. It's not really around where you guys do things," I say. "I haven't been down there in a while. They don't let us go down there either."

We pass the library, and I can see some of the changed standing in the halls, giving me the eye, like I don't belong here. With all the commotion going on the past two days, I think I'm starting to agree with them.

"So, there's not really much aside from the band room?" Kellie asks.

"Pretty much," I say, rounding a corner. Passing the auditorium, I point to the doors next to where the entrance is. "They're behind this door. But the doors locked. So we'll have to find another way in."

Kellie puts her paw to her chin, looking at the door up and down. She then turns to the door to the right, leading into the auditorium.

"You think it's linked to the auditorium?" she asks.

"What're you talking about?" I say.

"Think about it like this, right? It's the auditorium, this place is a school. They'd do plays, wouldn't they?" she says.

"I suppose."

"So, there'd be a backstage, and if they're going to put actors in a green room, it'd be linked to the backstage, right?" she says.

"Sure," I respond.

She walks to the other side of the auditorium entrance. Kellie then turns to me and points at the wall.

"Look, there's no other hallway connecting the auditorium to the outside. That means that if they're going to put a green room anywhere, it'd be in the band room hallway, since they'll put the kids in there for both concerts and plays." She smiles. "I used to be a band kid, so this is par for the course for me."

"So, then how do we get in?" I ask.

"Simple," Kellie says. "The projector room."

"Oh, I think I know where you're going with this," I say. "You want one of us to go up into the projector room and turn all the lights off. Making everyone blind, letting the other get to the hallway while everyone's confused?"

"Exactly!" Kellie exclaims. "It's a pretty good plan, right?"

"It could work, but who's going up into the projector room?" I ask. "You could do it, since you're a lot smaller than me."

"Actually, I think it'd be better if you did it," Kellie says. She starts pacing across the floor, formulating her thoughts into words.

"Because, if I were to do it, while I am smaller, and I could go, what happens if someone is in the hallways? What if I get into the hallways and there's guys there? That would make this whole plan a bust. If Carter were to go into the hallway to let me in and he got caught, then he could think up some excuse."

She turns to me again. "Yeah, I think it's better that you do it."

She holds out her paw. "Gimme your keycard. I'll head up into the projector room."

"All right," I say, grabbing my keycard. "But you should only keep the lights off for ten seconds. That should give me enough time to get backstage."

I hand Kellie the keycard.

"Sounds good. Once I see you in the auditorium, I'll turn off the lights," Kellie says, using my keycard to open the stairs to the projector room before slinking in.

Now, I'm on my own, and I don't have my keycard. So, I'd better make sure I don't get caught by someone who's going to start asking questions. Walking into the auditorium, I start making my way to the stage. There's a Wild West movie playing, and I can see a sizeable amount of changed sitting in the seats at the auditorium. I notice they're sitting in groups. Some large groups, some small. There's even two people in the back of the theater cuddling. I guess love can bloom anywhere, with anyone. As I turn my attention to the walkway leading up to the stage in front of me, the lights go out, as well as the projector with it.

Kellie must have seen me. Problem is, I'm not ready.

I start walking to the stage, counting in my head.

10…

9…

This walk soon becomes a racewalk, trying to make as little sound as I can over the commotion and yelps of people. I can hear someone cry out from the bleachers.

"I'm scared of the dark!"

8….

7….

6….

Now, the racewalk turns into a light jog. I can't really see where I'm going, but I know that if I keep going straight, I'll make it to the stage.

5….

4….

The light jog is now picking up, but while I'm moving, I end up double stepping and stumble, catching myself as quietly as possible. However, being one hand short, not only do I barely catch myself, but I can feel my shoulder ache in pain as the force causes me to jolt. I look in front of me and I can see where the hard wood of the stage turns into the painted floor of the stage.

3….

2….

I start crawling as fast as I can, beginning to round the corner to the backstage.

1….

The lights come on, as I swiftly pull the rest of my body into the backstage. The commotion calms down as the movie picks up right where it left off. Holy cow, I didn't think I was going to make it. Holding my hand to my chest, I can feel my heart beating rapidly. For a few moments, I calm myself down and walk to the door.

Opening the door and looking down the hall, I can see the door that Kellie and I were looking at before we started our plan. I'm in the right hallway. I notice the large doors where the band room is right down at the other end. All I have to do is go to the doors, let Kellie in, and check for any entry into the room.

Walking out of the doors, I start shuffling down to the double doors to let Kellie into the hallway. This is surreal. I feel like I'm doing something I'm not supposed to. Well, I am. But I can't shake the feeling that I'm doing something right. It's a lot easier to make my way back into the hallway where Kellie is and tell her that I couldn't find anything. It'd keep her out of trouble and my coworkers off my back.

Although, they'd be at square one. I don't know if I can do that in good conscience. I make my way to the door and push it open slowly. As soon as I can see the other side, I'm greeted by Kellie, with a massive smile on her face.

"Holy crap, dude, that was awesome," Kellie says, slinking into the hallway.

"I tripped. I didn't think I was going to make it," I reply.

"I wasn't tall enough to see much of it, but I did the ten seconds like you asked. I don't think anyone saw you. Still, though, that was super cool." Kellie smiles.

"Thanks, Kellie," I reply. "Now, let's get to this door and see what we can find."

Kellie and I walk down the hallway slowly. I keep checking over my shoulder to see if there's someone coming to throw us out.

Kellie stops dead in her tracks, eyes glued to one of the doors before the band room.

"What're you doing?" I ask in a whisper. "The door's right here!"

"Dude, look." She reaches down in front of the door and holds something in front of me.

It's a pack of gum, one of those small five-stick packs. It's missing two.

"Someone dropped their gum. How long you think it's been here?" she says, unwrapping the package.

"I don't know! It's gum! You're just going to eat gum left on the floor for who knows how long?" I ask.

"Why not? It's wrapped," she says, unwrapping all three pieces and then eating them all at once.

I shake my head. "You are something else."

"Hey, dude, free stuff is free stuff." Kellie replies. "Now, let's go check out this door."

Kellie walks past me and up to the door.

A massive double door stands in front of us. Kellie approaches the door and presses one of her ears to the wall, listening for anyone inside.

"Seems like no one is in here," Kellie says.

She then puts her paw onto the door and starts jiggling the handle. The door doesn't budge. However, it does make a surprising amount of noise.

"Quiet down!" I say. "I would like to not be caught."

"No one's in there! So it wouldn't hurt to try the door, right?" Kellie says. She looks around at the door and then starts heading down the hallway, towards the end of the hall.

"What's that door down there?" Kellie asks, pointing to the door at the end of the hall. It's made of metal; however, the glass on the door has been blacked out, leaving the only source of light in the hall coming from the florescent bulbs in the ceiling.

"It goes outside. Part of this reason this hallway is off-limits," I say.

"So, if I were to walk through the door right now, I would be able to escape?" Kellie asks.

"Hypothetically, I guess," I say. "But I don't know what patrols are, especially with Paul's previous escape."

"Interesting…" says Kellie.

Kellie pauses and continues to walk down the hallway.

"Where're you going?" I ask, starting to follow her.

Kellie doesn't respond and instead starts walking faster. She's seriously not going to pull this, is she?

I start slowly chasing her, gaining on her as she starts to run faster. She's making a break for it? Reaching out with my only good hand, I manage to grab her by the hood on her hoodie, stopping her in her tracks.

"Were you seriously going to run?" I ask.

She turns around with a big smile on her face. "No, stupid! I'm just playing a prank on you!" She laughs. "Now, if you'll let go of me, I'll show you what I'm really looking for."

"You aren't going to book it?" I ask.

"Yeah, dude, it was a joke. Ya know, L-O-L, L-M-A-O. A joke," Kellie says, imitating internet abbreviations.

I glare at Kellie. This chick is supposed to be helping me, and she's starting to get on my nerves now. I reluctantly let her go, and she starts walking to a door on the side of the hallway. The sign on the wall says "Green Room." Next to the door on the wall is a vent grate.

"Bingo," Kellie says, peering into the window in the door. "Carter, look."

I walk up to the window and peer inside of the room. On the other side of the wall is a grate similar to the one that is next to the door, and in the back of a room, behind some tables, is another door.

"See that door in the back of the room?" Kellie says. "That'll lead into the band room. I guarantee it, so, it'll take a little longer than I thought, but if I can get into the green room, which I should be able to, I can then get myself inside of the band room."

Kellie pulls herself from the window to look at the grate on the wall. I turn to the grate as well, and I find a set of four screws holding the grate into the wall. They're all Phillips head, which means that we need to have Lyla and James get Kellie a screwdriver.

The grate is smaller than Kellie height wise, but it's wide enough for me to sick my upper body in. I turn to Kellie.

"You think you're going to be able to fit through that?" I ask.

"Oh yeah, this is no problem. I'm a lot smaller than I was before, so I'm sure I'll be able to fit inside of the vent. It's not that long of a crawl, so I should be okay," Kellie says.

"Okay," I reply, "then we'll just have to find a locker and tell Lyla and James you need a screwdriver. You think you're going to need anything else aside from that?" I ask.

"Just a screwdriver?" Kellie replies. "I suppose that would do it. I can just go through backstage in the middle of the night, and then sneak through the green room to get the phones."

"Sounds like a plan. Let's get out of here," I say, turning to the door. "I could probably give you the screwdriver myself, since it's only one thing."

Kellie nods, and we start walking our way down the hall to the big door I let Kellie in. While we're walking, Kellie trips over some boxes on the way there, falling to the ground with a surprisingly loud thud. I scramble to pick her up.

"You okay?" I ask.

"Yeah... yeah, I'm fine, jeez, that hurt." Kellie groans as I pick her up.

"You seriously biffed it, Kellie. You sure you're not—"

Right as I'm about to finish my sentence, the sound of the double doors we were walking through swing open. Both of us freeze. Someone's here, and we're both right out in the open.

A single security guard in a SWAT uniform walks in. Oh no, this isn't good. We start to walk backwards to the nearest corner to hide from the man, but he sees us before we make it.

"Hey, you two!" the man shouts, increasing his pace towards us.

I can feel Kellie starting to shake as the large man approaches.

"What are you two doing in here? Everyone knows this hallway is off-limits and for security staff only." The man glares at us. I can feel Kellie starting to slink behind me.

"I...I..." I stammer, not knowing what to say. I can't think of a good excuse to give this guy for why we're both in here.

"You what?" the guard says, his expression hardening.

Without thinking, I say the first coherent thought that comes out of my mouth.

"This changed followed me into the hallway. She's been doing this all day and I can't shake her."

Wait... I didn't mean to say that! No, no, no!

"That so?" the guard says, peering around to Kellie, whose claws are now digging into my shins.

She's going to blow it, oh god, I just threw her under the bus.

"Yes… I'm sorry," Kellie says.

Kellie's… playing into it? *Oh god, no, this is terrible. I didn't mean for this to happen at all.* The security guard speaks once more.

"Well, looks like we're going to have to take you back to your room, since staff has lodged a complaint about you," the guard says.

"Can he just take me back?" Kellie asks.

"No, he said he's been trying to shake you all day. I'll take you," the guard replies.

"It's fine," I say. "I can take her."

"Too late, buddy, this situation is mine now," the guard says. "Come with me, now."

"Please don't yell at me," Kellie says. "Then I'll come with you."

"I'm not yelling at you, miss, but I'm about to." The guard readies his stun stick.

I stand in between the both of them, dumbfounded at how quickly this is going south. Kellie starts to stand up as the guard pulls his stun stick out.

"Faster," he says.

Kellie hurriedly stands in front of me. Now, I'm a pure bystander to whatever is about to start next.

Kellie looks at me, with the same expression that you would get from a grieving family member. Before I can open my mouth to say anything, the sound of crackling electricity, followed by a thud that emanates through the wall.

"Don't stare at him," the guard says looking at Kellie lying on the floor in pain. The guard looks up at me, and his expression turns from anger to smug.

"These things really pack a punch, don't they? I heard you had to use one on that bear guy." The guard chuckles.

He picks Kellie up like a football, holding her under his arm.

"They're still looking for him outside, by the way. Nothing yet, though. We'll keep this scuffle between the three of us, if you don't tell them I finally got to test out the stun stick," the guard says.

"…Sure," I say, fully committing myself to the story.

"Sweet," the guard says. "Now, I'm going to leave with this… creature. You be a good staff member and walk out a few minutes after I do."

The guard then starts walking out of the hallway. I turn away, not looking at the aftermath of my stupid mistake. I threw Kellie under the bus. She got hurt because of me. I reach down to my leg to feel the spot where she dug her claws in. It's tender and hurts. Worse now that she's gone. I lift my pant leg up and notice that she broke my skin. I'm bleeding slightly. Serves me right.

A few minutes pass, and I start to head towards the door. About to open it, I feel the door move a little easier than before. Examining the door from the corner of my eye, I can see a wad of gum holding the door's locking mechanism open.

CHAPTER 10

Kellie

LOOKING AT THE tiles on the floor move upwards, I can't stop thinking about what Carter said. He didn't really mean that, did he? Why would he spin some yarn saying I've been stalking him? Does he really care about my friends and me? Or did we rope him into this whole thing and he's trying to think of a way out? I can't really do anything now. I'm being carried by this security guard, and my back aches from where he hit me with the stun stick. Lying limp under the guard's arm, I watch as the tiles slowly stop. The voice of the security guard calls out from above me.

"Where's your room at?" he asks.

"I don't know where we even are," I say. "I'm in room D-9."

"We're in Hallway A, shit," the guard mutters to himself.

"Do you even know the layout of this place?" I ask.

"Shut up, I've got my landmarks," the guard says, muttering under his breath.

"Nice to be carried around by a big strong man," I say, making fun of him for carrying me like ball. "Should've taken me to dinner first, though."

"What'd I say to you? I'd rather be caught dead than with the likes of you. You're creeping on people. Plus, you aren't even human anymore," the guard sneers.

"And? I'm still human on the inside. That's what they're all saying here," I respond.

"Tell me that when we catch you eating out of the trash, Just like the raccoons I shot back home. So, shut up, or I'll test out the stun stick again," the guard snaps back at me.

I don't respond, letting this guy carry me all the way back to my room. He swings open the door and drops me inside.

"Don't go chasin' down people who don't wanna be near you. We've already got enough trouble as is. Luckily, I'm a nice guy. So in exchange for you letting me shock you earlier, I'm not going to let this go between the three of us. You got that?" the guard asks.

I nod.

"Good, better not see you pulling some shit like this again," the guard says, closing the door.

Now, I'm left alone. I can leave whenever I want. But the feeling of Carter making up that story about me following him around all day still sits with me. I can't see a window outside, but I know it's getting close to the evening. I don't feel like going back out. I lie down on my bed, looking at the popcorn textured ceiling. I have an inkling in my mind that what Carter said wasn't true. But I also feel like it's something he was thinking. Something that he wanted to say and finally found an excuse to really speak his mind.

If he feels that way, does he want to help us? Does he want us to go home? Go to our families? What about Lyla? Or James? I weaseled my way into their group, forced myself to do something.

Is... is it my fault? Do they all think the same thing? Do they all secretly hate me? Waiting for the moment they can kick me to the curb? Leave me alone by myself, to go on their grand adventure?

I can feel an aching feeling rising up from my chest and into my throat. It's a feeling I've felt before. Something that I haven't felt in a while. Closing my eyes, I can feel myself drifting in the bed they've given me. The mixture of this pseudo betrayal, and the thoughts inside of my head sends me into a trance, manifesting in the form of an environment I remember.

My home. The last place I want to be. I look down at myself. I'm slightly taller than I am now. Looking at my hands, I'm… human again. Looking at my attire, I'm wearing a teal dress, formal attire.

I… I remember what this is. I don't want to be back here. No… not now.

The sound of footsteps coming from the hallway sends shockwaves through my body. I know exactly what's going to happen next.

"What do you think you're wearing?" a snarky voice coming from the hallway rings through my ears like nails on a chalkboard.

Looking up, I see her. Lisa, my stepmother. The last person I want to see. I try to walk, but I can't move. I go to clap back. This conversation has played through my head multiple times before. I have several things I can say.

When I go to open my mouth, the words that come out aren't the words I want to say.

"I'm… I'm wearing the dress Dad and I picked out," my disembodied voice says.

I'm trapped inside of my own mind. Watching a conversation I've won thousands of times in my head play out the way it originally went.

"Your dad doesn't know how to dress himself. You really let him pick out your dress? Neither of you have fashion sense. You look like a fish, Kellie," Lisa says, walking up to me, looking me up and down.

"I think I look fine," I respond. Going out with my dad to pick up this dress was one of the few memories I cherished with my father. Something that's about to be broken down piece by piece.

"You look far from fine. Look at yourself. Maxis are so out of style. And for someone of your… height… you're not really fit for those, now are you?" Lisa moves the bottom of my dress around my legs.

"You look like you're wearing a candy wrapper. It's not what I would've picked, that's for sure," Lisa says.

"I don't… I don't really care about your opinion," I say. "I'm going out with friends. It's Celeste's bachelorette party. She said fancy. I won't be home tonight." A slight relief goes through my body. The calm before the storm.

"Wouldn't be surprised even if you did come back tonight, I wouldn't notice you come in with that trash bag covering you," Lisa says. "Just so you know, you're supposed to stand out in these kinds of events. I know Mommy Dearest wasn't always willing to give you the finer things in life, Kellie. However, it's like your mother to be someone who's always in the back corner of a room. So, go have fun, and maybe if you're lucky, you'll exchange glances with one of the homeless people on the sidewalk." Lisa chuckles. "Oh, who am I kidding, the only thing you're going to be exchanging glances with is your reflection in the wine glass!" Lisa chuckles to herself. "Be sure to stay out extra late. Your father and I are going to be gone for a couple days starting tomorrow. I'd like to not be late for our skiing trip, unlike last time."

"Have fun," I say. "Try not to freak out when the lift stops moving this time," I respond.

I can feel the insides of me shrivel up. I know what's coming next. I've heard it plenty of times before, but it hurts every time I replay it in my mind.

"Listen here, you little weasel." Lisa now gets in my face. "You ever wonder why we always take Charlie with us on these trips and not you?"

I go to respond. I know what she's going to say, and this is the perfect time to counter it, but just like it happened the first time, nothing comes out.

"Don't say anything. It's because we have an image. I know this, your father knows this, and Charlie, that little angel, she knows it. Ya know she's got all A's in high school, right?" Lisa sneers. "My little angel, and you… Levi's little… kid."

"Whatever you're planning on doing with yourself, your job, your hair, your…" Lisa gestures to all of me. "It's not working, it never worked, and frankly, with that little attitude of yours, I don't think it ever will." Lisa pauses. She's set all the pins up, and she's about to knock them all down.

"It's not like I'm calling you ugly or anything," Lisa says, supposedly reading my thoughts. "It's just that you don't have anything going for yourself right now, and that… well, it brings us all down with it. Your father, me, Charlie. We don't need it."

Lisa walks away, stopping in the hallway, not even looking at me. "Don't feel bad for yourself. It's just the cards you're dealt with, so wipe your face off, and… ya know, go have some fun. Good talk, Kellie."

I put my hands up to my face… tears. Grabbing some paper towel from the kitchen counter, I try to dab my eyes, but when I pull the paper tower from my face, I can see smears of makeup from the hour I spent putting it on. That feeling, like someone just stabbed me right in the middle of my chest, wells up inside of me. I collapse onto the floor, continuing to cry, destroying more of the carefully applied makeup. Looking up at the clock, I've got three minutes before I need to leave.

Then, I hear a pounding coming from every single wall. The pounding becomes more and more aggressive as I sit on the kitchen floor, weeping into a paper towel. Soon enough, the world around me dissipates into nothing. My body vanishes with every thud in the walls. Soon enough, I open my eyes, still lying on my back, looking at the popcorn ceiling.

The door, now a slight knock, rather than a massive thud, is the only sound in the room. I sit up in my bed and wipe my eyes. I'm still crying from reliving that memory. I take a deep breath before speaking.

"Come in."

The door creaks open, and Carter enters, closing the door behind me.

"Kellie… You… you okay?" Carter asks.

He looks at me and can tell that I'm not in the best of moods at the moment.

"I'm… I'm fine, it was just a bad dream," I reply.

"Kellie, I just… I just wanted to say that I'm sorry. I didn't mean for what happen—"

"Carter, it's fine," I reply. I don't actually know if it's fine. I don't even know if his apology is completely sincere. I just… I just don't want to hear it right now.

"What time is it?" I ask.

"It's the middle of the night. I'm coming to ask if you still want to… take a walk," Carter says.

I go to say something, but Carter interrupts.

"I've already walked around the facility. There's no one in the hall, and I'll leave your door unlocked. So… we won't see each other until tomorrow. I don't want to get caught aga—I mean, I don't want *you* to get cau—I mean—"

"I know what you mean," I respond. "Just give me a couple minutes, and I'll be out."

"Sure… Sure…" Carter says, sheepishly walking out of the room and closing the door behind me.

With the soft sound of the click in the door, I stand up and walk to the sink. Looking at myself in the mirror, I can see my face. I've been crying, but it's hard to tell. I can see wet fur running from my eyes down my face. Grabbing my hoodie, I wipe off my face, trying to make the tear marks go away. After a few seconds, I can't see them anymore. I can still tell I'm not happy. But deep down, I feel… content. Like I'm in a better place than I was before all this. Even though I look different, my nose, now dark, my short hair reduced to a tuft in between my pointed ears, my face now wearing a permanent mask… But for the first time, I don't feel like I'm wearing a mask anymore. I feel like in a sense, this is where I'm supposed to be. I feel like… an unfiltered, uncensored version of me. I don't think I was always supposed to look like this, but it's a fresh start. I feel new, I feel… cute for the first time in a long time, even if I spent the past hour weeping like a baby.

I pull myself together. These people I've met, Lyla, James, they need me to do this, and it was my idea. But as I walk to the door, a single thought runs through my head.

What if… I need them more than they need me?

CHAPTER 11

Kellie

OPENING THE DOOR, I walk outside, with Carter waiting for me. He hands me a single screwdriver.

"I talked with Lyla about the plan," Carter says. "She told me that her phone would have a grey floral case with her name etched into the body under it. It's a black smartphone."

"Got it, let's go," I say.

"I can't go with you, can't risk being caught together," Carter says.

"Gotcha," I respond dejectedly.

"I want to say I'm sorry again," Carter says.

"I know," I respond.

"You sure?" Carter asks again, I can feel remorse in his voice.

"Yeah," I respond.

"All right," Carter says. "I'll be here when you get back."

"Okay," I reply, walking into the darkness of the hallway.

Carter responds once more. "Good luck."

Walking down the hallway, it's a lot easier to see than usual. Surprisingly, having night vision is really helpful. Making my way down to the auditorium, I pass through the halls, checking corners to make sure someone else isn't going to be either following me or on patrol. I know I'm not supposed to be out here, but I know that I'm going to be in trouble if I am caught, and if they start asking around, word about

Carter and me being caught in the hallway earlier today is going to make sure they either put me in my room for a while or keep eyes on me while I do… anything.

I can't have that, not now.

Working my way back to the auditorium, the hallway is completely deserted. I walk over to the door and perform a light tug on it. It opens without issue. Looking at the door, I notice the gum I left from earlier today, still in place.

Carter didn't get rid of it. That's… that's good.

I sneak inside of the door and start making my way down the hall-way. The screwdriver still sits inside of my hoodie pocket. As I walk down the hallway, I can see boxes stacked in front of the door leading backstage, the door Carter snuck through before he let me in. Someone knows. I don't know if it's the guard who stunned me, or someone else who decided to box up the doors, but I'm glad that I made that quick decision while being carried off.

I finally make it to the green room, and I peer through the window. There's no one inside. Checking the hallway once more, I don't see any-one coming in. If there's any time to pull this off, it's now. I pull the screwdriver from my hoodie pocket and start going to work on the grate in the wall. Once the bottom screws are out, I set them in the corner of the nook hiding me, the door, and the vent from someone standing in the middle of the hallway. Now's the hard part, unscrewing the top screws. Holding the bottom of the grate with one paw, I start taking out one of the corner screws. Once the screw I'm loosening comes out, I catch the vent grate in my hand. Setting it down gently, I'm going to have to be very careful with this next one.

Taking the screwdriver to the second screw sitting on the other top corner of the vent, I go to work. Popping it out, I gently set the screws in the same corner and move the vent to the side.

Climbing into the vent, it's a bit of a squeeze, but I have enough room to move comfortably without getting stuck. I make my way through the short vent and find myself in front of the second grate. This one is metal, and where the air filter is for the room. Looking to my left, I see a junction, where the fan is for the vent. Just looking at it, even though it's off, gives me the heebie jeebies. The thought of my body being mangled in the vent, I don't know if I want to think about that.

I push on the air filter, trying to pop open the filter door. With enough force, I manage to pop the door open, and as it swings open, it hits a table, making a soft yet audible *clank*.

I cringe. Someone better not have heard that... Hurriedly, I pull myself out of the vent, close the filter door, and hide under a table. For the next minute, I sit in silence. I can feel my ears moving around to catch all sounds coming my way. But there's no one investigating the clang from this room. I breathe a sigh of relief and stand up in the green room, hiding in the shadows. I make my way to the door connecting the green room to the band room. Slowly opening the door towards me, I'm greeted with a bunch of metal crates blocking the door. There's enough room for me to squeeze through on top, but I don't know what's waiting on the other side.

Taking a deep breath, I jump up and grab on to the top of the crates. Looking through the gap into the room, I see rows and rows of hangers for SWAT gear, and boxes locked tight with padlocks.

I don't see any beds, or anything of that sort. But there's one thing that I do see... a Flashlight, beaming in the middle of the room. There's someone walking around the room. Of course, the one thing I don't need right now is someone finding me, especially this far. I climb up onto the cases and slowly climb down into the nearest corner. I'm out of this guard's line of sight. I don't think I'm going to be caught unless they come anywhere closer to me.

Looking underneath the lines of uniforms in front of me, I can see the feet of the guard. They're pacing the room, slowly getting closer and closer to me. I feel like he's coming this way; however, the melody of a ringtone goes off.

The guard, shifting his attention to the lit office in the back of the band room, starts walking towards there. Slowly, I sneak through the many boxes, clothing racks, and SWAT gear until I can get a reasonable look at what they're doing.

The guard sits down at the desk and picks up a cell phone from the box in front of him. He then opens the side of the phone and removes a chip from it. He puts it in another box next to him. I don't know what the guy just did, but whatever he's doing, he's tampering with what I can only assume is the box of cell phones.

Now, I just need to get in there somehow. Turning to the stack of helmets on the box near me, I have a perfect idea. But first, I need to know how to execute it first. Looking around the room, I notice another hiding spot in a clothing rack that's right near the door to the office. Now, to execute my plan.

I turn to the stack of helmets in front of me and tilt the top helmet just a little towards the front. Now, I need to book it. I book it through the shadows to the hiding spot, being careful to not let my claws click against the tile floor. Once I'm in my hiding spot, I look to the stack of helmets.

The top one, being tilted forward, made the stack top heavy, and they're going to fall at any minute.

Sure enough….

CRASH!

CLATTER!

The stack falls, startling the guard. Jolting out of his seat, the guard walks out of the office to investigate the fallen helmets.

Now's my chance. I rush into the office, behind the desk, and look out into the darkened room.

The guard is picking up the helmets. He turns on a radio on his shoulder.

"Hey, assholes, next time, stack your helmets properly. Nearly gave me a heart attack."

With the guard distracted, I peer into the box and look at the phones. Not finding either phone in the first box, I turn to the second box on the desk. Scanning the box for the phone I'm looking for, I notice a familiar blue case in the middle of the box. I grab it and instantly recognize the drawing of a cat on the case.

This is my phone. That's one.

Pocketing the phone, I start moving around the others in the box as quietly as possible. I see a grey floral case. This has to be it, right? I grab the phone. As soon as I do, one of the other phones in the first box goes off….

Catching the guard's attention. He frantically puts the boxes back together and rushes back to the office. As soon as he starts turning around to face me, I hide underneath the desk, taking the grey phone with me, pressing myself up against the front of the desk. The guard rushes up to the desk to silence the phone. The sound of clashing plastic fills the room as the phone's ringer is silenced.

A sigh of relief from the guard, as the sound of the phone being tossed into the second box is heard. I slowly start to peel the grey floral case from the phone in my hands. It pops open, quietly at that; however, I can't be so sure it's Lyla's yet. I must find the etching.

Lucky for me, the sound of clattering helmets once more is just what I need. The guard, now sighing rather than jumping, walks over to the fallen helmets to pick them up once more. With him out of the room, I fully pop the case off and find the name on the back of the phone.

"Delilah Anne Hagen."

It's hers. Now, time to get out of here.

Looking out of the room, I see the guard still picking up helmets. While he's not looking, I run to my previous hiding spot. Now, I wait. The guard, begrudgingly, takes his time to set up the helmets as they were. It takes longer than expected, but eventually, he walks back into the office.

Using this opening, I rush back to the boxes and squirm my way back into the green room. But I'm not out of the woods yet. I still have to get out of the green room, reattach the vent cover, and get back to my room.

Making my way through the vent, I close the air filter door behind me and crawl through the vent once more.

Making my way out of the vent, I start screwing in all the screws back into the vent cover. Everything is going smoothly. I'm almost done. I put in the final screw and am about to head out of the nook, when I hear the door open to the hallway.

Oh no.

The sound of boots. Two of them start coming down the hallway. However, one of them stops.

"Jeez, dude, you see this? Which idiot thought they could get away with this?"

I… I recognize that voice. It's the guard from earlier today.

Another voice is with him.

"What the heck is that?" the other voice asks.

"Gum, that's seriously gross," the guard says.

"Nasty," the voice replies.

Both of the boots start coming closer. Each step making my heart beat faster than before. I can feel my chest pounding in anxiety.

"Why're we down here anyways?" the guard asks. "Aren't we supposed to be outside looking for that bear guy from yesterday?"

The other voice responds, "Another team's picked up his trail. They said that he's up north, just past town. Should be another day or two before they get him."

"I should be out there getting in on the action, man. Instead, we're doing what?" the guard says.

"We're helping Jeff. Apparently he's getting scared in the storage room," the voice says.

"Jeff's weak," the guard responds.

"That's why he's here, we're just checking up on him," the voice says.

I hear a pounding on the door of the band room, followed by a shrill shriek.

"What a baby," the guard says. The sound of the door opening is heard, and the guard, Jeff, answers.

"You scared the buh-jeesus outta me, dude!"

"Heard you needed help," the voice responds. "Ghosts haunting you?"

"No!" Jeff says. "I just gotta feeling is all. Helmets are falling over. I'm sure I ain't alone!"

"Well, let's come in and find the specters spooking you," the guard says.

I hear the boots enter the room where I previously was, followed by silence.

Pure silence.

It's deafening.

Is the door closing?

Are they in the hallway?

Are they in the room?

Can I leave?

When is the door going to close?

Now?

Now?

CA-CHUNK.

Go.

Go.

Go.

GO.

Before I know it, I'm running. Not just running, sprinting, with the screwdriver in my hand. I see the door to the band room closed. I'm free, but I can't stop running. Looking at the door, I trip, but I don't catch myself. Instead of faceplanting on the tile, I close my eyes, and when I open them, I'm still running...

On all fours.

Catching myself, I hurriedly stand back up and look in front of me. I'm already at the door at the end of the hall... The screwdriver is in my mouth.

What the hell just happened?

Taking the screwdriver from my mouth, I slowly open the door and hurry as fast as I can back to my room, keeping myself on my two feet. When I get to my hallway, Carter is at the other end, nodding off.

I wave to him. He looks up and sees me, then starts walking back to my room. We meet in the middle.

"How'd it go?" Carter asks.

"I'm... I'm not doing that again," I reply.

"You might have to..." Carter says.

"Let's hope it's not until I'm well and ready," I reply, handing him the screwdriver.

I go to hand Carter Lyla's phone, but he stops me.

"Give it to her tomorrow. I don't have anywhere to hide it," Carter says.

"Okay," I respond.

"Get some rest, Kellie, you look beat," Carter says, opening my door.

"Thanks," I respond.

I walk into my room, and Carter closes the door behind me, a beeping sound signaling the door's locked, and now, I'm officially home free.

Now... I'm alone, and I have my phone.

I place Lyla's phone underneath the mattress cover they gave us, sitting at the bottom, where my legs don't reach. My phone, on the other hand, I power on, and somehow, it still has battery. But very, very little. Enough to notice one thing.

MISSED CALLS (13): DAD

Chapter 12

Kellie

Dad…

I tap on his name, and my phone goes to call him, but I don't get a dial tone, nor the robotic voice telling me that I can't call. I pull the phone away from my head and look on the screen. The place where my service would be is replaced by "NO SIM."

They… took our SIM cards? Why were they taking the SIM cards out of phones? That must've been what the guy was doing inside of the office where I got the phones from… The phones… they're completely useless! Even more, as soon as I try to back out of the phone app, it dies. Now, they're dead, and they're not even going to call anyone.

Did Carter know? Why did I go through this whole freaking plan just to not be able to use the phones? That doesn't make any freakin' sense!

Okay, okay, calm down, Kellie. Let's think rationally about this. The phones are useless… right now. But, if I can get out of here with Lyla and James, maybe we can figure out how to get our phones working again. That would make a lot more sense… Still, tomorrow, I need to get this phone to Lyla.

I lie down on my bed, my room dark, but I can still see around me, since I'm able to see in the dark now. It's weird. It's not like I'm looking through a filter, there's no direct light, and I can still see fine. Lying down once more on the bed, I don't feel tired. But as I lie down, I can feel my body relaxing, and I start drifting off into sleep.

I don't relive any memories this time. However, I'm in the middle of a grocery store. There's a phone ringing, and I know it's my phone. I don't know where it's coming from, but I'm running around the whole building, frantically looking for my phone, the feeling of something horrible happening to me if I miss this call eating away at my brain. All the while, there's people staring at me, who look either angry or disgusted at me. I don't care, though. My only focus is finding this phone. Before I find it, I end up waking up.

Not in a cold sweat, but just a weird feeling. I think last night took a toll on me. Carter, the whole sneaking around for our phones. I sit on my bed. There's a knock at the door.

"Kellie, it's me, Carter. Can I come in?"

"Yeah, I'm up," I reply.

Carter walks in my room, holding the same Ziploc bag I've been getting for the past week or so.

"Here you go, Kellie." Carter hands me my toothbrush and toothpaste.

"Thanks," I respond.

While I shuffle over to the sink to get around for the day, Carter tries to make small talk.

"You sleep okay?" he asks.

"I slept all right," I respond.

"You sure? You still look like crap," Carter says.

"Yeah, I'll live. Just woke up on the wrong side of the bed," I respond.

"All right then," Carter replies.

I give him back my toothbrush. Carter walks out of the room.

"I'll be outside when you're ready to go to breakfast," he says, closing the door behind me.

"Sounds good," I respond. With the door clicking closed, I walk over to the bed to retrieve Lyla's phone. Putting it in my pocket, I walk out of the room and follow Carter down to the cafeteria.

Walking down the hallway, I trudge along. The thoughts from the previous night swirl around in my head. I know Carter keeps apologizing for the whole issue down in the hallway, but I keep replaying the memory in my head, like the memory of Lisa. I know there was a better way out of it, but he chose the one story that not only got me dragged out of the hallway, but also tased. I can't help but think he did it on purpose. Why wouldn't he? It's the perfect way to get me out of the way. That just makes me think about Lyla and James. I didn't make the best first impressions on them either. They were apprehensive to get me in on this plan. Lyla said, "As long as we're not going to get caught, you can do it." Did she really mean that? Am I just expendable to them? Are they even my friends? Or are we accomplices to our little escape attempt?

These feelings, this doubt, anger, I don't know. It's welling. I can tell. I feel that pain in my chest again, like a knife being twisted right in my heart. They haven't even done anything, and I feel betrayed, lied to. It's like a cold hand, dragging me down. Carter and I stop in front of the doors to the café.

"Have a good morning, Kellie," Carter says, smiling. I can't help but think he's faking it. After everything last night, he has the audacity to smile to me? Tell me to have a good morning after the stunt he pulled? I feel angry at him, but I can't just yell at him.

"Thanks," I respond, walking into the cafeteria.

Stepping into line, I'm stuck, waiting. It feels like the seconds are minutes and the minutes hours. I can see Lyla and James sitting at a table together, smiling. Talking to one another. But, what about? The day? The weather? Me? If they're talking about me, what are they saying? Did Carter tell them about the whole thing with the guard in the hallway? Are they laughing about me getting hurt?

No, no, they can't be doing that. They're supposed to be my friends. I'm getting worked up over nothing. We're in this together, right?

As the line chugs along, I get this feeling like they're going to finish up before me and then walk out, leaving me alone. I don't even see them looking my way. But I have to get to them first. I've got Lyla's phone, and I'm not about to be caught trying to give it to her.

As these thoughts continue to swell around in my mind, festering, like a wound that hasn't been treated, I see Lyla look over to the line and make eye contact with me. She gestures to James, and they both wave.

That single action makes those thoughts disappear, or at least, I'm able to push them into the back of my mind, where I won't be surrounded by them. I smile a little and wave back.

The line seemingly moves a little faster now. As we move towards the line where they're handing out food, it's the same as yesterday. I grab my tray and walk over to the table, where Lyla and James are sitting.

"Hey, Kellie!" James says with a smile.

"Hey, guys," I respond, sitting down.

"You don't look so good," James says, his supposedly concerned expression scanning me.

"Yeah," I respond. "Long night last night, didn't sleep well."

"Carter mentioned it," Lyla says. "We heard about the issue in the hallway." Her expression shows concern as well.

"It wasn't pleasant," I respond. "I don't know why he did that."

"I don't think he meant it," James says. "He's a good guy, one of us."

"I don't know. It's been bugging me all night," I say.

"I wish we were there to help. If we knew that was going to happen, we could've helped you," Lyla says.

"I appreciate it," I respond. "But I guess it wasn't all for nothing." I reach into my pocket and then hold Lyla's phone underneath the table.

I feel Lyla grab the phone and then pull it from my hand.

"You gotta tell us about it," James says. "What was it like?"

"It was… scary," I say. Leaning in close, I drop my voice down a little. "The room was dark, there was a guy in it, I hid in the shadows, and snuck into an office where I got the phones. But I checked last night. They took the SIM cards out."

"So, we can't use them?" Lyla asks.

"No," I say. "They're useless. Mine died before I went to bed. We'll have to find a charger and another means of calling once we get out of here."

I look around to see if anyone else is listening before continuing.

"But I think I found a way out of here," I respond.

"Really?" James asks.

"What'd you find?" Lyla asks, her expression lightening up.

"There's a door, right at the end of the hall where I took the phones. I don't know what's on the other side, but I'm very certain it leads out of here," I say.

"So, we should go then, right?" Lyla asks.

"We can't now…" James says. "It's only been two days since Paul escaped. On top of that, there's also the fact that Kellie doesn't know what's on the other side. If we're going to make a break for it, we should be prepared."

"That's a good point," I respond. "Maybe we need to get some supplies and make our way out of here after we've made some preparations."

"I'm fine with doing that," Lyla says. "We'll just have to figure out what we need."

"How far are we from the closest town?" James asks.

I try to think. "I'm not sure. How long did it take you to get here, James?" I ask.

"I'm not sure. It was longer than two hours… I can't tell you the exact time."

"I know we were going south…" I respond. "I remember the road we took to get here once we left the town. Getting here didn't take as long as it did for you. So the best option is to find a road and then start walking till we get to town… If my car is there, we should be able to make more progress."

"You're not going home?" Lyla asks.

"Not really," I respond.

Lyla pauses, uttering one word after some thought. "Gotcha."

The heck does that even mean? *Gotcha?* Does she think we're going to split off once we get out of here?

James speaks up next. "I know that I need to get home after we get out. If you wanna tag along with us, I don't see any issue with it. We've made it this far, right?"

"He's right," Lyla says.

Lyla stands up, grabbing her breakfast tray. "Anyways, we should think about what we need to grab before leaving. Food should be first on the list, since we don't know how long we'll be walking. Once everyone's out of here, we can reconvene and figure out how we're going to pull it off." Lyla starts walking to the trash can.

James turns to me. "You think there will be a wall outside of that door?"

"I'm not sure. I'd say if there's a fence or a wall, it's going to be like the one in the rec area, so we'd need some way to hop the fence, ya know?"

James nods. "Good point. I think while Lyla thinks about how we're going to get some stuff for the road, I'll come up with some ideas on how to hop this hypothetical fence."

"You guys need me for anything?" I ask.

"Nah, I think you've done enough. You deserve some rest, don't you think?" James smiles. "Take a load off and let us pull some weight."

"I mean, I still wanna help," I reply.

"I'm sure we'll have something once we all meet up later. Wanna reconvene in the library around the afternoon?" James says.

"Sure," I respond.

"Awesome, see you in a few hours then!" James says, getting up and walking out of the room with his tray. Lyla meets him at the door, and the two of them leave. I'm by myself once more. Sitting alone, with my half-eaten breakfast.

I can't help but overthink things. I know in my mind that they're giving me some time to kick my feet up, but I can't help but feel like there's more to it. I think about what Lyla said when I told her I wasn't going back home. "Gotcha," she said. What'd she mean by that?

Does she not want me to tag along?

Does she not want me to come with them?

Does she just want me to pave the way for them to get out? Just to leave me here?

I get up, walking out of the room, tossing whatever I haven't eaten into the trash on my way out. Stepping into the hallway, I start walking. I'm not really focused on where I'm going. Passing people lining the walls, I feel like everyone is staring at me. I start to walk a little faster down the hallway. But the feeling of eyes continuing to be on me as I walk invades my head. Like I've been outed for a horrible crime, and everyone is waiting for my execution. Looking behind me, while still walking, I notice that the people in the hallway aren't actually looking at me. The feeling still remains, though, like two people sitting in a restaurant, exchanging glances with one another, yet neither has the courage to actually get up and talk to the other person.

While I'm walking backwards, I run into something. It's a person. I don't know who's behind me, but I freeze. I don't know if it's another person like me. Or another human, someone who's going to make a big deal about me bumping into them, like Carter, in the hallway.

I slowly turn around, and the first thing I see is a pair of shoes. It's a human. Looking up to see who's towering over me, it dawns on me. This particular human isn't wearing the same thing as everyone else.

He's wearing a lab coat.

It's, it's him.

I look up, and the glare of the fluorescent lights from the ceiling bouncing off his glasses obscures the eyes of the man I bumped into.

"Sorry, I didn't see you there," Dr. Thorn says.

"I'm… I'm sorry, I didn't mean to bump into you," I respond.

Thorn crouches down to my level, like an adult to a child, his face sporting a friendly smile.

"You all right? You look like something's bothering you," he asks.

I freeze. I've spoken to this guy before, but based on what Lyla's said about her first visit with Thorn, I don't think I want to talk to him. Especially since I just spent last night becoming an accessory to Lyla and James's escape.

"I'm… fine," I respond. "I just wasn't paying attention to where I was walking."

I go to step away. But Thorn pipes up again.

"Something is bothering you, isn't it? It's kind of my job to make sure you're all happy," he says, standing up. And taking a look at his clipboard.

"I have some extra time before my next appointment. Why don't you come to my office and you can tell me what's bothering you. Maybe we can figure it out together?"

He smiles again. Looking at this guy, I don't know how much he knows, but what I do know is that I shouldn't be talking to him, at least from what Lyla mentioned.

"I don't know if I want to talk about it," I say, starting to step away and continue down the hallway.

Before I can pass by Thorn, I feel a hand on my shoulder. Turning around, I see Dr. Thorn stopping me from continuing on. He reaches into his pocket and hands me a pen and a notepad.

Taking it from him, I ask, "What's this?"

"You seem like the kind of person who likes drawing. Thought you might get some use out of it. Something that you can take with you rather than having to go to the art room," he says.

"Thanks…" I respond, putting the notepad into my pocket.

Dr. Thorn responds, "Of course. I know how hard it is to find some good paper when you're in the art room. I'll have to make an order for some real paper. For you and the others."

Thorn pushes his glasses up before continuing.

"But, in the meantime, I know it's not much, but you've got the only pen and notepad allowed in the halls. Just promise me you won't take the pen apart. I don't want people to get the wrong idea."

"Sure," I say.

"Good to know," Thorn replies before walking away. However, he stops before rounding the corner, looking down at his watch and then looking to me.

"You sure you don't want to come over to my office and talk? Your next appointment is in a few days. You wouldn't have to come in then either," he says.

"I…. uh…" I reply, looking down at my hoodie pocket, where I put the notebook. I know this guy's bad business. If I talk to him, who knows what's going to happen. But then again, what does he know? If he knows about outside, he can't possibly know about the guy who tased me. We both agreed to keep it quiet. So he probably doesn't know about the phones either. And… he gave me a gift, like how Lyla got the sunglasses from him. He can't be that bad, right? If I don't say anything, I don't think it'll be a bad idea if I talk to him for a little while.

"Sure," I respond, shuffling towards him at the end of the hallway. Thorn's expression changes from a neutral one to a warm smile, as he guides me down the hallway and towards his office. Following him down the hallway, I notice that he's been following me this entire time, rather than leading me. Lyla might be right. There might be something more to this guy than I originally thought. If anything, I shouldn't slip up about anything that's going on.

Thorn walks me into his door and guides me into the office, gesturing to the little couch sitting across from his desk. I take a seat on the couch. No turning back now. Thorn opens a small mini fridge behind his desk.

"You drink coffee?" he asks.

"Not particularly," I respond. "I never liked it."

"Not because of your new body?" he asks from behind the desk.

"The doctor said we're pretty much the same on the inside. I could drink it; I just don't like it," I respond.

"Mhm, I see..." Thorn says. "Well, I've got water and an orange juice I never opened. You want that?" he asks.

"How old is it?" I respond.

"It's from this morning. I brought it back with the canned coffees here," he says.

"Sure, I guess I could have it," I say.

He rises from behind his desk and walks around to the front, handing me a small bottle of orange juice. Looking at the cap, it's still unopened. I open the bottle and take a sip. Thorn cracks open a can of iced coffee and takes a swig from it, before grabbing his swivel chair and sliding it to the front of his desk. Setting himself down in the chair, he grabs his clipboard, adjusts the seat height, and wheels the chair in front of the couch. Thorn, now literally looking down on me, initiates the conversation.

"So, tell me, what's bothering you?"

"Well," I say, "it's just been one of those days, ya know? I had a bad dream last night, and it's just kind of worked its way into the day itself."

"A bad dream, huh?" Thorn says, scribbling onto his clipboard. "Interesting, what was it about?"

"It was something that happened before all this," I say. "It wasn't anything crazy, just a bad memory about family."

"A bad memory about family?" Thorn says, looking up from his clipboard. "You mind if I ask what it was about?"

"I guess it wouldn't hurt to tell you," I say. "Basically, my stepmom was bashing me about a dress I was wearing to a friend's bachelorette party. She said some real nasty stuff. Made me late for the dinner."

"And this memory manifested in a dream?" Thorn asks.

"I guess. It wasn't really a dream, though, more like I was trapped inside of my own body, reliving the memory?" I say. "I know it sounds silly, but just being in that bad mood bled into the real world, and I haven't been having a good day since."

"It sounds like you don't really have much to go back to," Thorn says. "You could stay here, meet all sorts of new people, make friends."

"I wouldn't say it like that," I respond. "My dad loves me."

"Your dad..." Thorn says. "Is he the only one who is around? Aside from your stepmother, of course."

"Eh, they have a kid, Charlie," I respond. "A girl, she's about... three years younger than me."

"And you're?" Thorn asks.

"You have our files, right? From the doctor? I'm twenty-three," I say.

"Yes, I've seen your files. Pardon me for being so forgetful. You know how it is, with so many people coming in and out, it's hard to keep track of everyone," he says.

"Gotcha..." I respond.

"So, do you think you don't fit in with your family?" Thorn asks.

"I wouldn't say that," I respond. "I'm just... different. I don't do the things they normally do. I'm still part of the family. My dad knows that."

"I see. Tell me a little bit more about your family?" Thorn asks.

"Uh... okay. I guess I can. I'm pretty chill with my dad, but my stepmom is the one I have the most problems with," I reply.

"You mentioned that. What about her makes you upset?" Thorn asks.

"I guess just the way she treats me. She sees me as baggage attached to my dad rather than his kid. Like I'm dead weight she needs to get rid of."

"You know she thinks that of you? Or do you feel like she thinks that of you?" Thorn says.

"Oh no, I know that," I reply. "It's not hard to see she thinks that of me. I know for a fact she does. It's in the way she talks, the way she doesn't include me in the activities the family does. She tells my dad it's because she wants to spend quality time with him and their kid."

"You aren't included in anything?" Thorn says, raising an eyebrow and scribbling onto his clipboard.

"Well, she does include me in some things, but not everything. When I am included, it's usually just going out to eat, nothing super expensive like what they do with Charlie," I say, getting comfortable in the couch. "Usually, they're gone by the time I wake up. My dad leaves some money on the table, sometimes with a post-it note, but not really much else."

I can feel myself getting upset with every word that comes out of my mouth. The thought of Lisa, ostracizing me as part of the family, only to mock me in private when my dad wasn't looking. I started asking them not to take me places, as to not give her more ammo for the next time she wanted to blow off some steam in my face.

Thorn taps his writing utensil on the clipboard and looks up at me. "And this was what happened before you came here?"

"Well, yeah. They always go out of state for skiing trips, something my stepmom likes to do. They go all the time. This was one of the weeks it happened. I was left home alone when... all this happened." I gesture to myself.

"And you came to us then? You didn't call your dad?" Thorn asks.

He's right. Why didn't I? Why didn't I go out of my way to tell my dad what had happened to me? I just kind of… up and left. I don't know what came over me. I manage to make an answer up while I'm processing all of this.

"I didn't want to be a bother," I respond. "Didn't want to ruin the trip for my stepmom. I'm sure she's having a party now that I'm gone."

"That's a bad way to put it," Thorn says, "You don't think she has some semblance of love for you?"

"I'm not her kid. She's not obligated to love me like my dad," I reply.

"What about your mother?" Thorn replies, "Where is she?"

"Not in the picture. She left when I was young," I say.

"But going off of your logic, wouldn't she obligated to love you?" Thorn questions.

"I mean, I guess," I respond. "Partially why I'm still mad at her, despite never meeting her."

"I see…" Thorn says, leaning back in his chair. "Let me ask you something…"

"…Okay," I respond.

"How do you feel now? Since you're not with your family, minus your father," Thorn says, a puzzled expression on his face.

"I guess I feel better, unfiltered. Like I'm not hiding myself," I respond. "It's got nothing to do with my appearance, if that's what you're implying. It's got more to do with being able to be unabashedly… me."

Thorn scribbles on his clipboard, looking at me a couple times before setting it down and turning his full attention to me.

"I think I know what you need," Thorn says.

"What's that?" I respond.

"You don't need to go home," Thorn replies. "Not because you're unfit for society, but because you need a fresh environment, a place to start new, a clean slate if you will."

Thorn scoots closer to me. "Say… I let you out, you can take two people with you, whoever you want. Where would you go? What would you do?" Thorn smiles. "I'll be honest with you, we're still in the whole 'getting used to the changed' phase of the world right now. It'd be difficult to start working for someone, to be able to make money. People are apprehensive, especially with the uncertainty of how these instances of instinct sometimes crop up."

He continues, "I don't see much of that in you. You've been here maybe two weeks? We've spoken before, but you've seemed pretty human on the inside to me. But I don't know if it's in your best interests to go home. Aside from your dad, you've got nothing left. Am I wrong?"

He's… he's not wrong. I know that there's not much left for me back home… aside from my dad. But, even if he did let me out, what *would* I do? Would I go home and receive more ridicule from Lisa because now she thinks I'm even worse-looking than I was in the first place? For once in my life, I actually feel confident in the way I look. I hate to say it… but… he's right. I am in need of a fresh start.

"You're… you're not wrong," I say. I can't help but sound defeated. "But I don't think I want to be cooped up in a repurposed school."

Thorn nods. "I agree, this place is kind of drab, isn't it? It's very small, and not a lot of people here are very happy, especially with the whole closing of the outside."

Thorn snaps his fingers. "Tell you what, I think I have just what you need!" He gets up and walks over to his desk, pulling out a file and handing it to me.

"What's this?" I say, opening the file. Inside of the file is a facility, but it's not like the one I've been in; it looks like a resort, complete with a pool, full basketball court, tennis court, sauna, and everything else that would be included in a five-star hotel.

"This is a resort facility that's been built. It was supposed to be for another company, but we gained the deed for it relatively recently. It's open now. It has plenty of people already living in it, and it's reportedly the place with the highest morale on the East Coast! I think this would be a perfect place for you to get that fresh start!" Thorn replies, his expression is beaming.

"I'm supposed to be going there in two days. Of course, if you want, you can come with me and live here. I'll give you a clean bill of health, and you won't have to do anything we've done here; you can just live. You can live as you want to, until the world is ready for you. After that, you can go out and do whatever you want!" Thorn continues.

I flip through the pages of images from the facility. There's people there, all like me. And surprisingly, they're all happy. They're all enjoying themselves, spending time with one another, swimming, playing games, and just all around enjoying life like they never changed in the first place.

"This looks… this looks nice," I respond, continuing to flip through the pages. I stop. This new page I'm looking at isn't pictures of the facility, but two transfer orders. Inside of them are two names I recognize. Lyla Hagen and James O'Shaughnessy. I can feel the fur on the back of my neck stand upright as I read the names. They're going to transfer my friends? Does… does he know about the escape plan? While I'm still processing this, Thorn snatches the folder from me. His expression turns from jovial to cold, but he quickly regains his composure.

"Sorry about that, you probably shouldn't have seen those transfer orders. But since you've seen them. I've been selectively picking people who I think will benefit the most from this transfer. Do you know them?" he asks.

I'm still in a slight stake of shock, processing the information that I saw with my own two eyes. I manage to bring myself together enough to say something.

"Sort of?" I respond. "I've seen them in the halls."

"Oh good, you're not friends." Thorn holds a hand to his chest, sighing in relief. "I was going to say, you should probably keep it a secret between us. Since you three aren't all chummy, it's going to be easier for you to."

Thorn puts the file back in his desk and turns to me. "You'll be coming too, right? I think it'll be a wonderful idea for the three of you to get close during the ride there!"

I don't know how to respond. If I say yes, I'm locked into this whole ordeal, and then I'm moving to a whole new place, and I'm dragging my friends with me. We're trying to get out of here! But if we escape, will they still want me around? I don't know what to do… I'm not sure what to respond with, but before I can formulate a sentence, I hear my own voice come out of my mouth.

"I'll come with you guys. This could be good for me."

Chapter 13

Lyla

Leaving the cafeteria, I start making my way down the hallway, stopping only to see if James is following me. I pause for a moment, allowing him to catch up.

"Jeez Louise, Lyla, you could have waited for me," he says in between breaths.

We both start walking down the hallway.

"Sorry, but I'm on a mission right now," I reply. "We're almost out of here. We just need to prepare and then it's time for us to go home."

"We don't even know what we need yet!" James responds.

"We have an idea; I've been thinking about it all day," I say.

"We just have food and water on our list," James responds. "Don't you think that's not enough?"

"We're going to have to travel light, so just food and water, and a way over the fence," I respond. "You've seen those SWAT guys. They'll definitely catch us if we're too slow, so we're going to have to be fast."

I continue. "Kellie said it took her an hour by bus. You live near here. How fast do buses drive here?"

"I don't live near here, but if it took three to get from my town to here, and the bus normally goes around fifty-five miles an hour on back roads, getting to town is, what, around fifty-five miles? That'll take us all day," James replies

"So, we only need food for one day," I say. "We hop the fence, walk to the town where Kellie's car is, and then take it to your house, and then mine."

"I suppose," James replies. "Just a day's worth of food, and plenty of water for all of us."

We both stop talking as we pass a couple of guards in blue polos, who stare at us as we walk by. Once we're out of hearing range from them, I continue.

"Precisely. We could have it all together by tonight and be ready to go at the same time," I say.

"Don't you think it's a little risky to do that?" James inquires.

"It's been risky since we got here," I continue. "The sooner we get out, the sooner we'll be able to go home."

"Still, we have one lingering question," James says.

"What is it?" I reply.

"We need to find a way to hop this hypothetical fence," James mentions. "We don't know what's on the other side of the door Kellie saw, but if it's anything like the rec area, it's going to have a fence, and barbed wire. Maybe it's not even a fence and it's a wall. We still need a way over."

"Okay, so do you have any ideas?" I say, weaving through people as we walk down the hallway.

"Only one," James says. "But it's a bit of a stretch."

"I'm all ears." I respond. "What is it?"

"A grappling hook," James says.

"A grappling hook?" I respond. "How would we make one of those?" I ask.

"I'm sure it isn't hard. They've got the tools to do it in the workshop, just some bent metal, something to stick them together, and then some rope," James says.

"Where are we going to get rope?" I respond. "Assuming it's going to hold us all."

"I thought about that too," James replies. "The pool room has a broken volleyball net. Apparently it was busted from before we all got here. Thing is, they just have it stashed next to the other net, so grabbing the broken rope would be exactly what we need to get over the fence. I don't know if we can separate the rope from the net, but I do know that it's there. I've heard some people mention it."

"But why a rope from a volleyball net. You think it's going to hold us all?" I ask. "Why not one of those climbing ropes from the gym?"

"I thought of that too, but remember, but they'll know if we took the ones from the gym, so it'll be impossible to actually take it. If we take the one from the volleyball net, it should be fine, plus, it'll be easier to tie around the grappling hook," James replies.

"That's… not a bad idea," I say, stopping to think. "We could totally do that now, but where would we stash it?"

"What if we just built it on the spot?" James says.

"What do you mean?" I ask.

"What if we just set the stuff aside and then build it on the spot before leaving? There's no locks on the pool room door, nobody comes in after the lights are out. We find a way out of our rooms, we could snag the rope, tie it around the grappling hook, and then use it to throw it over the wall or fence or whatever," James replies.

"Okay, so when are we doing this?" I ask.

"We could do it now," James remarks. "It's still morning. At least we can check and see if the rope is a viable option, and I can see if there's enough supplies for hooks."

"Sounds good. I suppose we can check the rope and hook out, and then figure out food during lunch," I reply.

"Good idea. I'll go get started on the hooks in the workshop. Check out the pool room," James says, walking down the hall. "We'll meet in the library to reconvene with Kellie."

Seeing James disappear around a corner, I'm left to my own devices.

It's up to me to figure out how I'm supposed to get this rope… if it's even there. I start walking down the hallway, passing groups of people mingling in the hall. I can hear some people complain about how the outside isn't open yet.

"It's been two days, and they haven't done anything yet!" one of the people in the group says.

"I know, there's that massive pile of rubble in the middle of the rec yard, but everything else is fine. Why won't they just… keep us away from it?" the other one in the group asks.

"Probably because they don't want us climbing on it. You've thought about it, haven't you?" the third one chimes in.

"I guess so. I think I'm just becoming stir crazy with not being able to go outside. I just want to go home," the first one says.

I finally make my way to the pool room. Opening the door, the smell of chlorine is unmistakable. I make my way into the room. With it being the morning, I don't see very many people in here, and the ones who are in the room are just sitting with their legs in the water, not doing anything. I scan the room around me, and just like James had said, there's a net for volleyball in the back of the room, coiled up next to a locker filled with pool items. Walking up to the locker, the other people in the room don't seem to mind that I'm here. Which is nice, since I'm not trying to draw any attention to myself. Walking up to the locker, I notice the net, and bunched up on the floor below it is another net. I crouch down and start moving the net around, trying to find the end. The whole net seems tangled, for every time I pull on it, I feel like I'm getting farther away from the actual end.

The seemingly endless net keeps moving around as I pull and twist and try to make sure that this rope doesn't get any more twisted than previously. It's starting to test my patience. I can't see the people behind me, but I have a feeling they might be staring.

Finally, after enough time, I can see the end of the net. There's a piece of the casing torn open, with the rope sticking out. I take a deep breath, and I attempt to remove the supporting rope from the net itself. The rope gives, and it starts coming out of the casing. I redo the entire process of untying the net, as I stealthily remove the rope from the casing.

Looking over my shoulder, I see some of the people. They're not paying attention to me, so luckily, I'm fine. However, I end up making eye contact with someone who's sitting on the far end of the room. They get up and start moving towards me.

Okay, now it's time to keep a calm head, I can't be freezing up now, and the rope is almost completely out of the net. I have to think of a lie and think of it quick.

The footsteps of the person walking up to me draw closer, their claws clicking against the concrete floor. I stop what I'm doing and wait for them to approach me. Maybe they're not going to be suspicious.

The voice speaks up. "Whatcha doin' over here?"

I turn around and am met face-to-face with a coyote. They're staring me down with a neutral expression, but I'm unsure if they think I'm up to something.

I have to think of something to say. I don't know if they're going to keep my secret, so I need to bluff. Thinking about what I saw while trying to get that stupid rope out of the net, I craft a completely fabricated excuse.

"I was trying to open… the locker, but for some reason it's not budging. I was hoping to get something out of there so I could float in the pool," I say, forcing a smile, hoping this guy buys it.

The coyote looks at the locker and reaches out a hand. Crap, I didn't think he was going to actually try to open it! He's going to open the locker and completely see through my bluff! I start to take a step back as the guy reaches out to the handle and tugs on it.

CLANK.

The door… didn't open.

A confused expression befalls the coyote's face. He tugs on the door again, but it won't open. He squats down, right near where I was, pulling the rope out of the net. I can feel the fur stand up on my neck, hoping that somehow, he doesn't notice the bound-up rope next to the locker.

"Hmm…" the coyote says. "Looks like the doors jammed a bit. Let's try this."

He stands up, grabs the handle, and lifts up on the door, jiggling it. The door opens, and we both recoil at the fact that none of the items in the locker have been washed.

"Just… just close it," I say.

The coyote closes the door and laughs a little. "My god, that was disappointing, wasn't it?" He runs a hand over his head.

"Yeah… that was… awful. I don't think I'm going to be swimming now," I say, stepping back.

"I don't blame you. I think I'm going to get out of here and maybe try to find an open window!" He laughs.

The coyote starts walking away, leaving the pool room. With him gone, I'm alone again. Everyone else is still sitting, talking to one another. Before anyone gets suspicious, I need to be fast. Crouching back down, I start pulling out the rest of the rope. Finally, it comes loose. Coiling the rope up, I now need somewhere to hide it. I look at the locker. I kind of don't want to open it again. It's rank in there, but… nobody's going to suspect that's where I put the rope. I glace behind me one more time, and I see that nobody's looking. So, against my better judgement, I hold my breath, jiggle the door open, and put the rope in the bottom shelf.

Closing the door, I can finally breathe again. My job's now done, so I make my way out of the room and back into the hallway. Walking down the hall, I start making my way back to the library, hoping to find James there so we can continue our plan.

On the way there, I see Kellie rounding the corner. I don't think she notices me, so I walk up to her.

"Kellie, I'm going to the library, you want to come with me? I'm supposed to meet James," I say.

Kellie jumps slightly, letting out a tiny "eep!" when I walk up to her.

"Sorry, Lyla, I didn't see you," she says.

"It's fine. You okay? Something seems off about you?" I respond. Something about her does seem off, and she seems more on edge than she was this morning.

"I'm fine," she says. "Just been a bad morning."

"You wanna talk about it?" I ask.

"No, it's fine, just having one of those days," she replies.

"You sure? If it's something personal we can just talk about it. James doesn't need to be involved," I say.

"Yeah, it's nothing important," Kellie says.

"Oh, well, do you want to go with me to the library then?" I ask.

"…Sure," Kellie replies.

We both start making our way to the library. Maybe we'll make some progress with James, and with all three of us being able to get the food during the afternoon, we can be out of here tonight! I haven't told Kellie yet, but with James here, we can all be on the same page.

CHAPTER 14

Lyla

MAKING OUR WAY into the library, Kellie and I take a seat at a table in the corner, out of the way of everyone. We don't talk much. I don't know if there's something going on with her, but she seems like something's bothering her.

Kellie, shifting in her seat, decides to say something.

"Lyla," she says, "we're friends, right?"

I'm a little taken aback by this question, but I try my best to answer.

"Yeah, I'd say were friends, why do you ask?" I respond.

"I don't know, it's been a very weird couple of days. I've kind of been trapped inside of my own head until I met you guys, and then… I didn't really know what you guys were up to, and I just kind of got swept up into it. I guess, I don't know where I fit in this whole thing," she says.

She doesn't know where she fits…

"I guess I know how you feel," I respond.

"What do you mean?" Kellie asks.

"I didn't really have much going for me in the way of life. I was kind of living things day by day. Then, this whole thing happened to us, and now, I don't even know where I'm at, or where I'm supposed to go," I say.

Kellie nods, giving me a silent approval.

"Everyone's so on edge here, it's hard to communicate with anyone.

I'll be real with you, Kellie, I don't think I've actually gone up and talked to anyone first. Both you and James came to me. You guys made me your friend. I didn't come up to you guys and say, 'hello, my name is Lyla, nice to meet you!' I didn't do that. I woke up in this place, I was completely terrified, and I didn't know what was going on." I continue, "Now, though, I feel like there's something I'm supposed to be doing. I don't know what it is, or if I'm even doing that."

Kellie pauses, contemplating what I'm saying.

"Do you think this whole experience, being different, being here, made you think differently?" she asks.

"I… I'm not sure," I say. "I know you asked me something like this when we first met. I'll be honest with you."

I start to think back to how things were before all of this happened, where I was living a normal life, spending my time with my friends, working my dead-end job, and just trying to get by. I had plans, I had all sorts of things planned out for me; it was like a checklist. Get my own place this time, start my career this time, meet someone this time, get married this time. But now that's all gone. I've been thrust into this new world, this new experience, something that I didn't think I was going to be doing with my life. Mulling over it all, it feels like my life has ended.

"I'm… I'm kind of scared," I continue. "I had so many plans for myself, ya know? I was going to make something of myself. It was just waiting until my next big break. When everything would change for the better, and I could be proud of the person I've become. But now I don't think I'm going to get that chance. I feel like everything I've worked towards has been ripped from me in an instant. I don't even think we have control over what happened to us, and now I feel like life isn't going to go back to normal."

Kellie nods. "I know where you're coming from. It feels like things are a lot different. But I've noticed, even though things are different, this could be something good for us, right?" she says.

"Good for us?" I ask. "I don't know how things could be better for us. I mean look at me. I'm not normal looking. Who's going to talk to us? Who's going to be around us? We didn't ask for this, but everyone outside of here is going to treat us differently."

"Maybe…" Kellie says. "But after I changed… I don't know, I feel like I've been given a second chance."

"A second chance?" I ask.

"Yeah, a second chance," Kellie continues. "I feel like I can live, be… me. Where I grew up, it was all about image, you dress nice, you look good, you go to fancy places, and you spend all your time trying to be someone you're not. Now, I'm not there anymore, and that cloud of judgement I felt… It's gone. I don't feel like I'm tied down by the confines of the people who kept me down, and by that circumstance, the world around me. I'm free to be me. Now, I feel like I'm the master of my own destiny."

"I mean, I guess I can see where you're coming from," I respond. "I still can't get over the fact that I'm not… really human anymore. Like you said, it could be a second chance, but it feels like I've lost any semblance of what I used to be, like… I'm not me anymore. That, and I don't know how my friends and family are going to react to seeing me like this. Are they going to welcome me with open arms? Or are they going to shun me for looking the way that I do? I think that's what's the scariest."

Kellie shrugs, seems like talking about all of this is helping her mood. I know it's helping me. I don't think I really have had someone to talk about this with, besides James. Though it's never been this deep.

"I mean, yeah, I don't think we're going to get over being different for a long time. There will always be those memories of before. Being human, I'm not completely over it myself. But, when I see myself in the mirror, I still see myself. I still see Kellie, just a different version of her. It's still me up here too."

Kellie points at her head before continuing.

"But I know that things might get better for me, because I've met you guys. It may not be under the best of circumstances, but I at least hope that we're all going to be friends for a long time. I... I didn't get out much before all this."

"I know how you feel," I respond. "I didn't do much before all this. I spent time with my friends, but even then, it felt like we were going through the motions. Something that I didn't realize until now."

I sigh, before continuing.

"Now, I just want to get out of here and go back."

Kellie tilts her head, her expression becoming confused.

"Why do you want to go back?"

"It's just this nagging feeling. Like, I had friends before all this. I didn't speak to my parents after I left college. But now... this whole thing that's happened to us... I get this feeling deep down that I should've tried to talk to them before, that even if I come back looking like this, maybe... they'll still want to talk to me. I feel like that's the only real connection I have back to before, and I want to act on that," I say.

Kellie pauses, her expression changing to one of slight discomfort.

"You have a family?" I ask. "Do you... feel like that too?"

Kellie doesn't say anything, seeming to space out, lost in her own thoughts. She manages to stammer out a few words.

"Yeah... I do," she says.

"You want to talk about it?" I say, trying to ease the mood. "I just spilled my guts. I think if we're going to stay friends, you should at least spill yours a little."

"Just my dad," she says. "My dad was really the only one who cared about me. I saw he called me when I checked my phone last night. But I don't know if it's worth it to go talk to him."

"Well, what're you going to do when we get out?" I ask.

Kellie pauses again, seemingly constructing the new few words she's going to say.

"I… I don't know. I guess I was just going to follow you guys," she replies.

"Don't you think it's a good idea to call your dad?" I ask. "You said yourself that this is like a second chance."

"I guess you're not wrong," she says. Kellie stays quiet, thinking about something. Something's on her mind, something that I don't know about.

"You… you okay?" I ask.

"Yeah, but… I need to tell you something important," she says.

I start to respond, but James approaches the table with a cloth bag in his hand. He sets it down on the table lightly, the sound of metal clanking soft but not audible enough to draw any attention.

"Hey, guys, what'd I miss?" he asks.

"Well, I got the rope, and it's hidden in the pool room just like you said, almost got caught, but it's probably not going to go anywhere," I respond. "Kellie was just about to tell me something important."

I turn to Kellie, who looks up at me.

"Oh, yeah, did… did you try to turn on your phone?" she asks.

My phone? My phone! I completely forgot that I had my phone on me now. I look around, before trying to turn my phone on. To my dismay, the screen doesn't boot up. I put my phone back in my pocket.

"My phone didn't turn on. Looks like I'm out of batteries. Is there something wrong with the phones?" I ask.

"Y…yeah, they've taken the SIM cards out of the phones. I don't think they want us calling anyone outside of the facility," Kellie responds.

"Well, all the more reason for us to get out of here," I respond, before turning to James. "Is that what I think it is in the bag?"

James nods. "This is it. If I give it to Carter, he should be able to put it in the spot where you put the rope in. Then, we can get out tonight once we all go to the cafeteria for lunch and grab some extra food. Preferably non-perishables, something that will keep us full until we get to Kellie's town."

"So then that's all we have to do," I say. "We just go to lunch, and then make our escape tonight."

"You, don't think we should… leave tomorrow?" Kellie asks.

"Why would we leave tomorrow?" I say. "The quicker we get out, the quicker we'll be free. There's something about this place—more the people running it, I don't like."

"Lyla's got a point," James adds. "The faster we get out of here, the easier it's going to be for us to make it home, and then, who knows after that?"

"I'm not sure… if I want to go home," Kellie says.

"What, you're having cold feet?" James says.

"No, I just… I just don't think there's a lot for me to go back home to," Kellie responds.

James pauses until he gets an idea in his head.

"You can always stay with me," James says with a grin.

"Stay… with you?" Kellie replies.

"You're in too deep with us now, and you're our friend," James says. "I don't think my sister's going to care that you're coming back with me. We can be pals and not have to worry about all the baloney here."

Kellie shifts in her seat, possibly thinking about how this idea would pan out.

"I guess that wouldn't be too bad. We'll still have to stop in town so I can get my car, and…" Kellie glances up at me, probably remembering our heart to heart. "And… to say goodbye to my dad."

James gives a big smile. "Well then, it's a plan! Once we're out of here, we can get to town, make our way to my house, and we can start fresh there!"

Kellie seems to lighten up a bit now.

"That sounds nice," she says.

"Now, all we have to do is make our way to the cafeteria, grab some food, find Carter, and then we'll be able to get out of here tonight!" James says with a smile, grabbing the bag, lightly lifting it up, and then walking to the door.

Kellie looks at me and then gets up from the chair and starts making her way out into the hallway. I follow her, and as we watch James round a corner, it's just Kellie and me once again. We start walking down the hall towards the cafeteria as most of the people are spilling into the halls to go to lunch as well.

I turn to Kellie. "Hey, you sure that SIM card thing was what you wanted to tell me about earlier?" I ask.

"Huh?" Kellie turns to me, not hearing what I said.

"I said, was that SIM card thing you mentioned, was that what you wanted to tell me? Or was it something else?" I ask again.

"Oh, no, that was it. I just thought James might want to hear it too," she replies.

"Oh, okay, gotcha," I respond.

I don't know if I believe that.

Chapter 15

Lyla

Kellie and I walk to the cafeteria. We're not talking, but in reality, I don't know what to say to her. I feel like I should make conversation. But I don't know what to talk about. We had that heart to heart. I just… I don't know what to say. We're right at the tail end of this. We're almost free. I guess I'm just a little on edge. We're so close, I can feel it in my bones.

Kellie's the first one to speak up, cracking the silence between us.

"Hey, uh… Have you ever felt like you… don't belong?" she asks.

"I mean, I guess to an extent, sometimes," I reply. "I feel like it now."

"Now?" Kellie asks. "Why's that?"

I sigh, before continuing.

"I just kinda feel like this isn't real?" I say. "It's like a dream we don't wake up from. I don't really feel like I belong. I've kind of blocked it out of my head."

"Ah, I see," Kellie responds.

"Why'd you ask this anyways?" I say. "Didn't we talk about this already?"

"Sort of," Kellie responds. "I just wanted to keep talking."

"Gotcha," I reply. "What about you, do you feel like you belong?"

"I… I don't know," Kellie says as we approach the line to go into the cafeteria. "I feel like I do sometimes, but other times, I don't."

We both get in line.

"What makes you say that?" I inquire.

"I guess I just don't feel like I fit in with you guys?" Kellie says, looking away from me as we're waiting in line. "I kind of feel like I weaseled my way into this, but I like you guys, and I don't really want to mess that up, ya know?"

"I don't think you're messing anything up," I respond. "I know how you feel, though. I felt like that with my friends sometimes."

Kellie turns to me. "You did?"

"Yeah. I think everyone's got moments like that. Where you're not really getting that feedback from the people around you, and you can't do anything about it. It feels like you did something, but you don't know if that's the case. You feel like a parasite, or like some kind of pet people keep around, 'cause they feel bad for you."

I shrug my shoulders.

"But I guess life works out in a way where it'll filter out those people, the ones who didn't matter in the first place. You'll be left with the people who do care, the ones who want to see you succeed and be happy," I say.

I turn to Kellie, facing her now as we both move forward with the line.

"Like, take James for example," I say.

"Are you talking about him telling me to move in?" Kellie asks.

"Precisely," I reply. "If James wasn't a good friend, would he have given you that option, even though we've only hung out for a few days?"

"I guess not," Kellie reasons.

"So, he's one of those people who won't be filtered out," I say. "You keep those people close, the ones who do care about you."

"What about you?" Kellie asks. "Is the world going to filter you out from my life?"

Dang, that was kind of direct.

"I'd hope not," I reply. "I think we've got a decent posse going on right now, and you've been nice so far. Plus, it's nice to talk about these kinds of things every once in a while. It was hard with my friends before all this."

"You couldn't talk about this kind of stuff to your friends?" Kellie asks as we walk through the doors and into the cafeteria.

I rub the back of my head and chuckle. "My friends weren't too keen on talking about real feelings. I think we all kind of felt like we were going to bring everyone down."

"I know that feeling," Kellie says. "Do they even know you're here?"

"I don't know," I respond. "I like to think that they're probably worried about me, but until I get out of here, I don't think I'm going to know."

"I get that," Kellie says.

"What about you?" I ask. "You have friends?"

"Sort of?" Kellie responds. "We kind of all fell apart a year ago."

"Why's that?" I ask.

"I guess we all grew apart. People got jobs, started their careers, got engaged, married even," Kellie says. "After that, they really weren't too focused on hanging out anymore."

"Ah, gotcha," I reply. "You ever try reaching out to them?"

"Multiple times," Kellie says. "But they never returned my texts or calls. I haven't spoken to them in a long time. I guess they got filtered out."

Kellie laughs slightly.

"Well, you've got James, and you've got me," I say. "We can all stick together. Then, we can all be friends. Feels like we need each other anyways."

"Yeah, I think so too," Kellie says. "I know I didn't expect to make friends like this anyways."

"Neither did I," I respond.

We both work our way through the line and grab our lunch. Picking a table, we sit down and wait for James. Soon enough, we see him in line, and he waves at us. Kellie waves back. I do the same. Soon enough, he's sitting at the table with us. James now joins the conversation; his expression seems more confident than before.

"So, I got Carter to help us set up," James says, with a big grin.

"Really?" I say. "That's good, so everything's set then?"

"Yeah, everything's set," James says. "Now, all we have to do is wait for the lunchroom to clear out, grab some food, and keep it on us until tonight, and we'll be out of here."

"Look at you!" I laugh. "The man with the plan."

"More like chameleon." Kellie chuckles.

"It's true." James laughs with Kellie.

Everyone seems to be in high spirits now. We're having a good time sitting at the table, just laughing and giggling with one another.

As lunch continues, we see more people walk out of the cafeteria. There's only a few small groups left. We're all done with our lunches, but we're still waiting. However, we hear a familiar voice call out to us, and they join us at the table.

"Hey, guys."

It's Carter, the sling holding his arm gone. He seems to be in better shape now compared to the previous day.

"Oh, hey, Carter," James says. "What's up?"

"Nothing, just came to see how you're doing. And to tell you that I'm done doing what you asked," Carter replies.

Carter shifts in his seat; it seems like something is bugging him.

"What's up?" I ask. "You seem bothered."

"That's why I came here," Carter replies. He looks around the room before continuing. "I'm hearing some commotion from the people in the SWAT uniforms. They're saying that they noticed some phones going missing. Apparently, there's two extra SIM cards that don't have phones."

The jovial vibe of the room has suddenly been sapped.

We all look at Kellie, who slinks into her seat.

"Guys, I didn't know that they checked for both of them…" she says.

"I know," James replies. "I don't think any of us expected this."

"Yeah, that's not the worst part," Carter says. "They're going to be doing searches of the rooms, tomorrow. They didn't tell us what time, but they said that they're going to be looking tomorrow."

"So, that gives us all the more reason to get out of here. We go tonight, just like we planned," I say.

"I don't know," Kellie responds.

"What do you mean you don't know?" James asks.

Kellie sits up. "Listen, we don't know how security is going to be tonight. They could expect something."

"I guess," James says. "But if they search your rooms, they're going to find the phones. They'll probably search all of us too."

"That could happen," Carter replies. "They catch you, it's a possibility that you're going to have to say goodbye to the outside world for a long time."

"I… I guess, I just don't know," Kellie says. "We should try to leave tomorrow morning."

"Before everyone wakes up?" I ask.

"Yeah," Kellie says.

"But they'll see us take off. It'd be extremely dangerous," James replies.

"But then security might be less," Carter says.

"That's true," James replies. "But all three of us can take on a guard, right?" James asks.

"If you're going to chicken out and go all color changing on us, I don't know if that's going to help," I say.

"Well… what if we got the prods?" James asks.

"The… stun sticks?" Kellie asks.

"Yeah. Those," James says. "Carter, could you get those when you let us out?"

"I'm already doing enough favors for you," Carter says. "I'd love to help more, but if I want to help more than just you guys, I seriously need to keep my head down. Letting you out is going to be the last favor I do for you."

"Jeez," James says. "Guess we're on our own tonight."

"It's now or never, isn't it?" Kellie asks.

"Seems to be the case," I say. "We leave tonight."

The only thing for us to do is to get the food. Looking around the cafeteria, we don't see as many people as before. It seems everything's all but cleared out. Looking around the cafeteria, it seems like most of the staff has left as well. There's one or two more people in the back, watching over the cafeteria.

"You think we could… just… ask?" Kellie says.

"What makes you say that?" I reply.

"Well… look," Kellie proclaims, pointing to the person behind the counter. One of the few people left is the deer who makes breakfast in the morning.

"Seems like we could ask him. He's one of us, I think," Kellie says.

"It's not a bad idea. You could just tell him you're sneaking food into the theater for a movie night," Carter says.

"It's worth a shot, and if not, we can just… I don't believe I'm saying this… steal," James says with a shiver.

"Who's going to do it?" I ask.

The three of them look at me.

I sigh. I guess it's been decided. I stand up and start making my way to the counter. Working my way through the cafeteria, I come up to the deer behind the counter. He seems to notice me and leans over the counter.

"What can I do for ya, miss?" the deer asks with a snort.

"Uhh. Hi, I was curious if you happened to have some…. like… snacks back there?" I say.

"Like… chips? Or granola bars or something?" he asks.

"…Yes," I say. "We're going to bring some stuff into the theater for a movie night, and we'd like something to snack on."

The deer looks me up and down, seemingly judging me.

"I dunno… I might, but they're for the facility too," the deer says.

"I'm not asking for much, maybe enough to last a small group a few hours," I say.

The deer ducks behind the counter. "How many people?" His voice echoes.

"Uh…." I respond. I'm thinking in my head. Assuming that we spend at least a day walking from the facility to the town, we'd need at least enough food to last a day. I have no idea what he's about to give us, but I know that we're going to need something.

"Six people?" I respond.

I turn around and look at the group. Kellie nods, and James gives a slight wave before pointing at me. I turn around, and the deer is above the counter.

"Here's all I got to give away. Stuff that won't be missed…" he responds.

It's some fruit, a few granola bars, a can of nuts, and a Ziploc bag of bacon.

"So, we got some apples. I like 'em, and I keep some for myself, but you can have a few. I've got some mint chocolate protein bars that everyone seems to hate, so I don't think anyone's going to care if they're tossed, some cashews that one of the polo guys left a week ago, they're yours now, and a Ziploc bag of bacon from this morning. I've got some saved for the more carnivorous people here. They seem to like it, and it keeps 'em in high spirits. Doesn't have me on good terms with the farm types, though. I think it's giving them an identity crisis." The deer chuckles; his expression says otherwise, though.

"Gotcha…" I say, taking the food.

"Wait a second," the deer says, going under the counter once more. He comes back up from the counter, holding a small bag.

"Throw 'em in this," he says, handing me the bag.

"Thanks again," I reply, taking the bag and throwing the food in it.

"No problem. If anyone gives you trouble, just tell 'em Ted gave it to you," Ted says.

"Thanks, Ted," I reply.

"'Course, I'm only doin' it 'cause ur cute." Ted laughs. "I'm joking, you're cute, but it ain't the reason I'm doing it. I just like helping out. I do, however, expect to have some of that bacon when the movie night comes around."

I can't help but feel a little warm inside. This deer said I was cute. But, I'm a possum. I'm not even a human anymore. Yet somehow, it doesn't bother him. He's not doing it to humor me… right? I don't know, and I'm not sure I want to know. But the fact he said it at all made me… happy.

"I'll… I'll give you some," I reply with a smile.

"Good to know. Nice actually meeting you, miss…" Ted says.

"Lyla," I say.

"Nice to actually meet you, Miss Lyla," Ted responds.

"Nice to actually meet you too, Ted," I respond.

I walk back to the group and set the food on the table.

"Well, here we are," I say.

"Fantastic, all we have to do now is… wait," James says.

He's right. That's all we have to do. We just… have to wait. And then, we'll be out of here. And I'll… I'll be able to find out what's left of my old life. As we get up from the table and start to walk back to the hallway, I keep thinking about the few days I've spent here. I've gotten into fights, I've met people I never thought I would meet, I've felt almost every range of emotions, and even more than that, my whole life has been flipped upside down since the moment I woke up in that room. I still don't have the full picture, but… I look at James, and Kellie, and Carter, and the more I spend time with them, the more I feel like I've known them my whole life.

For a moment, I don't think I want to find out what's left of my old life. We could all just leave and go wherever we want, be completely new people. Live life off the grid as a group of walking, talking woodland critters. Like in those movies I used to watch as a kid. Somehow, a life without anything from my previous life weighing me down feels better than anything else right now. Just living in an infinite vacation with this newfound group of friends, who I get the feeling would do so much for me.

The only issue is, I don't know if I'm going to be able to reciprocate that.

CHAPTER 16

Lyla

AFTER WE ALL left the cafeteria, we split up. I made my way into my room. Putting the bag Ted gave me underneath my bed, I sit down for a moment. I can't help but let my mind race. I keep thinking about how close we are to getting out of here. It's the only thing on my mind. I feel like I'm just running through the same thoughts in my head like a broken record. What do I do when we leave? How long does the walk take? What'll I say when I get a phone? Who do I call first? Where do I go from here? Can I go back to normal? Is there even a normal to begin with?

It seems like an insurmountable task, like something I would have only read about in books or seen in movies. But it's real. I'm going to be breaking the rules. But I'm not a bad person. I've done silly things like this when I was younger. I've snuck out, I've skipped school, I've faked being sick to skip my job. Typical stuff, but they don't have major ramifications. You get caught skipping school, you get a slap on the wrist.

Problem is… if we get caught, I don't know what's going to happen. Something bad, obviously. But how bad? I keep thinking back to Paul, his rant against Carter. How he said they kept him here despite him being ready to go home. I don't want that to happen to me. Or… my friends.

We need to leave. No matter what happens, we're getting out… tonight.

I lie down in bed. I'm going to have to wait until the time comes tonight. I should try to sleep. I close my eyes, my head still racing with thoughts of what could and couldn't happen when I leave this room for the final time, thinking about all possibilities… but as my mind races, one singular thought is still prevalent throughout all of this.

Freedom.

Soon enough, I find myself drifting off into sleep. I don't know if I dreamt about anything. I fell asleep and floated in a void of nothing. My mind, clear. Yet, I didn't realize it was. It felt like no time, and too much time all at once.

Soon enough, the faint sound of a door opening permeates the void my consciousness floats through, and that sound brings me back from the confines of my mind. Sitting up in the bed, I see James and Kellie, both in my room. Carter is standing by the door, looking around the hallway cautiously.

"You up?" James asks.

"Yeah, I'm up. Is it time?" I reply.

"Yeah…" James says. "It's time."

I get myself out of bed and grab the bag from underneath. It's time for us to get out of here, for good.

I slowly exit the room, Carter closing the door behind us three. He takes a deep breath in.

"Well, end of the line, guys," he says. "This is as far as I can take you."

"Thank you for the help, Carter," James replies gratefully.

"Yeah," Kellie adds. "If it weren't for you, we wouldn't be here."

I nod. "Yep. You've helped us a lot these past few days."

"It was bound to happen," Carter replies in a quiet tone. "I'm just glad I'm helping some people get out of here."

"Hopefully…" James says, "we'll see you on the outside."

Carter nods. "Maybe someday, just… don't get caught, or else you'll be seeing too much of me."

He starts to walk away, whispering, "I gotta make sure nobody sees me. Good luck guys!"

Carter then disappears into the dark hallways of the facility, leaving us alone.

"Now to get the hook," I say, starting to walk towards the direction of the pool room. James and Kellie follow behind.

I feel someone reach out and grab my arm. It's James. I can hear him whisper to me, "Sorry, I can't see in the dark."

"It's fine. Kellie and I will get you there," I whisper back.

We all slowly make our way down the hallway, the clacking sound of our claws on the tile flooring the only thing the three of us can hear.

Making it to the door in the pool hallway, we go inside. The smell of chlorine is diminished compared to the daytime, as the pool is covered. Our only source of light is the moonlight coming in from the windows on the ceiling.

We slowly make our way to the locker where our makeshift grappling hook is hidden, our footsteps reverberating throughout the room. Working our way over to the locker, the three of us are standing in front of our final stop before our escape attempt.

"Okay, hold your breath," I say, handing Kellie my bag and approaching the locker. I place my hands on the locker's handles and start to jiggle them, recalling the trick the coyote used when I was getting the rope. The locker's doors creak and swing open, louder than we anticipated, but knowing that we need to remain quiet, we all listen to our surroundings for the sound of anyone who's decided to take a late-night stroll.

With the locker open, everyone winces. Running out of air, I snatch our supplies and close the door, leaving it ajar as to not make another sound.

I nod to the others, and we all exhale.

"Okay," Kellie says. "Now, it's my turn. Let me take you guys to where the door is."

Kellie starts heading to the doors. James grabs my arm once again, and we leave the pool room, going back into the hallways of the facility.

It's nerve-wracking, passing all of these rooms as we work closer to the place where Kellie is taking us. Each one of these rooms houses one of the other people like us. I have a feeling that I need to do something. I need to make sure all the people in this building don't end up like Paul, kept here for weeks, even months. But right now, that's not on my list of priorities. Right now, the only thing I'm thinking about is making sure that I get out of here. Hopefully without any pushback from the staff.

We finally make it to a door. I recognize what this is. James showed it to me on my first day here. The auditorium.

"This is where we're going?" I whisper to Kellie.

"Yeah. This is how Carter and I got to that room where I found the phones," Kellie says.

I nod and gesture for Kellie to lead the way.

Kellie opens the door, softly, and the three of us sneak inside.

The auditorium is a lot darker than I remember, most likely because there's not a movie being played on the projector in the middle of the room. Fortunately, I'm able to see in the dark. Something that I didn't think I'd need but am extremely glad to have.

Kellie points to the walkway leading onto the stage and gestures for us to follow her. We all walk as quietly as we can, making sure to make as little noise as possible. The closer we get to the stage, the easier it is to hear footsteps on the wooden floor. This is what the auditorium is made for. I didn't think that it would be so much of an issue.

Continuing to sneak onto the stage, I look back to see if James is okay. He's still holding on to me. He can't see me or Kellie, but he's looking around, as if he's trying to force his eyes to see what we do. I want to say something, let him know we're almost there, but talking now would be a jail sentence.

Quickly enough, we make it backstage, and Kellie points to a door on the far side of the backstage. The three of us approach it. Walking up to the door, Kellie looks at it before attempting to open it. But it's not opening completely.

Kellie looks at me and makes a square with her hands, then points to the door. I tilt my head in confusion. Kellie frowns and makes another gesture. She makes the box shape again and then imitates someone putting the shape down in front of the door. Oh…. I understand now. There's something blocking the door. I nod and let go of James, who starts moving his hands around, trying to feel out where we are.

Kellie makes a motion, telling me to help her push the door open. I walk up to the door next to Kellie, and we push the door. It moves a little more, but it's not open enough for us to fit through. Kellie steps back and looks at me again. Her expression changes from confused to pained, like she knows what she's about to propose is a bad idea.

She then does a gesture of her walking towards the door with her shoulder. I know exactly what she's proposing. She wants to bash the door open.

I look at the door and back at Kellie. She points to the hallway and nods. I know what she's saying. "We're almost there."

Nodding in approval, I walk back to James, who's standing behind us, still looking around at nothing. I grab him and walk him to the door, put his hand up against it, and then put him in the pose Kellie was doing. He seemingly catches on and nods.

I interlock my arm with James, to prevent him from running into anything, and Kellie stands next to me.

She holds her hand up and counts down. 3… 2… 1…

We all charge at the door. After a *thud*, it moves more this time.

We all step back, light now seeping into the room. Whatever's on the other side of the door, the lights in that room are on. James blinks a few times and looks directly at us. He removes his arm from me and nods. Kellie counts down again.

3… 2… 1…

We all charge.

THUD.

The doors are opened more, more light coming into the room. Kellie raises her hand again as we ready ourselves. James finally can see what we're doing. Letting go of me, getting into position, he gives me a nod.

3… 2… 1…

We all charge.

THUD…

CRASH.

KLANG.

Oh… Oh no.

Something fell over. Kellie tugs on my arm and points to the door. It's open enough for us to fit through. Once we go through this door, we're going to have to start running.

We all squeeze through the door. Kellie first, then myself, then James.

Once we're through, we see a long hallway and a set of double doors, with the windows blacked out. That's it… That's the outside.

Kellie looks at us.

"Run," she says.

She doesn't have to tell me twice. James, assembling the grappling hook, looks up and starts running with us, rolling up the rope, getting it ready to throw.

Booking it down the hallway, we get closer and closer to the door. Closer… and closer… to freedom.

We make it to the doors, and Kellie pushes the first one. It's open. That's one, but there's another right after, inside of the little room that most schools have. Spending so much time in this place, I started to forget that it used to be a school.

Shaking the thoughts from my head and refocusing on our goal, Kellie pushes the second door open.

I grab James, who's tying the final knot on the grappling hook, and pull him through the doors with us.

Kellie opens the second door. We all walk out, and we're greeted with an open area and a brick wall at the end of a yard. The wall's constructed fairly quickly, built over the parking lot of what was once the school. A large metal door is sitting on the side leading out to what's presumably the road, while the wall directly in front of us leads into a wooded forest.

Being hit with fresh air for the first time in days, it feels… good. Finally, we're at the final stretch.

THOOM.

THOOM.

THOOM.

Lights, bright lights. Three massive spotlights illuminate our position, and the doors we just exited out of swing open.

"Ah, you're… right on time," says a familiar voice.

It's him. Dr. Thorn.

"Hello, hello! You guys going camping?" he says with a laugh as we're surrounded by the men in SWAT uniforms.

"Thorn." I groan. This guy, how did he know we we're leaving?

"I'm sure you're quite surprised," Thorn says, pacing around the outside of the circle of men surrounding us. "Just how did Dr. Thorn know we were going to be leaving tonight? What tipped him off?"

Thorn laughs.

"Seriously? You think I wouldn't find out. You're all sloppy," Thorn says, his tone becoming more direct.

"I knew something was up the moment you stepped into my office, Lyla. Your demeanor, your fight with Paul, your friendship with Carter? But I needed proof. I can't just confront you without enough information to know exactly what you're up to."

Thorn peers between the heads of the men who encompass our trio.

"First, the cell phones. You have them, I know. Why would just two cell phones go missing? Why not the whole box? Doesn't matter, they're useless."

Thorn paces around us.

"Just a reminder of the lives you used to lead. I've known about the phones since the morning they were taken. Just because you make deals with guards, Kellie, doesn't mean they keep their end of the bargain."

Kellie shudders.

Deal? What deal? What the heck is this guy talking about?

"Oh, and of course, Lyla, you remember my friend, right? Nice fella, calls himself Ted. We talked about him before."

Ted? Oh crap, that guy. That was him!

"You know," Thorn says with a sly grin. "He's really bummed out that you didn't bother to come in for movie night. It's a shame really."

"You're not going to let us go, are you?" James calls out from the chaos.

"James, James. I thought we were pals! You've done nothing but be a good resident! Why are you letting yourself get caught up with such... bad influences," Thorn retorts.

"I have a family," James says, "I need to go—"

Thorn interrupts him. "Ah, ah! You *had* a family. They're not a part of the life you're living right now. In fact, you three... you three don't even exist!

"We... don't exist?" Kellie asks. "What're you talking about?"

"I'd rather not spoil it. Especially since you've been very good at not spoiling surprises." Thorn chuckles.

"Surprises?" I ask, turning to Kellie. "What're you talking about?"

"Lyla... No, wait. It was about—" Kellie tries to speak but is interrupted by Thorn once more.

"Wait, I'd like to tell her. You see, I've planned a bit of a trip for the four of us. We're going to another facility on the East Coast. It's much nicer than the one we're at right now. I told Kellie about it, she saw you two were invited, and agreed to come along!"

"You… you what?" James asks, turning to Kellie.

"NO! Wait, you don't understand! It's not like that!" Kellie says.

"Oh, but it is. You put everyone right where I need them, and under the perfect cover too! Not only can I move you troublemakers somewhere else, farther away from your 'homes,' but I can also make an example of you as well. All I had to do is wait until it was put right into my lap." Thorn laughs.

Thorn gestures to the guards.

"Just rough 'em up. I still have a lot to talk about on the drive, so… Nothing severe, make sure they know their place."

The guards start closing in on us.

Kellie…. What did you do?

CHAPTER 17

Lyla

WE ALL GO back-to-back with one another, James reluctantly readying himself for the guards coming to us. Kellie attempts to run in between the guards. She makes it through but is swiftly grabbed by two guards, who surround her and start wailing on her with their stun batons.

The guards finally close in on both of us. A swing from one of their batons comes towards my head. I try to block it with my arm, but all it does is change where the pain was going to end up. The loud *thwack* of dense rubber meeting flesh rings out through the commotion, as James is knocked down to his knees. Three guards take him on, while I'm left with the other three.

I attempt to get some punches in, but with my fists against their SWAT gear, it's not doing much. It feels hopeless. I'm fighting with all of my strength, but nothing is working. Another swing. I'm hit in the leg. Stumbling backwards, I ready myself for another blow, trying to remember when the last time I've been in a fight was, and how that could help me.

But reminiscing isn't going to help, as I'm thrown down once more. The guards continue to circle in on the three of us. Kellie is still holding strong, fighting against the people who have taken joy in beating her senseless. Another blow, this time on the head. I collapse onto the floor, a loud, unbearable ringing in my ears the only thing my mind can process. Lying on my side, trying to get up, I'm hit again, but not with one of the stun batons that I've been beat down with. Instead, the sharp pain of electricity is being forced into my body, from one of the cattle prods that was used by Carter when he was confronting Paul. I can feel every muscle in my body tense up, as the feeling of electricity crawls through my nervous system like barbed wire.

Looking outside of the circle of guards, I can see James, in the same position as me, being hit time and time again with stun batons and cattle prods. I can see the look on his face; it's indistinguishable from the thought that's slowly forming in my mind.

"It's over... we lost."

But I won't let it be. It can't be. We've got too much to live for to be condemned to this facility, to be stuck inside, never to see the light of day again. If Paul can escape, then we can too...

I attempt to stand up, getting on all fours, readying myself to take a stance and fight back, but I'm hit again in the back by the cattle prod. I collapse again. I can see Kellie, now sprawled out on the ground. She's completely given up. We both make eye contact. Her expression is different. James's was one of sorrow, but Kellie's is one of regret. Tears billow down from her face. I know she's sorry about something. But what is it? Did she set us up? Why didn't she tell us about Thorn's plan? Why didn't we leave as soon as possible? Why did we bring her with us? We could've done this alone! I know we could have!

I'm hit once more with the cattle prod. This time, though, I don't feel like my blood is replaced with barbed wire. Instead, I feel... warm.

It must be the adrenaline in my veins now, but I feel like I've been given a second wind. I start to get up, and the cattle prod hits me again. That warm feeling strengthens. I get back on my hands and knees. Looking down at my hands, I don't believe what I'm seeing. Arcing onto the ground from my fingertips is... electricity.

It must be the adrenaline.

There's no way that what's happening is real, but I'm looking at it, and it is. This is… this is like Paul. He controlled the ground…

I'm hit again with the cattle prod, and the warmth from the electricity inside of me increases again. I feel like I'm invigorated with more energy. I need to use it. I need to help my friends escape. I stand up, pushing my hands outward towards the guards surrounding me. The electricity from my hands transfers its energy to their bodies, causing them to cease all movement, knocking them to the ground.

Now, I've got the attention from everyone else. The guards on James and Kellie turn towards me. Arcs and bolts of blue emanate from my body. Standing up, I'm filled with a new vigor. The air around me smells clean, sweet, mixed with a burning metal.

With everyone's attention drawn to me, I can see James finally starting to get up. Kellie isn't moving. I look at James, who nods in agreement.

The guards charge at me, and I start fighting back, the same way I was doing before, but now I'm able to hold my ground. One aims to swing their stun baton at me, but I'm able to catch it this time, sending shocks through their body, as their free hand swings directly at my head.

I'm hit in the head, but now, I'm angry. That unbridled rage, the need for freedom, and the electricity combined make me tank the brunt of the blow.

Using my newfound powers, I'm able to push him off me, sending the guard through the air, and into the bushes beside the door that they came in.

Two more come at me and attempt to grab me by both of my arms. They're stopped by my grasp, completing a circuit of flesh and bone. I expel enough electricity to push them off of me and leave them groaning on the floor.

James stands up and runs over to Kellie, picking her up and running to the wall. He starts undoing the grappling hook, attempting his escape, while Kellie lies on the floor, still refusing to move.

The door opens again, Thorn stepping out into the parking lot once more, but instead of seeing us incapacitated, he sees me and the majority of his guards unconscious.

"This is… unexpected," Thorn says.

"I'm not having it," I reply.

Thorn shakes his head. "It's only going to get worse from here on out. You and your friends jump that wall, you're going to be running for a very long time."

"At least we'll be free," I say.

"Free, but hunted," Thorn replies. "Like prey. You're dangerous, Ms. Hagen. Even now, with this… light show you're doing."

"It's not light show," I say.

"I'm well aware," Thorn says. "Just like Paul's stunt was no fluke either."

Thorn pulls out a walkie talkie. "Last chance, Ms. Hagen. You either come with me and live a comfortable life, or you run, and you don't stop, until either we find you or someone else who's not as kind as us does."

I can only see red now. This guy, who does he think he is, giving me an ultimatum? This piece of shit, this one guy who thinks that he's better than us because, what? He's the same as we were before all this? He's somehow better? I'm still me! I'm still able to live my own life!

I notice on the ground that one of the screws holding the guard's armor plating in place is on the floor. Taking it in my hand, I look at Thorn once more.

"I'll take my chances," I reply, before hurling the screw as hard as it can at him. I reach out and can feel the heat from my chest move into my arm, and then into my hand, electricity sparking out of my fingers, arcing onto the screw, which is mere feet away from Thorn. This arc of electricity diverges right into Thorn's body, and a loud crackle is heard, followed by Thorn's pained scream.

He collapses onto the ground. His arm clenches his face. He picks up the walkie talkie, sputtering words out.

"S-s-s-shoot… on… sight…. Outside."

The sound of doors opening all around the facility are heard.

I'm still in a haze of red. My breathing is heavy, and I taste metal. The muffled sound of someone yelling starts to come to me.

"LYLA!"

I turn around, and James is staring at me, his expression one of worry. Kellie's now moving again, readying herself to climb up the grappling hook.

I start running to where they're at, Kellie making her way to the top of the wall. Standing on the top, Kellie waves to me while James is climbing, only to hear gunfire and jump off the wall. I turn around and see some medical personnel helping Thorn up, who's slumped over. Surrounding them are guards, who are aiming at us with weapons and starting to open fire.

James scrambles up the rope, and now it's my turn. I climb as fast as I can up the rope, the sound of whizzing ammunition and crumbling concrete all around me. I make it to the top and jump down. Once we're down, we see flashlights appear over the wall.

It's time to run.

The three of us start booking it through the woods, trees expanding as far as the eye can see. We don't know where we're going; we just know one thing.

We need to go, now.

James is being led by Kellie, as I'm following behind them both. The sound of snapping twigs and crumpling leaves is the only thing the three of us can hear.

I'm brought back to the first thing I remember before all of this… wandering through the woods. Not knowing where I am. That feeling terrifies me. I know that I'm not going to wake up somewhere new when this is all over, but if I don't run now… I don't think I'm going to wake up at all.

Flashlights follow us into the woods. We're not spotted, but we know that they're closing in. I hear Kellie yell something to us.

"Look! Up ahead!"

Some lights! And not flashlights. They're streetlights. We must be close to the road! I feel slightly more at ease, but the flashlights are still chasing us.

The road becomes closer and closer, until we see a van approach the road, brandished with the same symbol that's sewn into the shirts and gear of the facility staff.

This isn't good. The three of us turn to the right and start running parallel with the road before the doors open.

Kellie looks at me. "Can you do something? Use whatever super-powers you just found out you had?"

I reach my hand out to expel more electricity, but nothing happens. I feel cold, like I've been standing outside in the freezing rain for hours on end.

"I… I can't!" I say.

"We need to hide!" Kellie says, looking around.

"Why… why don't we hide… hide in a tree?" James replies between breaths.

Kellie looks around, James still being dragged behind Kellie. Kellie points to a massive tree deeper into the woods.

"Go there!" Kellie shouts to me.

I follow Kellie up to the tree, who places James's hand on the tree. As he starts to climb up the tree, Kellie does the same, scampering up to one of the branches hidden amongst the leaves. Once I have enough room, I join them, climbing up the tree and positioning myself on a separate branch.

All of us remain quiet, as the sound of boots rumble through the woods. Flashlights poke holes in between the branches, however, I can't see anything, the leaves blocking my vision of the ground.

I can hear James whisper from above us.

"You… you guys okay?" James says.

"Yeah, I'm hidden," Kellie replies.

I go to open my mouth, but I can't say anything, I'm starting to feel woozy. The air brushing up against me is freezing. I-I think the adrenaline is wearing off.

"Lyla?" James asks.

The world begins spinning.

"Lyla?" James asks again.

I go to speak again, but nothing comes out.

Everything starts to fade away…

"Lyla!" Kellie whisper yells.

The last thing I remember is feeling like I'm losing my balance.

CHAPTER 18

Lyla

I CAN FEEL my senses coming back to me. I half expected to feel the horrid pain of falling two stories to the ground. But I don't feel that.

As I open my eyes to see where I am exactly, I find out that I'm nowhere near the ground at all.

I'm upside down.

I start panicking, waving my arms around. How am I upside down? Why am I not falling? I look up, or... down, to the ground. James is down there, staring up at me, confused, although I don't know how well he can see me. It's still dark.

I start to shift my gaze upwards to where I fell from the tree. I see Kellie on the branch I was standing on, whispering to me.

"Stop flailing around! You're actually going to fall if you do!"

I stop moving and realize that the only reason I'm not falling is because my tail is wrapped around the branch, holding me upwards.

This is it, isn't it? Getting superpowers, planning an escape from an insane rehab facility, those didn't feel weird or unnatural. But this, hanging upside down from a tree like an actual possum. This is what's weird. I feel disgusted, exposed, like my friends shouldn't be seeing me like this. But there they both are, staring at me like I'm more of a freak than anyone else around here. It's that same feeling from when I first woke up. It's muted, but it's still there, hanging in the back of my mind.

Kellie reaches out to me with her hand. I grab her hand, and she helps me up onto the branch.

"Jeez, dude, you almost fell there," Kellie says.

"Almost," I reply.

"You like… passed out there for a second," Kellie says, "Did you… do that thing with your tail on purpose?"

"If I did, I wouldn't be waving my arms around, freaking out," I say.

Kellie and I start making our way down the tree. Kellie goes first, and I follow.

"Why're you so bent out of shape about it? It saved your life…" Kellie says. "Well, maybe not saved your life, but you didn't get hurt because of it."

"'Cause it feels weird," I say. "I shouldn't be doing that."

"You also shouldn't be shooting lightning from your hands either," Kellie replies.

"I guess, but at least shooting lightning out of my hands isn't me acting like a freaking woodland creature. That's what makes it weird," I respond.

"I guess," Kellie responds. "But… that's just kind of who we are now. You're going to have to get used to it sooner or later, and let's be honest, if you weren't a possum, you probably would have fallen on your head, and who knows if you would wake up from that."

"I guess," I say.

We both jump off the tree and make it to the ground, James is standing there waiting for us.

"I'm glad you're okay," James says. "I could have sworn you fell."

"Yeah, I'm fine," I respond. "Now that we've got some time. Kellie." I turn to her.

"Yeah?" Kellie says.

"What's up with this whole transfer thing you forgot to mention to us?" I ask.

"Oh… That," Kellie says, stepping back a little.

"You were hiding something from us. He mentioned a deal with a guard," James chimes in. "Why?"

"It's not like that!" Kellie says, stepping farther away.

I close the distance. "Were you setting us up to be caught like that? Are you working with the facility?"

"No! No! You have it all wrong," Kellie replies, stepping back.

"Then tell us," I say.

Kellie looks terrified, like a kid about to get picked on by someone who's way bigger than them. But she takes a deep breath and starts talking.

"I was in Thorn's office," Kellie begins.

"Why?" James asks.

"I was just… asked to go," Kellie says. "He gave me this notepad and stuff." Kellie pulls a notepad out of her hoodie. "I guess it was kind of like your glasses, Lyla. I didn't want to be suspicious, so I went."

I reach to the top of my head, the glasses remaining there. So, this guy gave her a "gift" too?

"I don't know how he knew I draw, but he did," Kellie continues. "But I just kind of ended up talking to him. I didn't think he'd know about the phones or anything like that, so I thought I was in the clear. I go in there and start talking to him, and he mentions that I should have a "change of scenery" since I don't really have that much to go back to."

"Which was the transfer," James says.

"Yeah," Kellie says. "I saw you guys in the file, in the transfer. He had the whole thing planned out and invited me to go, saying that we could all be friends in the new facility."

Kellie pauses.

"But the transfer was supposed to be tomorrow morning. And since we were leaving tonight, I thought if I told you guys, we'd rush, and things would go south. But it happened anyways. I didn't think he'd play me like that."

"So, you're not working for them?" James asks. "What about the deal with the guard?"

"NO! Why would I?" Kellie snaps at James. "That was the thing I was actually trying to tell you about earlier!" Kellie turns to me. "That was it, but I thought about it, and I thought it'd be worse if I told you."

We all sit in silence, contemplating Kellie's confession.

Kellie continues. "When Carter and I scouted the location for the phones, he spun some yarn, saying I was following him. So the guard hit me with one of those stun sticks and said he wouldn't report me if I didn't tell anyone he used it on me unprovoked…"

Is she telling the truth? Was she really going to tell us and then decided not to? What would have happened if we did find out? Would things have gone better if we knew first? Or would things have turned out the same?

"I have one more question," James says.

"Sure," Kellie replies.

"Can we still trust you?" James asks. "I'd like to go home as much as anyone else, and you've helped us throughout this whole thing. But you kept something from us. I guess I can understand why. And we don't really know what would have happened if you had told us. But I just want to know if you're going to do something like that again."

Kellie sighs, standing there. The three of us in a circle. I have… mixed feelings. I want to believe Kellie. She's our friend, right? But her showing up, getting involved so quickly, helping us. Now, we find out she's hiding information. Can we really trust her?

"Yes," Kellie says. "What I did sounds… selfish. But I did it 'cause I wanted us to get out of here without being reckless. It didn't go that way… I know you guys can't… really trust me right now. But I'm asking that you guys don't just… leave me out here."

James looks at me. I can tell by the look on him that he's asking me to give her another chance. It seems that he knows that we should still take her along. I agree with him, but I don't know what the ramifications of taking Kellie with us is going to be.

I step back.

"All right, I believe you," I say.

James nods. "You were in a tight spot and made a quick decision. We don't know what would have happened if you told us. But now that it's over, there's not really anything that can be done about it."

Kellie nods. "I promise you guys I did what I did to help you guys. I wouldn't try to sabotage our escape."

"I believe you," James says.

"You'll have to prove it to us," I say. "Next time."

"Okay." Kellie nods.

"Let's go," James says. "We've got a ways to go before we make it to the town, and Kellie's car."

I nod. "Which way did you guys come from to get here?" I ask.

"We went south," Kellie says. "So, if we're going back into town, we need to go north."

"Yeah," James says. "The road's right here. So if we start going right like we have been, we should make it to the town by afternoon tomorrow."

"Sounds good," I say, as we all start walking in the tree line, following the road but remaining out of sight.

We spend hours walking through the woods, ducking behind cover and hiding from any car that passes on the road. We can't take any chances. We've been alone with our thoughts for what seems like forever. I keep replaying the confrontation with Thorn inside my head.

I don't know what came over me when I attacked him with my abilities. I've never been one to hurt someone like that. Even people I don't like. I don't even remember my thought process when I attacked him.

I know that I was angry. I know that I wanted to escape. But I didn't think I'd physically injure someone. I just used my powers to push those people away… right?

I can't help but dwell on it. What I did back there; am I some kind of monster? Am I continuing down a path that's removing me from my humanity? Further separating myself from what I once was, and what I am now?

Again, I'm brought back to the first time I saw myself in the mirror. It's not me, but it's me at the same time. This thought, that feeling. It's been the one constant thing that I've noticed throughout our whole journey. Being both me and not me at the same time. A fractured version of myself. Telling myself that things won't ever be the same, but they'll return to some form of comfort and normalcy. Now, as things become more and more strange, I can't help but think that this isn't going to be the case.

Things are going to continually get stranger as we continue our path, making it farther and farther into our journey home. But I can't help but think about what's going to happen when I make it back to my town. Are my friends going to remember who I am? Is my family? Are they going to see a version of me that they don't recognize? Yet will still try to love me despite the person or… thing I've become?

The thought of being rejected is the hardest thing to think about. I keep replaying conversations in my head, not real ones but hypothetical ones. People telling me that they can't have me around because I look "unnatural" or they try to, but it's all a façade. They tell me that they still accept me, but they don't actually. They talk about me behind my back, complain about things I can't control.

I want to go back to what once was. It's all I can think about when I'm left alone like this, and yet, despite the fact that I can now look at my own reflection and not feel fear or disgust, it still doesn't get any easier. Now, I'm hyper focused on what others think of me. I don't even know if I've conquered my own insecurities. I've talked about them, but talking about them only gets you so far. Do I have to take them on by myself? Or do I have to have others help me through them? Do I ask James for help? Do I even trust Kellie?

What do I do?

I'm pulled out of my own thoughts by James.

"Hey, look," he says to Kellie and me.

We both look up and can see sunlight coming in through the trees. Light finally hitting our faces, real light, for the first time in days.

Something about the sun coming up makes me feel better. Like a sign that things are going to get better for all of us. Telling us that we're going to make it, no matter what happens to us. We're still going to make it home.

It's comforting, a feeling of comfort I haven't felt since I woke up here.

"You feel that too, right?" Kellie asks.

"Yeah," I respond.

Chapter 19

Kellie

"Let's take a bit of a break," James says, finding a non-damp place to sit on the ground.

I sit down with James. Lyla's the last of us to sit down. Taking the backpack from her shoulders, she sits in front of us.

"Anyone want anything from this?" Lyla asks.

James is the first to open the bag, grabbing some of the food Lyla gave to us from the cafeteria. I reach in and grab whatever I can find. It's a small Ziploc bag of bacon.

Lyla reaches in and grabs some trail mix.

"It's not a lot, but it's something, I guess," Lyla says, eating some of her trail mix.

The warm sun rising over the horizon beams onto the three of us.

"We're almost to town," I say.

"I would complain about my feet hurting," James says, "but they don't." He chuckles.

"What're we going to do when we get there, aside from getting your car, Kellie?" Lyla asks.

I hadn't actually thought about that. What would we do when we got there? Then I remember… my dad.

"I'm going to call my dad," I say. "Maybe he can get me some new clothes. Plus, I should still see him while we're in town. I'm sure that he'd like to know where we're going."

"I'm fine with that," James says. "What do you think, Lyla?"

"Sure, we'd just have to keep our heads down, make sure we don't draw the attention of anyone who knows the facility," Lyla responds.

I nod. "Of course. We should be fine."

We all sit in silence for a little bit longer. I can't help but think that James and Lyla are still upset at me. What I told them about the transfer, that was the truth. I wouldn't lie to them like that. But I know that what happened wasn't what I thought was going to if I told them.

They've already told me that it's okay, and they're willing to let me go along with them, but I don't know if they're doing that because they really want to keep me around or if they're using me. I hope it's the former. I feel bad about what happened. I do!

I keep yelling to no one inside of my head, before I decide I should probably say something. Make some conversation.

"So… Lyla," I say.

Lyla turns to me, mouth full of trail mix. "Yeah, what's up?"

"What're you going to do when we get into town?" I ask.

"Sheesh, uh… I'm not sure," Lyla replies. "I guess just find your car, help you see your dad, and then we all head out. We're still pretty close to the facility, so I don't think we should be sticking around too long, ya know?"

James adds to the conversation next. "I agree, we should still be able to go see your family, but we shouldn't stick around too long, just in case people want to contact the facility."

I nod. "Makes sense. I just want to talk to my dad and get some new clothes."

I tug at my red hoodie I'm wearing. The bright red has been replaced with pine needles, leaves, and grime that no article of clothing should be covered in for someone like me. I do need a change of clothes. We all do.

James is the next person to strike up conversation.

"So, I don't know if it's a good idea to talk about," he says. "But… what was up with that electricity thing you did?"

We both look at Lyla, who realizes we're talking about her.

"I… don't know," she replies. "It just kind of happened. I guess it's like Paul's thing? Like a superpower?"

"You don't think it was a one-off thing?" I ask.

"Why would it be?" she says. "I shot lightning out of my hands. I don't think that's going to just happen once."

"Can you do it now?" James asks.

Lyla reaches a hand out, attempting to make electricity appear from her hands. Electricity arcs between her fingers for a moment, but then it dissipates.

"Huh," Lyla says. "I guess I can kind of do it. But it's not as strong as earlier."

"Do we need to shock you again?" James asks.

"I don't think so," Lyla says. "Ever since we hopped the wall, I've been… really tired. Maybe that has something to do with it."

"Maybe," James replies.

"That'll be the next thing I figure out once I get home," Lyla says.

We all continue to eat whatever's left in the bag. Lyla then gets up, followed by James.

"All right, let's get a move on. We should be in town by noon," James says.

"How're you so sure it'll be noon?" I ask.

"What, you've never told time with the sun before?" James replies, a grin on his face.

"No, I guess not," I reply.

"Oh, it's easy," Lyla says. "I used to be in this scouting troop when I was little. They told us about it."

I get up, and we all start walking again.

"Okay, so. Everyone knows that the sun rises in the east and sets in the west," James says.

"And based on the season it is, the sun will usually set at specific times," Lyla interjects.

"But there's always one constant," James continues. "The sun will always be directly above us when it hits noon."

"Exactly." Lyla says. "So since it's… still summer. The sun should set around eight p.m. And since the sun just came up, it's around six or seven in the morning. We'll definitely make it there by noon."

They both start talking to each other about time, going on and on about how they learned the things that they did. It's interesting to hear them talk about it all. Even though I don't remember much of the details pertaining to it. Hearing them both go back and forth, as the conversation changes while we're walking, it seems like we can retain morale, despite our situation.

We continue walking, and as the hours go by, the trees start dissipating. More road is being revealed. Lyla and James are being cautious about when we move and how fast we do, making sure we don't get caught by any stragglers from the facility.

I can sense it, though. We're close to town. The surrounding area's becoming more and more familiar to me. I know we're getting closer. Soon enough, I'll find a way to call my dad. It's exciting. But I'm also terrified. What if he doesn't know that it's me on the other end? What if he doesn't recognize my voice? Did my voice change? I don't know. I feel like it didn't. What if he doesn't want to see me? What if he's scared by the way I look? Is he still going to want to come see me? He's my dad; of course he's got to pick up the phone. Why wouldn't he?

It's all I can think about. The conversation between Lyla and James has been drowned out, and the only thoughts in my head are versions of what could happen when I call my dad, and what'll happen afterwards.

Every possible outcome my brain can conjure up, every possible sentence, every possible expression. It's like a blender of possibilities.

Before I can make any concrete thoughts about my future, I hear one of the two in front of me calling out.

"Kellie, look."

Glancing up through the two of my friends. I can see my hometown. Small, yet enough to do for a day or so. Living there, it's dull. Shops of all kinds line the main street that winds through the town. Houses line the outside of the town, with the main highway splitting off into exits to the suburbs.

We're here. All we need to do is find my car and find a working phone.

Making our way into the town is the easy part, cutting through backyards, avoiding the main roads, and hiding whenever cars come by. It makes me feel like an escaped felon. The feeling that if another person sees me, I'm going to be sent right back to the facility.

During our walk from the suburban area and into town, we don't see very many people like us.

"You'd think we'd run into maybe one or two people who are like us," James says.

"Well, I'm not sure, but maybe they're scared?" I say. "Maybe they're at the facility too."

"Maybe," Lyla adds. "I don't know if everyone is that dumb to fall into whatever they were telling us."

"Authority can convince a lot of good people to do stupid things," James says. "It's happened before."

"Maybe," Lyla says.

We come up to a four-way intersection, and, hiding in the bushes, we plan our route.

"Where is your car, Kellie?" James asks.

I peek out of the bushes, looking for landmarks to help figure out where we're at.

"It's really close," I reply. "See that coffee shop there?" I point to the coffee shop on the corner.

"Yeah," Lyla replies.

"We just need to go down two blocks. It's in the parking lot."

"That's in the middle of the open," Lyla says. "We've been sneaking around so much. You sure we'll be fine in the open?"

"If those people haven't found us yet, you think they would have already searched the town?" James questions.

"I don't know," I say. "But we can't get to my car without going that way, so we're going to have to risk it."

"All right," Lyla says.

The three of us emerge from the bushes and look down the road. We don't see anyone coming, and whatever cars we see have already passed us. It's a good opportunity. So, the three of us take a deep breath and start crossing the street, into the open.

Walking down the street, we're keeping our eyes out for people who might be walking down the road. Some people are sitting in the coffee shop as we pass, but they're all staring down at their phones or laptops.

One lady, working the register, makes eye contact with me before we disappear. I could see her expression change into one of either confusion or... worry.

We continue down the block, maintaining a decent pace. Lyla breaks the silence.

"Is there... anyone else here? You'd think there'd be more people like... walking down the road," she says.

"The town's super small. And it's in the middle of the day. Most people are at work, or driving," I reply.

I point to the parking lot right in front of us.

"There it is," I say, pointing to the red sedan sitting in the parking lot.

"Is that your car?" James asks.

"Yessir," I reply.

The three of us approach my car, sitting just where I left it.

I walk to the back wheel and stick my hand inside the wheel well, feeling around.

There it is.

Pulling out of the wheel well, I retrieve a small black plastic box with magnets on one side. Opening the box, I find my one spare key.

"Glad this is still here," I say, walking to the driver's side door.

"Why do you have your spare out in the open like that?" Lyla asks.

"'Cause I always lock myself out of the car. My dad gave it to me as a Christmas present one year, and it's saved me from being locked out multiple times. Plus, nobody ever checks inside the wheels," I reply, opening the door.

I get into my car. Sitting down in it after weeks is a strange experience. I feel like I've lost my ability to drive. I spent so long not behind the wheel, it takes me a moment to get used to it again. I put the key in the ignition and start the car.

Even after sitting in a parking lot for weeks, this beater car I own rumbles to life. I unlock the other doors, and both James and Lyla get in.

"Calling shotgun," Lyla says, jumping into the passenger seat.

James reluctantly gets in the back seat. I hear the sound of several plastic bottles shifting around as he climbs in.

"Why do you have so many water bottles in your back seat?" he asks, buckling up.

"Uh... 'cause I don't clean my car," I say, putting the car into gear.

I step on the gas, and the three of us drive onto the road and start heading north. For a moment, I can feel the weight of everything that's happened to us lighten.

We're free... but we're not out of the woods yet.

"We need to find a phone," I say.

"So you can call your dad, right?" Lyla says.

"Yeah," I respond. "I know that some of the old gas stations have pay phones still. We'll stop at the first one we find."

As we drive, I keep my eyes glued to the windshield. There's a gas station not far from here that should have a pay phone. I just have to find it first.

We make a left and then a right around a bend in the road. The town slowly dissipates into suburbs, with houses replacing the coffee shops and used bookstores.

We don't drive for very long, until we find a gas station sitting off on the side of the road. It's a bit out of the way, not many cars coming down the road either. This one must have a pay phone.

We pull into a spot at the gas station, and I check my cupholder for some kind of change, finding a single quarter and a dime. Grabbing the two coins from the cupholder, I step out of the car and walk to the side of the building. On the outside of the building lies a graffiti-covered pay phone. Picking up the receiver, I go to put in the quarter. But I stop. What if this pay phone is busted? If I drop my only change in, I can't call for anyone; it'll eat my change.

I decide to put the dime in first. I hear a metallic clink… and then, another one.

I check the pocket where the machine returns change. The dime is there. So, I guess it either doesn't take dimes, or it's broken. I'm going to have to use the quarter then. I take my only quarter and then put it in the slot.

I hear the clink of coin on metal.

And then…

Dial tone. It's working.

I take a deep breath and recount my dad's phone number.

Punching the phone number in on the keypad, I wait with bated breath, hoping that I dialed it in right.

Ring…

Ring…

Ring…

Silence.

"H…Hello?" I say into the phone.

Silence. For what seems like minutes.

"Kellie… Is that you?"

The voice on the other end is unmistakable. It's my dad.

"Yeah, it's me," I say, choking up. Finally, someone I genuinely know, someone I haven't heard from in weeks.

"Where are you? I tried to reach out to you weeks ago! Your phone wasn't receiving calls! Are you okay?" My dad fires question after question at me.

"I'm fine, Dad…" I say. "I need you to come to the gas station on Parkland Road. Can… you bring me another outfit too?"

"Kellie, sweetie, what're you talking about?" my dad questions. "Are you being held hostage? Are you okay?"

"Yes, I'm fine," I respond, still choking through my words. "I'll explain everything when you come here. It'll make sense, I promise."

"Kellie, we saw on the news, all those people… Is… Is that why you—"

The phone hangs up. My time on the phone is over.

I told my dad where I am, and now… I just have to wait for him to show up.

I walk back to the car, where Lyla and James are still sitting inside.

"So?" James asks. "Did you get a hold of him?"

"Yeah," I say. "He should be here soon."

CHAPTER 20

Kellie

WAITING IN THE car with Lyla and James, the minutes feel like hours. We sit, waiting, with the A/C on. I check my gas tank; it's just under half. Just as I remember leaving it.

We're not really saying anything. James is asleep, and Lyla's staring out the window, watching the cars go by.

Lyla decides to break the silence first this time.

"What car does your dad drive?" she asks.

"I dunno, a blue like… Trailblazer," I say. "Why'd you ask?"

"Just keeping an eye out for it," she responds.

We both sit in silence, before Lyla says something else.

"You scared?" she asks.

"Scared?" I reply.

"Yeah, scared of what your dad is going to say when he sees you. Did he see you before this? Or is this going to be the first time he's seen you since you were human?"

"It's the… it's the only thing I've been thinking about," I say. "Ever since we started walking through the woods last night, it's been the only thing on my mind. I don't know what he's going to say. I'm not even sure what he expects. But from what he said in the phone call… I think he knows."

"What do you think is going to happen?" Lyla asks.

"I... I don't know," I reply. "He's still gotta care, right? I'm still his daughter. I didn't choose to end up like this, ya know?"

"Yeah, I've been thinking about it a long time," Lyla says. "Thinking about what my parents are going to think of me when they see me like this."

"I'm sure it'll turn out okay. I'm sure I'll be okay. I'm sure you'll be okay," I say.

"Possibly," Lyla responds. "I still don't see it that way myself. It lingers in the back of my mind. The thought of being rejected by my own family. I haven't been good to them. For the first time, they're going to see me, like... this? What's going to happen?"

"I'm not sure. But I'm sure they'll still love you," I respond.

"Maybe, but you've got a good relationship with your dad, from what you've told me," Lyla retorts. "Whatever happens here, it's the bar for what'll happen to me. But whatever does happen, it'll be lower, worse, whatever you want to call it."

We sit in silence for a bit, contemplating her outlook on our situation.

"Is that him?" Lyla asks, drawing my attention to the blue Trailblazer pulling into the parking lot, sitting at the other end of the parking lot.

The door opens, and the man steps out from the driver's seat. Tall, large beard, curly hair. It's him. It's my dad. In his hand are some clothes.

"Yeah," I say.

James sits up in the back seat. His voice sounds tired. "You... want us to get out with you?" he asks.

"No, that's fine. I'll do it on my own," I reply. Opening the door, taking a deep breath, and stepping out of the car, I'm standing in front of the car door. I take another deep breath and close the door. Now facing my dad.

We both start moving towards one another. His expression seems confused, yet slightly relived.

We meet halfway in between the cars. He's staring down at me, looking me over, like it's his first time meeting someone new.

Before I know it, I'm caught in his embrace; he's hugging me.

"I'm so glad you're safe," he says.

I can feel myself tearing up. I wrap my arms around him, returning the gesture.

"I'm so sorry," I say through my tears.

He sets me down and wipes away his own tears.

"You look different," he says through some chuckles, lightening the mood.

"Yeah… I do," I say.

"Where have you been?" my dad asks.

"I've been… somewhere bad," I say. "Some people wanted to help… people like me. But it turns out that was all a lie."

My dad nods. "I see. I'm just glad you're safe, Kellie. I blamed myself ever since we got back from that stupid ski trip. We should have taken you."

"It's not your fault, Dad," I reply. "I didn't expect… this to happen to me."

"We saw it all on the news, people becoming like you. It even happened at the resort. People refused to leave their rooms. It became chaos for the few days we were still there. That's when I tried calling you, but it kept going to voicemail. What happened?"

"They took our phones, they kept them hidden from us. They're not good people, Dad, we… we had to escape," I reply.

"So… what are you going to do now?" he asks.

"I… I don't know," I say. "I have friends now, James and Lyla. I met them in the place we were all at. They both need to get home as well."

"Are they… like you?" my dad questions.

"Yeah," I respond.

"So, you're… not coming home?" my dad says.

"No, I don't think I'm going to," I reply. "I've found friends, and I can't abandon them. They need me. I need to help them find closure, help them get back to their families, as they did for me. Help me find myself even though I don't… look like me anymore. It's a second chance. With my friends, for the first time, I actually feel comfortable, I feel happy. I don't think I want to stay here when there's more opportunity out there for me now."

My dad's expression turns from content to worry.

"I guess I can understand that. I just worry about you, sweetie, you're my kid. I worry about what you're going to do for money, where you're going to live. Yeah, you feel happier, but you're not the same you I saw before I left. At least, on the outside, how're you going to find work? How're you going to support yourself? I know that I can at least take care of you until all this blows over, and everyone out there is ready to see you succeed, even though you're different… You really want to go through all this hardship by yourself?"

We stand in silence.

"I mean, I just got you back. I haven't heard from you for weeks. Someone came to our house and said you… you died. That's… that's when I stopped calling," he says, starting to tear up again.

Someone… someone said I died? That doesn't make any sense.

"Who… who told you that?" I ask.

My dad sighs. "Some people came to the house, men in suits. They looked professional. Said that they were with a private company who's been monitoring this whole situation. I don't remember the name, but they mentioned you, said that they found dead in the forest, mauled by one of the people who were… different."

"You didn't ask them anything else about me? Like what I looked like?" I ask.

"No, they had so much information about you. They knew me, they knew Lisa, they even knew we were gone on vacation and left you here.

They mentioned that dental records matched you, and they just told us they'd be in contact about paying for funeral arrangements… They… never got in touch with us." My dad continues, "I just… I couldn't believe them, and then… a week later. You call."

I approach my dad and hug him.

I had this inkling in the back of my head that… I wasn't good enough, that my dad, despite everything, didn't care about me that much. Sure, we were friends, sure we got along. But that small seed of doubt still remained, with his fixation on… Lisa, and always being gone, it felt like he forgot about me, or… got tired of me.

But standing here, listening to him talk about how he really felt when I was gone… I don't feel that anymore. I can feel myself getting choked up. These emotions I've kept bottled, hidden behind the smile, the mask I wear every day, it's gone.

"I'm sorry, Dad," I say. "I'm sorry I ran, I'm sorry I didn't call, I'm sorry that I disappeared. But I'm here."

My dad hugs me again.

"I should have been there for you more," he said.

"You did your best," I reply. "We tried our best."

We both let go of each other and take a deep breath.

"You sure you want to do this?" he asks.

Before I can open my mouth to respond, an unfortunately familiar voice rings out.

"I think this could be good for her!"

Her.

Sauntering over to my dad like a cartoon villain is Lisa. My stepmom. The one person I hoped I'd never see again.

"Kellie, you look different," she says, slightly taken back by my appearance.

"Why's she here?" I ask my dad, paying Lisa no attention.

Before my dad can respond, Lisa answers for him.

"When you called your dad, he started running around the house and into your room. Said that you called, said you weren't dead, and that you needed clothes or something. I decided to accompany him, in case you were being held captive for ransom or something. Something certainly did happen to you, though," she says, looking me up and down like usual.

"I'm sorry, Kellie," my dad adds. "I know you two don't really get along, but she wanted to tag along."

"Anyways, as I was saying," Lisa continues. "This could be good for her. Going out, seeing the world. You certainly needed to get out of the house anyways. Seems like this is the break you were looking for."

"Not like this," my dad says, turning to Lisa. "What's she going to do for money? Where's she going to stay?"

"You worry too much," Lisa says. "She's been fine every time we've gone somewhere. It's obvious she can handle herself."

"She stayed with us, at home. Don't you think that she needs to come back and at least wait until all this is over, and people will treat her with respect?" my dad says.

Lisa pauses. I can tell by her expression that she knows that it's going to be tough out there for me, but she also knows that I'm not going to be a problem if I leave, and she'll have my dad all to herself, at least, for a while. She's taking this opportunity, and she knows that I'm well aware.

"She's got friends, doesn't she?" Lisa continues. "The people in the car over there." Lisa points to my car, where Lyla's sitting in the front seat, looking out the window. She notices the three of us looking at her. She smiles and waves, albeit awkwardly.

"We don't know these people," my dad says. "They could be bad."

"They're not," I interject. "They're good people, they helped me get out of here. Now, I'm going to help them."

My dad looks at me, then at the car, then back at me.

He sighs.

"Okay," he says. "I just want to make sure you're being safe. I want to hear from you soon. Call me, do whatever you can. Just… Don't get into any trouble."

He approaches me and hugs me one more time.

"I love you."

"I love you too, Dad," I say.

He hands me a crumpled set of clothes. "Here, I got you some new clothes, like you asked."

"Thanks, Dad," I say.

"Be safe," he says, walking back to the car, leaving Lisa and me the only people left outside.

"He's not happy about it," she says.

"I know," I respond. "But this is what you want, isn't it?"

"I don't know what you're talking about," Lisa says.

"Oh please, you can't be serious." I sneer at her. "You *never* stand up for me. So, why now?"

Lisa doesn't make eye contact with me. She stares off into the distance, but I know she's trying to formulate another one of her snide comebacks.

"Well… you're a grown…" She looks at me. "Thing, you can do what you want. Your father doesn't realize that."

I can't help but laugh.

"You almost did it," I say. "You almost said something nice, before you went right back to your passive-aggressive crap."

"Passive-aggressive?" Lisa exclaims. "Since when?"

"I'm not going to argue with you about this. Just say you don't want me around and get it over with," I say. "I'm already leaving anyways. You don't need to waste your breath trying to justify your actions."

"I'm not trying to justify anything. You're the one who's putting words in my mouth," Lisa says.

"Same could be said about you," I say. "Always insulting me, always finding the most minute flaws in me. You hate the very fact I'm here right now. I'm sure you were ecstatic when I left."

For a moment, Lisa cracks, like I saw through her "carefully crafted façade of a mother figure."

"How dare you assume something like that." She grimaces. "Your father cried his eyes out when you disappeared."

"I'm sure he did. But I'm not talking about him. I'm talking about you," I say.

"I did," she said.

"For show maybe," I say.

"There's no reason to be so crass, Kellie."

"Get a grip, Lisa," I say. "I'm just dishing out what you dealt me, and you know what. I finally feel confident enough to tell you what I really think."

"Please, I'm sure it's nothing I haven't heard before," Lisa says. "We always butt heads, we always argue, but at the end of the day, we're still family."

"No. We're not," I say. "We've never been family, you've made sure of that."

"You sure whatever happened to you hasn't messed with your head?" Lisa scoffs. "You're talking crazy."

"Actually, I haven't seen clearer until now," I snap back. "All the times you guys leave without telling me, all the times you run your mouth about me, all the times you treat me like some tenant just renting my own room. You treat me like some kind of animal!"

Lisa can't help but chuckle to herself.

"Well, at least you look the part now." She sneers.

"There it is," I say. "Finally, you show your true colors. Come on, spit it out!" I say. "Tell me how you really feel."

I point over to my dad, sitting in the car, looking at us before looking to his phone.

"He can't hear us."

"You wanna know how I really feel?" Lisa says. "Fine."

She takes a breath.

"You've always been so up your own ass, Kellie. You're always talking about how you can 'do great things,' but they never come, you refuse to face the facts, and you'd rather pretend like you're living with your own mother than us. It's been my house, my rules for the past… how many years? And you still act like I'm just some woman your dad dragged in from the bar. You act like I ruin your life, like I treat you like crap, but that's not true! I've been looking out for you. I've been trying to get you to see your full potential this whole time. I might be a little blunt, might be a little rude. Might say things I shouldn't, but it's stuff you need to hear if you want to be a better person."

She steps forward, leaning down to scold me in my face.

"You don't take my advice, you don't like me, you've never liked me, so I gave up! I stopped bringing you places, because you always kept bringing your dad down. One moment, we're having a great time, the next your father acts like you're top priority! Even when you're gone, when you pretended to be dead, your father kept talking about you. Saying how he could've done better, how he should've been there for you. It's maddening."

She pauses, before rearing up again into another tirade.

"Then all of a sudden you come back, but now, you're not even human anymore! After all that pissing and moaning from your father, he finally stopped. Things *finally* went back to normal. Except you had to call, you had to not be dead, and now you're here, looking just as horrid as you are on the inside."

"Wow," I say. "It feels so good to be right," I snap back. "Every little thing I thought about you true. You're an awful person, Lisa."

"I only say these things because they're true. You made me this way." She sneers.

"Oh, I made you this way?" I say. "You made me this way! Every time you said something about me, every little nitpick, every little insult, every little snide comment crushed me on the inside. You've never even shown a shred of interest in my life. You just wanted me to fit your ideals of a person!"

I step forward, making her take a step back.

"I didn't matter if I was making plenty of money, or if I was doing well. If it wasn't what you thought was right, it wasn't worth it. You sit there and you tell me that you wanted to look out for me, make sure I reach my full potential, when the truth is you wanted me to be like you, live your little happy fantasy. When you realized I wasn't going to do that, what do you do? You insult me, right to my face! That crushed me, that made me cry myself to sleep, that made me hide in my room and only come out when you weren't there. I avoided you so I didn't have to deal with you. Now, after everything that's happened, I finally have some people who confide in me, people who like me for me. Unlike *you*."

I poke her, like I'm drilling my point into her. As I step back to take a breath, I see her brush off the part of her shirt I touched, like I have some kind of disease.

"The funny thing is, I'm actually content. I'm actually happy that we're having this conversation. Because no matter what you can say to me, I finally feel comfortable. Like I belong somewhere. You've been nothing but a bully to me. Rude, mean, and spiteful once you realized I wouldn't conform. It's ironic, isn't it. I can't even conform to your standards now even if I wanted to."

"Fine by me," Lisa says. "I'm sorry you feel that way. But I guess it's neither of our problems now. You're leaving, and we can put this all behind us."

"Oh, I'm leaving. But not forever." I sneer.

"What're you talking about?" she asks.

"I'm gonna come back. You're married to my dad, after all, the last flesh and blood person who still loves me. You think I'm going to abandon my dad? I'll call, and I'll text, and I'll come back to visit. Who knows, maybe tomorrow, maybe the next day. Maybe I'll pop in unannounced. I've still got things at home. I'll have to get them someday."

"Doesn't bother me," Lisa says.

"I know it does," I reply. "Doesn't matter to me. You're not gonna get rid of me anymore. I'm not going to let you push me around anymore either."

I start walking back to the car, clothes in hand, leaving Lisa standing alone.

"Goodbye, for now… Mom," I say.

Lisa doesn't respond.

I climb into the car and start the engine. Looking out the windshield, I can see Lisa walking back to the car. We make one last moment of eye contact, and for a moment, we both know that things are going to be different between us. Whether or not that's reality, I guess we won't find out for a while.

I pull out onto the road, looking for the nearest highway exit to get us going north. Our next stop is James's house.

Lyla breaks out of whatever trance she was in while looking out the window and turns to me.

"So, how'd it go?" she asked.

"Better than I thought it would," I reply.

"You all right? You seem like you're upset about something?"

"Yeah, I'm fine," I say. "I just finally got some stuff off my chest I've been meaning to."

"That's good," Lyla says.

"Yeah," I reply.

As we continue our drive, the road changes from a winding trail to a dense forest, with the road parting the trees in a straight line.

James finally wakes up. He sits up in the seat.

"How long was I out?" he asks.

Lyla turns around to check on James, as I watch through the rearview mirror.

"A while, you slept like a rock," Lyla says.

"I needed it," he replies. "We've been walking for… how long?"

"I think I need a nap next," Lyla says. "We might need to stop somewhere soon."

"Good idea," I say, as I look back on the road.

As soon as my eyes move from the rearview mirror to the windshield, I see a figure shambling onto the asphalt. The figure grows bigger and bigger as I try to decipher what it is.

Whatever it is, we're going to hit it.

I slam on the brakes, everyone jolting forward as the screeching sound of my car's tires skid across the pavement. We all come to a stop, as the large figure stands before us. Whoever they are, they're big.

Lyla seems to make the connection, and what she says surprises all three of us.

"…Paul?"

The figure shambles towards the passenger side door, as Lyla lowers the window.

They lean down to peer inside, as I realize that it's him. Paul, the massive bear from the facility who escaped a few days ago. He sticks his head partway through the window, his expression slightly pained.

"Howdy, miss, didn't expect to see you out here." He chuckles, before groaning in pain.

"You wouldn't mind… giving me a ride home, would ya?"

CHAPTER 21

Lyla

"GET IN," KELLIE says, gesturing to the back door. Paul nods and shuffles from the passenger side. James slides over to the other side of the car as Paul squeezes in behind me. I turn around to face Paul.

"You look terrible," I say. "You okay?"

Paul nods. It's obvious he's been running since he left, his clothes torn, fur ruffled. He's been through some shit.

"Could be better, miss," Paul responds, lifting his hand on his abdomen, showing something we didn't expect to see.

A bullet wound.

"Jeez, Paul! You got shot!" James exclaims.

"I'll be fine…" Paul says. "I'm pretty sure it didn't hit anything vital; it's just… stuck in there is all."

Paul chuckles, which then turns into a pained groan.

"It's been like this for a day. We need to get back to my place, pronto," he says. "The Mrs. will know what to do."

"Where is it?" Kellie asks, putting the car into gear and starting down the road.

"Ain't too far from here, lady," Paul replies. "Maybe another half hour by car. Should be fine, beats walking."

"Did… did those facility guys do that to you?" I ask.

Paul nods. "Yeah, took 'em a few days before they wised up to my tricks."

"Tricks?" Kellie asks.

"You're talking about the whole moving ground thing?" James says.

"Yep, you got it right," Paul responds. "I thought it was some kinda fluke that I made the ground push me up like that few days ago. Turns out I got some kinda superpower, right outta one of them comic books."

"Lyla's got one too!" Kellie says.

"That's not important," I respond. "We gotta focus on getting Paul home."

"We're driving there, ain't we?" Paul says. "We got time. Tell me about your little superpower then."

"Uh…. Okay," I respond. "It's like, uh… I can… uh…"

I can't think of the words to describe what I can do. It's like it's embarrassing. I don't want to talk about it. Something inside of my head tells me it's not okay to talk about them.

"Lyla shoots lightning from her hands," Kellie says.

"Oh, does she now? …That's pretty cool." Paul chuckles. "Show it off!"

Show it off? He wants me to show it off?

"…All right," I say.

I fully turn around to face them and hold my hand out. I attempt to focus on making lightning come from my hands, like I did back at the facility. I can feel that same feeling I had, that tingly feeling from when I got them inside of my chest. I watch as small arcs of electricity run across my hand. I try to focus and make them bigger, but it fizzles out before anything can happen.

"Sorry… that's all I can do right now," I say, slinking back into my chair, thinking about the poor display of my abilities. I can't believe I embarrassed myself in front of everyone like that.

James chimes into the conversation, turning to Paul. "When she used them the first time, she was throwing electricity around, shocking those guys in SWAT uniforms…"

He pauses.

"She even blasted Thorn, too," James finishes his thought.

Paul laughs again, toughing out the pain.

"You really got the doc, eh? That's impressive!" Paul says.

"Yeah," I reply, "but I don't know how I did it. Now, I can't do it anymore."

"That's an easy fix," Paul responds. "You're just tired."

"Tired?" I reply.

"Yeah, tired," Paul responds. "It's kinda hard to explain. I'll show it to you once we get back." Paul leans over to look through the windshield.

"Make a right here," he says.

Kellie turns right onto a dirt road.

"So, your family is back at your house?" Kellie asks.

"They watched me leave," Paul responds. "They probably don't know I'm back, though."

"Did you try to call your family?" Kellie asks.

"No," Paul responds. "I've been wandering the woods since I escaped. Surprised I made it this far."

"Gotcha," Kellie says. "We met up with my dad on the way here."

"Did you now?" Paul says. "What'd he have to say?"

"They never saw me leave," Kellie says. "The facility told them I… died."

"Oh," Paul responds. "That's not good. Wonder if they told my family that too."

"Possibly," Kellie responds.

The conversation about Kellie and Paul's time makes it sound like they've been good friends. At least, enough so that Paul isn't focusing on the bleeding hole in his side. Staring out the window, I start to nod off, watching the trees go by. I close my eyes. Paul's voice brings me back what feels like minutes later.

"It's coming right up…. Now," Paul says, pointing to another dirt road.

"Left, here," he says.

Kellie turns left onto the one-lane dirt road. The road extends way longer than anyone thought it was going to, as we drive down the dirt road, the trees seemingly taking over all sides of the car. The late afternoon sun beams on a single slice of the path with just enough room for the car to fit. Then, the trees open up into a cleanly cut lawn and an older house at the end of the path, the trees surrounding all sides but the front. It's not big, but it's homey.

"We're here," Paul says.

We all pull into the driveway of the house, parking the car in a safe spot. All of us step out of the car one by one, as we finally stretch our legs. Paul stumbles out of the car last, standing up.

"Finally… Home," he says, turning to the sidewalk.

We all go to face the sidewalk, but someone's already standing there. An older woman, she looks like she's in her mid-forties. Standing next to her is a small girl.

"You're… home," the woman says.

"Lynn…" Paul says, walking up to her.

The woman hesitates but walks up to Paul, looking him up and down. The little girl follows her mother, reeling back at the woman's next statement.

"Oh my god, you've been shot!" she says.

"I'll be fine," Paul says warmly. "Can you fix me up?"

"I can try. Come on," the woman says.

She turns to the three of us. "You three can come in too."

The three of us walk inside and enter Paul's home. A set of stairs head up to the second floor in the foyer, while the rest of the first floor splits off in the other two directions from the same spot. Next to the stairs is a hallway that leads into the kitchen. The three of us follow Paul's groans into the kitchen, where Paul, the woman, and the kid are.

The woman has Paul sitting in a chair. On the table is a bag of medical equipment, and the woman is hunched over with some tools, opening Paul's wound. Paul, holding a towel covered in medical disinfectant, dabs it on the wound.

"Penelope, you don't need to see this. Go play with your toys or something," the woman says.

"But... I want to know if Dad's going to be okay..." the kid replies.

"I'll be fine, sweetie, just... go play with your toys, and I'll come see you," Paul responds through the pain.

The kid turns to Kellie, James and me, looking the three of us up and down.

The kid points to Kellie. "Can you come with me?"

"Me? Why?" Kellie asks.

The kid smiles, clearly missing some baby teeth.

"'Cause you're a raccoon, and raccoons are my favorite," she says.

Kellie looks around and then up to us for approval.

James and I shrug.

Kellie turns to the girl. She'd kneel down if she could, but she's only a half foot taller than this nine-year-old.

"Sure," she says with a big grin.

The two of them walk out of the room, leaving James and me to help tend to Paul.

The woman speaks up.

"You... uh... green guy," she says.

"Me?" James says.

"Yeah, you, hold this for me," she says, gesturing to a retractor in Paul's abdomen.

James walks up and grabs on to the retractor, looking away from the blood that's dripping out onto the floor.

"Make sure I don't lose... too much," Paul says, wincing in pain.

"You'll be fine, honey," the woman says, then turns her attention to me. "You, miss, take the towel from Paul."

I walk up to Paul and take the towel from his hand.

"Thanks," he says, relaxing his arms.

"Good, good," the woman replies. "I think I'm about to grab the bullet now. Once I get it out, you need to press onto the wound until I can get the suture kit."

"Got it," I respond.

"No time like the present, right, honey?" she says.

"Get… it over with," Paul replies.

We all wait in silence, the sound of squelching innards and blood dripping all anyone can hear in this moment.

I see the woman pull out the bullet. I spring into action and put the towel on the wound as James and the woman remove the tools.

The woman drops the bullet into a plastic dish with a *CLUNK*.

"We're done. I'll be right back," the woman says, leaving James and me, our hands covered in Paul's blood.

"Quite a reunion, huh?" Paul says. "I'm just glad that damn thing is out of me."

We all breathe a sigh of relief as the woman comes back.

"Sorry about that. I have the suture kit," the woman says.

The woman kneels down on the ground and starts applying stitches to Paul.

"Sorry for the poor introductions," Paul says. "This is my wife, Lynn."

"It's nice to meet you both," Lynn responds, "though I wish it was under better circumstances."

CHAPTER 22

Lyla

"IT'S FINE," JAMES says, keeping his hands to his side, trying not to get any of Paul's blood on them.

"We're just glad Paul's okay," I add.

"If it wasn't for you three… I don't know how much longer I could have lasted," Paul responds. "I felt like I was nearing the end of my rope."

Lynn doesn't look up from her work as she continues to patch Paul up.

"You definitely lost a lot of blood. That kind of shot would've killed any normal man," Lynn responds.

"I ain't no normal man anymore." Paul chuckles.

"Certainly not. Now, hold still just a bit longer," Lynn responds with a smirk. She continues her work but aims her words towards us, remaining focused on the stitching.

"I have to admit, I was pretty scared when I saw Paul like this," Lynn says. "Imagine thinking some kinda animal from the forest broke into our home, only to find out it was my husband."

Lynn lets out a humored sigh. "It was strange at first. But once I realized that Paul was still the same inside, I warmed up to it. Then, he wanted to leave."

"Leave?" I say. "Go to… the RCC?"

"Yup," Paul responded. "I was just as terrified as Lynn when I woke up, felt like something out of one of the movies Penelope watches. I didn't know what to think. I couldn't tell if I was still me. Lynn said that I was. But… I wasn't sure myself. I saw on the news that this RCC place was letting people like us get acclimated. Realized that if I could figure myself out in a safe environment where I didn't put you guys in danger… I could come back a better person."

Lynn looks down solemnly. "I knew something was up after two weeks. I could feel it in my bones. Paul didn't fit any of the descriptions we saw on the news, of how these 'affected people' acted. He was still the same in my eyes, but he didn't come back. I called, and I called, and I called. Penelope started asking when you were coming back, and they kept telling me you were safe."

"So, nobody tried to contact you about him?" James asks.

"Not at first," Lynn responds. "They told me that his condition was worsening, something about instinct, said he attacked someone. That was weeks ago, though. They told me that he wouldn't be back for a while, possibly never. I didn't believe it. I told them they were full of lies. They told me to continue to 'hold out hope' if you can believe it."

Lynn pauses for a moment before continuing.

"Then they stopped responding altogether. Nobody would give us information," she says.

"That's… strange," I respond.

We turn to the hallway, hearing the sound of footsteps as Kellie reenters the room, holding a stuffed raccoon.

"They did something similar to me," she says, adding to the conversation. "I couldn't help but overhear what you guys were talking about."

"How's my kid?" Paul asks. "She give you that?"

Kellie looks down at the stuffed doll, as if she's looking into a tiny, stuffed mirror. "She's having fun, She told me to hold onto it for a bit, said it looks like me."

"Yeah, that was always her favorite." Paul chuckles. "But, back on track, you mentioned it in the car, something about being dead?"

Kellie takes a deep breath before continuing. "Before we found you, we met up with my dad. I talked to him, he said that some men representing the company found him, told him I had died. They said I was found mauled to death by another one of us. Didn't ask my dad to identify, nothing. He just… accepted it."

Lynn looks up from the conversation in shock.

"Wait… They told your family… you died?" she asks.

Kellie nods.

"Sounds like they're trying to make sure nobody comes back," Paul adds. "Makes a lot more sense considerin' that they were trying to keep us there longer than they were supposed to."

"I don't know why they'd do something like that," Lynn adds. "It doesn't make any sense."

"Maybe some ulterior motive?" I ask. "They found me on the side of the road, told me that they found me… and… I know this is going to sound dumb. But they said I was playing dead."

"Well… to someone like you, I suppose that'd make sense," James says.

"I don't think I've ever actually… done that," I say. "I've frozen up, but I've never actually played dead."

"Maybe that's what it is," Paul responds. "That's what they're calling it 'cause you're a possum."

"I don't know… maybe," I add. "But I don't know who they could have told about me. My friends? Maybe my aunt? I don't talk to my parents anymore."

"They must have told someone," James says. "Maybe you can call them? We still have the phones."

The phones…. I totally forgot about that. We still have the phones. I just need a charger to see if anyone's contacted me!

"I'd need a charger," I say.

"Let me finish up here and I can get you a charger, if we've got the same phone," Lynn responds.

Lynn looks at her work for a few short seconds before taking the needle to Paul once more.

"And... done. There, now, don't move for a minute while I go get some bandages, and I'll help you out in a bit, Miss..."

"Lyla," I respond... "It's Lyla."

"All right, Miss Lyla. And you?" Lynn says, turning to James.

"James," he says, with a slight smile.

"And you?" Lynn asks.

"It's... Kellie," Kellie replies.

"Well... Lyla, James, Kellie. Let me finish up here and we can get you all sorted and find out what to do next for you three." Lynn walks out of the room, leaving us with Paul.

"She did a good job, don't you think? Starting to feel better already," Paul says with a grin.

"I mean, you're alive," James says.

"Eh, it's nothing I can't handle, 'specially now." Paul chuckles softly, taking care to not ruin his wife's handiwork.

"How'd she learn to do that?" Kellie says.

"Funny enough, she was a park ranger when she was in her twenties, dealt with this stuff all the time. Hunters shooting one another during hunting season, wild animal attacks too. Probably why she ain't terrified of me," Paul says.

Paul sighs. "Penelope, though, she was scared at first. It still hurts thinking about the first time she saw me. She thought I was some kinda monster. Took her a few days to realize that her pop was still inside all along. I still think about it. Seems like she's warmed up to the idea. Probably Lynn talking to her about it while I was gone. I don't know if she thinks it's temporary, or why it was only me who was affected. I'll be honest… I'm too afraid to ask. But she seems to be fine with it now, and as long as she's happy, I'm happy," Paul says, then turns his attention to Kellie. "She seemed to really take a liking to you."

"Me?" Kellie asks.

"Yup, she's always liked raccoons for some reason. I dunno if it's 'cause of us always seein' 'em, living out here in the middle of nowhere. Or if she just thinks they're cute. But they're her favorite animal. Now, one just walked into our house. Probably feels like meeting a cartoon character or something to her." Paul chuckles.

Paul leans back in the chair a little, still keeping an eye on his injury.

"Might even help take the weight of what happened to me off of her… I dunno, I'm not even sure myself." Paul continues, "I'm just hoping that now that I'm home, things can go back to some kind of normal.

"How did you make it back anyways?" Lynn asks, walking in with a large roll of gauze. "Did the four of you leave together?"

"Nah," Paul replies. "A few days ago, I made my grand escape. They were planning on keeping me longer. But somehow, I managed to make it out. I must've been given a gift or something from the lord, 'cause I was moving the ground like Moses moved the Red Sea."

"You can move the ground?" Lynn asks.

"Yeah, it's like some kind of magic," James says.

"Look," Paul says, turning our attention to the window looking out into the backyard.

Paul raises a hand and focuses on the ground, and we all watch as a piece of the lawn shakes and then rises in a perfect rectangle, creating a small plateau in the middle of the yard.

"Wow," Lynn responds. "That's… incredible."

"I don't know how I've done it, but it helped me get out of that godforsaken hellhole," Paul says. "Once I made it out, for two days, I was chased down by men in soldiers' uniforms. I spent those two days running, hiding, and defending myself from them."

Paul's expression becomes one of remorse. He sits in silence for what seems like a few minutes. As if he's thinking about something horrible he saw in those woods before continuing his story.

"After that… They got a good shot on me, and I lost track of them. That's when I ran into these three, who managed to make it out on their own."

"Can any of you do that?" Lynn asks our little group.

"Only me," I respond. "But if it wasn't for James and Kellie, I don't know where I would be."

"I see. Well, I'm glad you're all safe, and I'm glad you helped bring my husband back. I'm extremely thankful for that. Please, as long as you like, make yourselves at home," Lynn says, snipping the roll of gauze she's applied to Paul.

"Thank you," James says.

"We won't be here long," Kellie adds.

"Thank you," I say.

Paul stands up from his chair, able to freely move once more.

"Don't try to do anything crazy," Lynn says. "You've got a while before those stitches can come off."

"Thank you, honey," Paul says. "I think I'm going to lie down for a bit. We've got a guest room, if you guys want to bunk in there."

"Sure," I say. "I don't know how long we're staying."

"We've still got a ways to go before my town, and then Lyla's," James adds.

"Stay a little while," Lynn says. "Clean yourselves up, and we'll take care of you until you're ready to go again."

"Thank you again," Kellie says. "We seriously appreciate it."

"Anything for helping bring Paul home," Lynn says with a warm smile.

Kellie hands Lynn the stuffed raccoon. Lynn takes it out of Kellie's hands gently and heads upstairs, leaving us all alone with Paul once more.

"Miss Lyla," Paul says, turning towards me.

"Uhh… yeah?" I say.

"Take these last few hours of the day to rest. Tomorrow, I think I might be able to help you with your gift. I don't know much, but I think I might be able to show you how to use it effectively."

I nod. "Thank you," I say.

Paul nods back. "Just don't try to use 'em on me if we get in a fight again." He chuckles. "I understand that you were stickin' up for that Carter fella back at the facility. How'd that work out for ya?"

"He actually… helped us escape," I say.

"Did he now?" Paul's face turns to confusion. "I really thought he was one of the spineless ones. Seems like he might have a backbone in him after all… I'm surprised he didn't join your little group."

"No, he didn't. He said that he wanted to help some others make their way out," I say.

"Sounds like a noble cause. Wonder how far he'll go before he's caught doin' that. Can't imagine what they'd do to a guy like that, especially if he ain't changed like us," Paul replies.

Paul expression changes from confused to concerned. As if he's recollecting the possible outcomes of someone like Carter.

"Well, can't do much about it now. I know we didn't see eye to eye at first, but I do hope I can at least help you three get back on track. The guest bed, bath and the washer is in the basement, if you wanna go down there and hunker down for the night. Penelope ain't allowed down there, so you should be safe, lil' miss." Paul turns his attention to Kellie.

"…Thanks," Kellie says with a slight grin.

"Oh, and just to warn ya, before all this I did a little shootin' back in my day, and it's kind of my space. If you're squeamish, uhm…. be prepped," Paul says.

"Got it," James says.

Paul gestures at a door in the hallway. "This is the way downstairs.

Again, make yourself at home. I'll see you guys tomorrow." Paul looks up the stairs, as if he's waiting for his wife to allow him to go up there.

"Have a good night, Paul," James says, as we all descend down the stairs.

The room turns from a beige set of walls into a basement, the walls painted navy from ceiling to floor, except for the wood paneling running on the lower half of the walls. It's homey, shag carpet, full bar, and each wall lined with taxidermized heads of all manner of hunting wildlife.

That's what he meant by "did a little shootin."

"I see," James says. "Seems like he did a lot of shooting."

Kellie lets out a little giggle but stops herself, as if to make sure Paul didn't hear.

We all work our way into the basement farther, up to a couch and a massive TV.

"No way," Kellie says. "Look at this."

We all look to the massive couch in the basement. Right in between the TV, and the couch, is an entire...

Bearskin rug.

Oh, the irony. I hold in my laughter. James rolls his eyes, and Kellie is covering her face with her hoodie, trying not to break down. The irony of the situation pulls us away from all the insane crap we've been through for the past few days. For a moment, this single funny thing has brought us together even more.

We all regain our composure, and we investigate the basement even more. Paul wasn't lying when he said things were all set up down here. I can see a bathroom, and right down the hall from it is a washer and a dryer for clothes. That would definitely come in handy. I look over to the other side of the basement and see a bar, with another hallway leading to a bedroom, which Kellie is walking out of.

"Seems like there's only one bed in here," Kellie says.

"I can sleep on the couch," James says. "Anything's better than the facility."

"They've got a bed down here," Kellie says. "Who wants it?"

"You can have it," I say. "I can find somewhere else to sleep."

Kellie looks back at the bed, an idea forming in her head.

"We could probably share," Kellie says. "I don't have a problem with it."

"Oh," I say. "I mean, I guess that could work."

"It could be fun," Kellie continues. "Like a sleepover!"

"I haven't heard that word in ages," I say. "Sure, why not."

"Nice," Kellie replies.

Our conversation is cut short, as the door to the basement opens. We all look to the stairs as Lynn comes down the steps, holding a small pile of clothes in her hands, as well as a phone charger.

"Hello, I'm not bothering you three, am I?"

"No of course not," James replies. "We should really be the ones asking that."

Lynn smiles warmly. "Of course you're not. Anywho, I came down to see if you guys needed anything, and... Paul asked me to give these to you three."

She sets the clothes down on the recliner in the middle of the basement.

"Clothes?" Kellie asks.

"Yep, before all this, someone went shopping and forgot what size they were." Lynn looks up at the ceiling, as if she's glaring at Paul.

"It's nothing special, just some sleepwear, should be something clean to wear. If you decide on using the washer, you're more than welcome to. Oh, and here's a phone charger for your phone, Lyla. I don't know if it's the one you need, but it's our extra one."

"We appreciate it," I reply.

"Oh, you're perfectly fine," Lynn says. "I can't thank you three enough for bringing Paul home. Please, feel free to keep them. They're yours; it's the least we can do."

"You've already done more than enough," James says. "We don't want to take advantage of your hospitality; we won't be here for long."

"Stay as long as you need. You're our friends now," Lynn says, heading back to the stairs. However, she stops just before leaving.

"One more thing," she says. "Paul told me to tell you that if you want something to drink, you're more than welcome to use the bar. There's water in the mini fridge, but if you decide on making something, just be sure to clean up after you're done."

The three of us nod. "Thank you again," I say.

"Of course. We'll see you all tomorrow!" Lynn says, before walking upstairs.

After Lynn walks up the stairs, our attention is turned to the pile of clothes on the recliner.

James walks up and starts separating the piles of clothes.

"There's a few pairs of sweatpants, and some shirts," James says.

"They said we could use the washer," I say. "It wouldn't hurt to wash our stuff and have it ready for tomorrow."

"I've got my clothes in the car, so… I'm set, you guys can take whatever you want," Kellie says.

James fumbles through the clothes and grabs a pair of sweatpants and a shirt.

"I'll take these then," James says, putting his clothes on the couch.

Now it's my turn. I walk up to the few remaining pieces of clothes. Is it weird that I'm taking clothes from these people whom we've barely met? They said we could keep them, so I know I'm not doing anything bad. I've had friends borrow my stuff, but... They're my friends; I know them. I also know that I need to clean my clothes. I've worn the same outfit for almost a whole week, and I'm not about to continue that trend, especially when I have access to a washer and dryer right here.

Looking at the clothes, I grab a grey pair of sweatpants and a grey tank top that's meant for me. Picking up the clothes I have, I look down the hall to where the laundry machine and bathroom are. Carrying my clothes down to the bathroom, I peer inside.

The bathroom looks completely clean, all of the essence of Paul's man cave stripped from the bathroom, with the walls adored with inspirational quotes and colored towels. I look down the hall and call out to the others.

"Hey, uhh… who's going first?" I ask.

"You can if you want," James calls back.

"I'm going to get my stuff, so you can go!" Kellie replies.

Guess I'm going first then.

Chapter 23

Lyla

I step into the bathroom, setting my clothes on the counter next to the sink. I pull back the curtain on the shower and examine the faucet. I turn the handle, and the shower springs to life, shooting water out of the head. I wait a few seconds and reach out to touch the water. It's cold. I turn the faucet farther. It's still cold. I crank the faucet all the way to the end and touch the water again. Immediately, I regret this decision, as I reel my hand back. It's too hot.

I spend the next few minutes attempting to find the perfect amount of hot to cold water mixture before actually getting in. After I've finally deciphered the shower's controls, I discard my current outfit and climb into the shower.

As soon as I'm covered in the water, an immense weight feels like it's been lifted off of my shoulders. I relax as I lean against the wall, letting the water run down my back, warming me from the outside in. How long has it been since I've done something as normal and mundane as take a shower? It feels like forever since I woke up in that facility, since I met James and Kellie, since I fought Paul, since I watched him hop the fence, since we escaped ourselves, since I shot lightning out of my hands. Since... I was human.

I keep going back to that, over and over again in my head, comparing my life before all this to my life now. It's only been a few weeks, maybe a month. But… it feels like years. It feels like I've been like this for way longer than I have. I don't know if it's because we've been in a constant rush from one thing to another, or if it's because of something else. But finally, being able to relax and really let my guard down, doing something that's familiar… It feels like I've taken the longest nap possible, and I've just woken up. Refreshed my mind, maybe even my soul.

Regardless, it feels nice. I take a deep breath and let out a genuine sigh of relief. For a moment, nothing else matters, and I'm all by myself, alone with my thoughts, in a way where I don't feel like the weight of the world or my situation is pushing me down in any way.

Pulling myself out of my trance, I glance up at the rest of the shower. Luckily enough, there's soap and shampoo. Good enough for me.

I quickly finish taking my shower and step out. Grabbing one of the towels from the rack, I dry myself off. But I'm not dry yet. I still feel damp. I grab a second towel and try again. I'm drier, but still a little damp. Stupid fur. I'm not going to take a third towel. I grab the new clothes from the counter and put them on, slipping my dead phone into my pocket. Finally feeling clean for the first time in a while, I grab my old outfit and leave the bathroom, heading over to the washing machine, I dump my clothes in the washer. As I walk out to the basement again, James and Kellie are at the bar. Kellie is sitting on one of the stools, and James is standing behind it, grabbing a water from the mini fridge.

"Well, you look clean," James says.

"That's the point, isn't it?" I reply, sitting down on the stool next to Kellie.

"Yes, it is," James says.

"What else do they have in there?" Kellie asks, peering over the bar.

James ducks down into the mini fridge again and looks through the contents.

"Mostly the normal stuff. Water, soda, beer," James replies.

Kellie looks up at the back of the bar and sighs. "I kinda want a drink."

"Like a water?" James asks.

"No, like a *drink* drink," Kellie replies. "But there's nothing here, it's all whisky and liquor."

"You've never had like a hard drink before?" I ask.

"I have, but like… I don't care for it," she replies.

"They have cola in there?" I ask.

James glances down.

"Yeah," he says.

"You could always mix it," I say.

Kellie ponders my suggestion and shrugs.

"I guess, but only if you do it with me," she says with a cheeky grin.

"Guess I'm going to shower next then?" James asks, stepping away from the bar.

"Yeah," Kellie says. "I've already grabbed my clothes, so you go first."

"Suit yourself," James says as he walks down the hall to the bathroom.

"You're not going to have one too?" I ask.

"Eh," James responds, "I don't really drink."

"All right," I reply.

As James disappears down the hall, I take his place behind the bar, grabbing one of the bottles of whisky from the back of the bar.

"They did say we could do this, right?" I ask Kellie.

Kellie looks up, trying to remember what Lynn said about using the bar.

"She said we just gotta clean up afterwards," Kellie responds.

"All right," I say. Opening the bottle and grabbing a can of cola from the mini fridge, I then pick up a glass and put some ice in it, and finally mix the two together. I slide Kellie her drink and make one for myself.

Kellie looks at the cup and then begrudgingly decides to take a drink. She takes a small sip and then sets the cup down.

"That's strong," she says, grimacing.

"Well, I don't want to ransack the bar. So, you'll have to put up with it if you want to share a drink like adults." I chuckle. "Besides, you'll probably be able to tolerate it about halfway through."

I take a drink next. Yep, this is exactly what I made. Is it good? Not particularly, but it's better than taking shots of straight whisky.

We both take a drink again.

"Why'd you make it so strong?" Kellie says.

"I'm not a bartender. What, you can't handle strong drinks?" I reply.

"I've really only drunk with friends, sangria, wine, whatever really."

"Not much of a party person?" I say.

"I was normally the designated driver. I usually started having fun once we all got back to a place. So, I guess not," Kellie says.

"That sounds like a real bummer lifestyle," I say.

"I mean, I was doing it for my friends, ya know?" Kellie says. "That's what friends are for."

Kellie takes another drink. I follow.

"I guess," I say. "You think that they would plan that kind of stuff out so you could participate, switch off on drivers? Maybe ask for a cab?"

"I didn't mind," Kellie responds. "I was just happy to be out of the house."

"When was the last time you talked to your friends, like… before all this happened?" I ask.

Kellie stops, pondering the question.

"I don't know… Maybe a few months?" she replies.

"You didn't reach out to them at all?" I say.

"I mean, all this stuff happened," Kellie says.

"No, I mean before this." I add, "Between then, before this."

"Oh… I mean, I did a few times," Kellie responds. "But they don't really respond to my messages."

"That doesn't really sound like they were your friends," I say.

"What're you talking about?" Kellie asks.

"Have they ever asked you if you wanted to hang out?" I ask.

"Maybe once or twice," Kellie says.

"Were you always initiating the conversation?" I continue.

"Now that you mention it… Yeah," Kellie replies.

"Were you always working around their schedule, and they didn't wait for you?" I ask.

Kellie stops, her expression changing from defensive to one of realization.

"Oh…." she says.

"Listen here," I respond. "Those kinds of people aren't your friends. Those people take you for granted, and they don't consider that you've been putting in much more work than anyone else."

I take a second to refill my glass.

"You want another?" I ask.

Kellie pauses but hands me her glass begrudgingly. I take it and refill it for her.

"Those kinds of people are the people who wouldn't blink if you vanished," I say. "I've had friends like that. I've had some people that I've just kind of… cut out of my life. People that I didn't think were going to help me when the times got tough. People who didn't really care."

I pause, thinking about the people whom I was with before this all started. I never even plugged my phone in. I never even checked to see if any of them messaged me. A single thought crosses my mind: Who am I really telling this to? Me? Or Kellie? Or… is it both?

"I'm sure someone's told you before, maybe even me," I say between drinks. "But friends who're like the ones you mentioned, those people are the ones you can live with, but also live without. But every once in a while, you come across a friend who's not like that. Someone who's always got your back no matter what, someone who's looking out for you at every turn."

"Are... are you that kind of friend?" Kellie asks.

"We've had our rough patches," I say. "Sometimes I think about what happened, back at the facility."

"Lyla I—" Kellie begins to say.

"Hang on, I'm not done," I reply.

The truth is... It's been hanging in the back of my mind. What Kellie did, selling us out like that. But looking back on it all, I don't know what I would've done in that situation either. We knew something that she didn't. I was in a similar place when I woke up. If I didn't run into Carter, James, Paul, or anyone before I tried to get out of here, I probably would've taken that deal too, just to be able to feel connected to someone.

"Yes. I know, but... After everything... I can put myself in your shoes and... I can see myself doing what you did," I say. "I don't know what you're thinking, and I don't know what you've been through, but seeing you meet your parents, watching you tell us how sorry you are, seeing you play with Paul's kid. It... I know you're not like that. I know you wouldn't do that."

"Lyla," Kellie responds. "I still feel really bad about all that."

"Kellie, it's fine," I respond. "The important thing is that we're all out together. But enough of that. We're free."

"We are," Kellie says. "We... are friends... right?"

"Yes," I say. "We're in this together now."

"Gotcha," Kellie says.

"Anyways, changing the topic, how's that drink of yours?" I ask.

"It's fine, now that I've had one. It doesn't taste as strong now," Kellie says.

"Cool," I say. "I'll keep 'em coming."

"Okay!" Kellie says with a grin.

We both sit in silence for a moment, before we both finish our drinks a second time. Kellie hands me her glass, and I make us a third one.

"Should we still be doing this?" Kellie asks.

"What're you talking about?" I say.

"Like, drinking. We're not human anymore," Kellie clarifies.

"I don't know," I say. "I remember hearing something from the guy in the facility that we're relatively the same on the inside, so I'm sure we'll be fine."

Kellie looks around the room, as if she's searching for something to say.

"Oh! I have a question for you," Kellie says, excitedly.

"Okay," I respond, handing her back a glass. "What is it?"

"So, let's say that you got to pick which animal you became," Kellie says. "Nothing changes, but you get to choose."

"I get to choose what animal I become?" I respond. "Hmm... I'd be a wolf."

"A wolf? Why?" Kellie asks.

"I dunno, they're cool, everyone likes 'em, and they're strong, I guess," I respond.

"It's always wolves or dogs..." Kellie says to herself.

"What?" I ask.

"Oh yeah, sorry," Kellie continues. "I asked James this when you were taking a shower, and he said he'd be a dog. I wonder if everyone chooses that."

"Maybe," I say. "What about you?"

"Me?" Kellie asks, pointing to herself exaggeratedly. She's definitely more comfortable now.

"Uh... I don't think I would change anything," Kellie says.

"Really?" I ask. "Why?"

"I guess I was so used to not really liking the way I looked?" Kellie ponders.

"But you could be any animal in the world," I reply. "And you'd choose to stay as a raccoon?"

"Well, it's me, isn't it? I'm happy with the way I look now. I think I'm pretty darn cute," Kellie responds with a big grin.

"I guess. I dunno," I respond.

"Oh, come on, Lyla, you could've had it worse." Kellie laughs. "You're still cute."

"I dunno," I say. "I still kinda think about what life could've been like if I was a human," I respond.

"Oh, boo hoo!" Kellie says. "You're clinging to the past. Thinking about what could have been when you should be focused on what's happening now."

Kellie sits up and gives her full undivided attention to both me and her glass.

"You need to open up a little, focus on what's happening now. You said it yourself, a friend is someone who's there for you through thick and thin, highs and lows, and whatever else."

Kellie takes another drink from her glass. She's definitely a lightweight.

"So what if you think about what could have been but you can't change it! You gotta deal with what's going on now! You have superpowers! That's awesome! I'm extremely jealous! Plus, you're not like some kind of animal that prevents you from doing normal things. You have hands and feet, and you can talk and hear and see."

"I… I guess," I respond.

"Plus, on the inside, you're still you… Right?" Kellie says.

I don't say anything.

"Right?" Kellie asks again.

"Yeah. I guess I am."

Kellie leans up on the table, almost standing on it.

"So, why're you complaining? You worry so much about what other people think that you don't stop to realize that nothing about you in here"—Kellie pokes me in the chest—"is different! You're still you. We all look different, but look at Paul and his wife. They're still happy, despite the fact that Paul now is what he shoots!"

Kellie points to the bear skin rug on the floor.

"I… I guess," I say.

"Listen to me," Kellie says. "You're cool. I'm glad I met you guys, and I'm sure that even if we were both human, we'd still be friends. But I met this version of you, and I don't give a single crap about what you used to look like, 'cause it doesn't matter. You're you, and I know for a fact that if it wasn't for you, I'd still be locked up in that stupid facility pretending like everything is okay. Got it?"

She's right, isn't she? I've spent the last few days getting used to all this, thinking about how things could have been different, how they could have been better. But I didn't realize what I've created throughout all that. James, Kellie. They're my friends, and they care about me. They don't care about what I look like. They like me… for me.

But still, that voice in the back of my head, telling me that I don't belong like this. Telling me that I'm not normal… It remains. Lingering in the back of my mind, doubting everything I've been through.

"…Got it," I say.

"Nah, I don't like the way you said that," Kellie responds. "You gotta open up! You understand what I'm saying?"

"Yes," I say.

"Good," Kellie says. "You gotta get in touch with you! Release all those bottled-up feelings… and face the real you head-on!"

"Face the real me, head-on?" I ask. "What're you talking about?"

"Tomorrow, I want you to look at yourself and say you're cute," Kellie says.

"Say I'm cute?" I ask.

"Yeah, you heard me," Kellie replies. "Learn to love yourself a little. That's literally all I'm asking."

I sigh. "Okay."

"Nice," Kellie replies. "Also, I would like another drink." She holds out another empty glass.

"One more," I say.

"All right, all right," Kellie replies. "But you gotta do something for me."

"What is it?" I ask.

"Let me fix your sweatpants," Kellie replies.

"What? What're you talking about?" I ask, handing her another drink.

"Just let me see your pants," Kellie says. "I'm going to modify them for you."

"Why?" I ask.

"Come on, trust me, as a friend. Go into the bedroom and just hand 'em out the door if you're going to be such a pansy about it."

I sigh. "Whatever."

I walk out from behind the bar and head to the bedroom, closing the door and handing my only pair of clean pants to Kellie through the crack.

"Okay, there," I say.

"Just gimme a moment," Kellie says, her voice drifting away from the door.

I hear the sound of… snipping? What the heck is she doing?

Kellie's voice comes back.

"Okay, here, take 'em, and put 'em back on, you big baby," she says, sliding the pants through the crack.

Taking the pants back into my hands, I notice she's cut a hole in the rear. It's for my tail.

"Why'd you do this?" I ask.

"'Cause you're an idiot if you're going to walk around with your pants sagging. Plus, you gotta get used to it, Lyla. You aren't human anymore. Think of it as a step into loving yourself. I dunno, dude, I'm trying to do something nice!" Kellie's voice replies.

I don't know, but I think I should have probably stopped Kellie sooner. Regardless, these are my only pair of pants, and now they have a hole in the back. I put them on, and just like Kellie said they would, they fit now. Maybe she was onto something? I'm… not really sure anymore.

I step out of the room, Kellie waiting for me, drink in hand.

"There she is. How they fit?" Kellie asks.

"Better than earlier, actually," I respond.

"Nice!" Kellie says. "I did that to all my clothes earlier while you were in the shower."

The door to the bathroom opens, and James walks out in a fresh new set of clothes.

"I heard you guys talking. Kellie do the thing to your pants too?" James says.

"Yes," I respond.

"Hey! You have fitting clothes now. I know I wouldn't go outside like that," Kellie responds.

James disregards Kellie's comment and turns to me.

"I threw my clothes in the washer with yours," James says. "Should be done in a bit, and I'll dry 'em afterwards."

"Cool," I say. "You going to shower, Kellie?" I ask.

"Sure am," she says. Setting her cup down, she disappears down the hall.

James takes a seat on the couch. I head back to the bar and start cleaning up everything Kellie and I touched.

"I needed that," James groans.

"I think we all did," I reply.

"Hard to believe it's been, like, what… a week?" James asks.

"I think?" I reply. "Maybe just under."

"I feel like I've lost all concept of time." James continues, "Ever since we've gotten out, it's felt like today was just three days."

"I know that feeling," I reply. "Ever since I've woken up, it's been one thing after another."

"Well, it's almost over," James says. "We stay here till the day after tomorrow, and then we go find my sister."

"That's the plan, isn't it?" I say.

"Then, my adventure is over," James says.

"You're not coming with us?" I ask.

"I have my sister to take care of," James replies. "Things may be different, but I gotta put my family first. Doesn't mean I won't stay in contact with you."

"I guess I can respect that," I reply.

"How can I forget about you and Kellie anyways. If it weren't for you two, I'd probably be living the same vicious cycle inside the facility," James says with a chuckle.

"That's what Kellie said about us," I reply.

"Yeah, I think… we've all helped each other to the point where we're kinda stuck with each other," James says.

"I agree with that," I respond.

"Of course. We've had each other's backs since the beginning. Even since you screamed when you found that hole in the wall." James laughs.

"Can't blame me for that. I just woke up, and I was completely terrified," I snap back playfully.

"No, of course not," James says. "Believe me, I would've done the same thing in your shoes."

"Yeah," I say.

We both sit in silence. I can feel myself getting tired. I don't know if it was the drinks, or if I'm completely exhausted. I finish cleaning and sit on the recliner across from James.

"Gonna be weird, splitting up," I say.

"It won't be so bad," James says. "Call me whenever, and I'll come running."

"That's… awfully nice of you," I reply.

"It's what friends are for." James grins.

"Same here," I say. "We gotta stick together, no matter how far we apart we are."

"Definitely," James says. "If we didn't, well, I don't know what we'd do. Don't know how much help I'd be."

"What're you talking about?" I say.

"I don't have any of those powers that you do."

"You did more than enough with the planning and stuff. I don't think I would've come up with that grappling hook idea if it wasn't for you," I recount.

"That was a pretty smart idea," James says.

"Don't discount yourself, dude," I say.

"Okay, okay, you got me," James says with a laugh. "So, if I'm the brains, and you're the brawn, what does that make Kellie?"

I pause. "Hmmm," I say. "She'd be the… agility?"

James thinks about it for a moment.

"Doesn't really roll of the tongue, but I get what you're saying." James grins.

The door to the bathroom opens once more, and Kellie steps out in a pair of sleepwear as well. Seems like it's the one her dad gave to her, 'cause her red sweatshirt's been replaced with a teal t-shirt and orange shorts.

"Okay, I think I'm beat." Kellie says.

"I think we all are," James replies. "Time to sleep comfortably tonight?"

"I'm going to sleep like a freakin' rock," I reply.

"You said it," Kellie says, heading into the bedroom.

I grab the phone charger from where the clothes once were and head to the bedroom with Kellie. I find the light switch and fiddle with the switches until the lights turn off.

"Thanks," James says. "I didn't want to get up."

"Good night, James," I reply.

"Good night, Lyla," he responds.

"Good night, James!" Kellies voice comes from the bedroom.

"Good night to you too, Kellie," James says.

I head into the bedroom, where Kellie is already splayed out on the side of the bed, though there's plenty of room for me.

I plug the phone charger into the wall next to the nightstand and grab my phone. Plugging it into the wall, I half expect it to spring to life. But it doesn't. Guess that's a problem for tomorrow's Lyla.

I collapse onto the bed, not even bothering to put the covers on.

"I'm so tired," I say.

"Me too," Kellie replies.

I readjust into a comfortable position and start to close my eyes. The feeling of sleeping on a real bed for the first time in a week cradles my body as everything starts to drift away. Soon enough….

CHAPTER 24

Lyla

THE SOUNDS OF the outside slowly fade into my consciousness, lifting me up from my sleep. The slight breeze, the chirping of birds, the sound of the wind on the curtains. I can hear it all. Compared to sleeping in the silence of the facility, it's almost too much. I try to open my eyes, but I can feel sleep pulling me back in.

The sounds of footsteps walking through the basement permeates the walls. I can hear them getting closer.

"You up?" James says.

I roll over on my side, forcing my eyes to open. Light beams into my retinas, forcing me to squint. Through my half-closed eyelids, I see James standing outside of the room, holding my clothes in his hand.

"Yeah, I'm up," I respond.

"Good, it's almost eleven. You slept like a rock," he says, throwing my clothes onto the bed.

I look around and notice I'm the only one who hasn't gotten out of bed yet.

"You two already up?" I ask.

"Yeah, only for a while. Kellie's upstairs talking to Paul and Lynn. I decided to come down and get you up," James replies.

"All right," I respond. "Gimme a few to get around."

"Sounds good," James replies. "Lynn brought down the usual amenities, so go clean up and come upstairs." He grins.

James then makes his exit from the room. I rise from the bed like a zombie. Flinging my legs onto the floor, I stand up for the first time today. Stepping out of bed, I grab my clothes from the end of the bed James tossed them on and ignore the siren's call of the mattress. I make my way back out into the basement living room and down the hall into the hallway. I sluggishly work my way back to the bathroom.

I enter and lock the door. I then proceed to go through my normal morning routine, as if the last week didn't consist of living inside of some insane facility. There's comfort in normalcy. Something I didn't quite miss until now.

Once I'm done brushing my teeth and making sure I look presentable, I put my clean clothes on and walk upstairs.

Entering upstairs, it's still morning, but not early to where it feels like a work day. I don't remember what day of the week it is, but it feels like a Saturday. The light shines in from the sliding glass door leading out to the deck in the back of the house, and everyone seems to be in good spirits. James and Kellie are sitting at the table, conversing with Paul.

Lynn is in the kitchen, standing in front of the stove. She notices me and turns around.

"Oh, James managed to wake you up! I thought I'd do something nice for you three," she says with a smile.

Penelope chimes in, "We made pancakes!"

It feels like something out of an old television show my mom and I used to watch. I don't remember the name of it. But there's a feeling of comfort seeing all of this.

"Thank you," I say, giving away a tired smile.

I work my way to the table and pick an open seat next to Kellie.

"Ah, you woke up!" Kellie says, grinning. "I was just telling everyone about how I thought you'd never get out of bed."

"Oh yeah?" I say.

"She said she poked ya, pushed ya, shoved ya, jumped on ya, just 'bout everything. You didn't budge," Paul replies, digging into a comically large-sized plate of pancakes.

"You seriously did sleep like a log," James says. "I even tried talking to you earlier."

"Did she say anything?" Kellie asks.

"Did I?" I add.

"Not really," James replies. "You said, 'Not now.' And 'Get out.'"

"Par for the course," I reply. "Sounds a lot like me."

"Well, don't be heading back to bed just yet," Paul says. "We've got work to do."

"Work?" I ask.

"Yup," Paul says, shoveling a whole pancake into his mouth. "Gotta show you how to use yer gift."

"Oh, that," I say. "Sounds like it'll be fun."

"I dunno about that," Paul says. "It ain't like I'm going to make you go through some rigorous training or anything. It's just about patience and whatnot. I'll explain later. If you got some unfinished business to take care of, then you got till I'm done with this breakfast."

As Paul mentions breakfast, a stack of pancakes slides in front of me. I look to my side and see Penelope pushing the plate onto the table.

"Thank you," I say with a grin.

"You're welcome!" She smiles, before heading back to her mom.

"Ain't she precious," Paul says.

"She seems like she's been raised well," I say.

"'Course, she's my daughter." Paul grins.

I nod and start taking to my breakfast. It's strange… the moment the fork connects with my mouth, it's like I'm transported back to when I was a kid. My mother made me pancakes from scratch once. The light fluffy texture, the warm butter, the hint of vanilla, and the flavor of store brand syrup. It's not much, but it's something that's etched itself into my mind since I was young. That memory, dragged back into the front of my mind as I sit here, making a new memory with friends, in an unlikely scenario. That continued feeling that everything's gone back to normal.

Before I know it, I'm done with my pancakes. I stop, dumfounded that I ate them so quickly.

"That hungry, huh?" James asks.

"Can't blame her," Paul responds. "They're good."

"They were," I say.

I pick up my plate and walk it back to Lynn, who's now cleaning up.

"Let me see that," she says, taking the plate from my hands.

"I can clean it if you'd like," I reply.

"Oh, don't be silly, you've got plans already. I can take care of it," she says with a warm smile.

I nod. "Thank you."

"Anytime," she says.

I step away from the kitchen, until I remember something important I wanted to do when I woke up.

My phone. I need to check my phone.

I walk downstairs and head back into the room where Kellie and I were staying, and immediately pick up my phone in the charger.

I attempt to turn it on, and to my surprise, it does start up. I wait patiently as the phone boots. Then, my phone opens to my lock screen.

I'm… surprised. I half expected my phone to be flooded with texts from my friends asking where I was. But my messages app is empty. My phone also says no SIM either. Figures.

My phone, on the other hand, has ten calls missed.

Two from my friends, and eight from my aunt Jessie.

I don't really know what to say about my friends only calling me twice. Are they worried sick? Or do they just not care? I start to think back to what I told Kellie last night. That real friends are the kinds of people that will have your back no matter what.

But my friends only called me twice, then gave up? Or did they call me after my phone died? Did they try to find me? Or did they give up after looking? Did they get into contact with the facility, and do they think I died? Or that I'm still trapped there? Did they contact my aunt? Did they contact my work? What happened?

I don't know, but I get this feeling that they didn't do very much to try to find me. I feel a pit in my stomach, that feeling that these people whom I regarded as friends abandoned me. I don't even know if it's true, but from what I've seen, I can't help but think that they're not really looking out for me as much as Kellie and James have. But my aunt calling me. She must be worried sick. I need to get in touch with her right now.

Grabbing my phone from the charger, I go upstairs. I don't see anyone at first, until Lynn rounds the corner, spotting me.

"Oh, there you are! Paul was just looking for you," she says.

"I thought as much," I reply. "Before I go out there, do you have a phone I can borrow?" I ask.

"Oh yeah, we've got a landline in the kitchen, a little old-fashioned, but it should do the job just fine," Lynn says.

"Awesome, thank you," I reply.

"No problem!" she says with a smile. "I'll tell Paul you're coming out real soon."

Lynn walks back around the corner, disappearing from the hallway. I look into the kitchen and spot a corded phone on the wall. She's right; it's old. Not rotary dial old, but old enough to where I can tell. I pick the receiver off the wall and look at my cell phone in my other hand. I tap on my aunt's contact and type the number into the keypad.

The phone starts ringing.

Rrrring....

Rrrring….

Rrrring….

Rrrring….

Rrrring….

Rrrring….

Click.

"H…Hello?" the voice on the other end says.

"Aunt Jessie?" I respond.

"Oh… Oh my god," the voice responds. "It's really you, isn't it."

"Yeah, it's me," I reply.

"Oh, thank god you're safe. I haven't heard from you in weeks! I… I tried calling, but once it started going to voicemail… I was sure the worst had happened," Aunt Jessie says. I can hear her choking up over the line.

"I'm… fine… sort of," I reply. "Has anyone asked about me?" I say.

"Your friends called me once to see where you were," she says. "I told them that you were supposed to be with them, but it seems like you vanished from your trip to the cabin. Where are you now? I need to know. I'll come get you this instant," she says, stammering, talking a mile a minute. I can barely understand her.

"Calm down, calm down. You don't have to get me. I'm on my way back," I say.

"You are? When will you come back?" she asks.

"I… I don't know. A day? Maybe two?" I reply.

"You're not in any danger? You haven't been kidnapped, right? How're you getting home?" Jessie asks.

"I'm fine, I'm not in any danger. It's… It's a long story…" I say.

"That… that *thing* happened to you… didn't it?"

Her voice rings out through my head. That *thing*… She's talking about me being changed, isn't she… But the way she said it… *That thing*… like it's some foreign concept to her, like she doesn't want to believe that it did. Like she doesn't want to see me… like this…

Do I lie and say no and let the issue slide or possibly get worse when I get home? Or do I rip the bandage off now and tell her the truth?

"Hello? Answer me," she says.

I try to say something, but… I can't. That feeling, I thought I got rid of it, but it's back. I can feel myself freezing up again.

"I…I…" I try to speak, but it's just stutters. I don't know what to say.

"Lyla, you need to tell me. Please," my aunt says. I can hear her worry in her voice.

I manage to squeak out something.

"Y…yes," I say.

I'm still frozen. All I hear is a soft whimper from the other end of the phone. I have no idea what she's going to say next, and it feels like I've just been caught red-handed committing murder. I feel flustered, embarrassed, and terrified, all at the same time.

"That… that explains a lot," my aunt says, her tone unchanging.

"Are… are you okay?" I ask.

"I'm… fine," she replies. "I just… I didn't think this would happen to you."

"I don't—" I go to say, before I'm cut off by my aunt.

"It's okay, I know it's not… not your fault. I… I still love you."

"I… I love you too," I reply, "But I nee—"

I'm cut off again.

"I'll see you when you get back. I'm gonna call your mom."

"No, wait!" I say, but before I can finish my sentence…

Click.

CHAPTER 25

Lyla

THE PHONE CALL ends. I'm still standing in shock. That feeling that came back lingers but slowly dissipates. What did my aunt say… she was going to call my… mom?

Why would she do that? I haven't spoken to my parents in ages. She knows better than anyone that I just… don't talk to my parents anymore.

It feels like she's taking that away from me. She's scooping up my opportunity to do that myself and taking it. I know that it's not the case. I assume she's only doing it to let my parents know I'm still alive, and that I'm coming back. But I should do that myself. I'm an adult. I know that I'm able to deal with these things on my own.

Still, I feel robbed, like a kid who got their lunch money taken. I put the phone back on the wall and my cell on the counter. Turning around, I see Paul standing in the hallway, looking at me. I jump back and then regain my composure.

"How.. long were you there?" I ask.

"Not too long, caught the end of the conversation," he says. "That family?"

"Yeah, sorta," I say. "It's my aunt."

"That's family," Paul says. "What'd she say?"

"I'm… I'm not sure," I reply. "She sounded taken aback. She knew that I've been gone for a while, and that I've… changed. She said she's going to contact my mom."

"Sounds like she's looking out for you," Paul says.

"Maybe?" I say, "But I can't tell if she's okay with me… being like this." I gesture to my body.

"Well, she's gonna have to. You can't change that about yourself," Paul says. "Lord knows I didn't ask to be turned into a bear."

"I guess," I say. "I just feel like she should have let me talk to my parents first."

"Why's that?" Paul says, gesturing to the door.

I start to follow Paul out of the house.

"I just… haven't talked to my parents in a while," I reply.

Paul opens the front door and steps out to the porch. I follow and step out into the warm sun. Lynn is outside, sitting with Penelope on the grass. Penelope is playing with some toy, I can discern. James and Kellie are off to the side, tossing a football. James seems to know what he's doing. Kellie… doesn't. I turn my attention back to Paul.

"You don't talk to your parents?" he asks.

"Yeah," I say.

"You should," he says.

"I know that now," I snap back. "They were just too busy to pay me any mind, so I spent most of my time with my aunt."

"No parent is too busy to spend time with their kids. Least, the good ones aren't," Paul says.

"I don't think my parents are bad people," I reply, following Paul to a tree out in the front yard. "They were just busy a lot of the time, only ever really saw them on weekends."

"What'd they do for work?" Paul asks.

"My mom used to be a banker, and my dad was an electrician," I say.

"They aren't anymore?" Paul asks.

"Nope, since I moved out, they didn't have to work to support me, so they started supporting themselves. They had this dream. They both wanted to start a restaurant," I continue.

"What kind?" Paul inquires.

"I don't… remember. I think they wanted something small, like a sports bar kind of place," I say.

"Oh, I know what you're talking about, love them places," Paul says.

"I don't think the kind of restaurant mattered to them. They just wanted to create something to share with people," I add. "But I only know about this 'cause my aunt told me they finally opened one when I was in my third year of college. That was… maybe three years ago?"

"Did you ever try to reach out?" Paul asks.

"Not since I moved out. I just got busy with schooling," I reply.

"Sounds like the shoe's on the other foot now," Paul says. "They didn't have time when you were young, and all of a sudden you don't have time for them."

"I'm well aware," I say.

"I hope you're going to find them when you go home," Paul says, "Can't imagine my life if I lost Lynn or Penelope."

"I'm going to," I say.

"Good to hear. You're a smart woman. I know you'll make the right choice," Paul says.

"Thanks," I reply.

We both stop walking. The shade from the tree keeps my body cool, but the air is warm. I'm in temperature limbo, and it's perfect.

"All right, time to make you learn," Paul says.

"Yep," I reply. I got so caught up in the conversation that I forgot Paul wanted to help me understand my newfound abilities.

"Take a look in front of us," Paul says.

I look in front of us, and there's an archery target positioned about twenty feet away from us. The sun shines down on the target, revealing the glistening chicken wire it's wrapped in.

"What's this?" I ask.

"That, miss… is a target, and I'm going to have you electrocute it," Paul says.

"All right…" I say, psyching myself up.

I reach out my hand to shoot electricity just like I did at the facility. That same feeling from the night it happened, that warmth in my chest swells up. I think about attacking the target with my powers, electricity arcs on my fingers, as I reel my hand back and push forward. A small burst of electricity shoots from the palm of my hand, but… it's not enough to reach the target.

Paul leans back and then puts a finger to his chin.

"Hm…" Paul contemplates.

"Sorry," I say.

"No need to be sorry," Paul responds, still lost in thought.

Paul then snaps his fingers and turns to me once more.

"What're you thinking about right now?" he asks.

"Hitting the target," I say.

"No, no. I mean, what're you *thinking about*, not focusing on," Paul says.

"I don't know," I respond. "I'm thinking about a lot of things."

"Let's try this then," Paul says. "Clear your mind."

"Clear my mind?" I ask.

"Yes, just try to not only focus on the target, but visualize it, really think about hitting it," he says. "Like this."

Paul takes a deep breath and holds his hand above the ground, pulling the earth out in a spherical shape.

"What I've come to understand is that you need to visualize what you want to do. Focusing is one thing, but working together with visualization is like givin' it a running start. I visualize this ball I've made from the ground, I visualize it's shape, I visualize me pullin' it from the ground. Then, I do it."

"Okay," I say.

"Don't try to force yourself," Paul says. "It doesn't work."

I nod, and I hold my hands out together. I close my eyes, and I imagine myself throwing both my hands forward, watching as the electricity arcs from my hands to the target in front of me. I take a deep breath. But I hear the wind, the birds, I hear a lot. I try to drown it out. I open my eyes, and I push my hands forward just like I did in my head. The electricity I generate from my hands arcs out and heads towards the target, but zigzags to the side, singeing the ground.

"I missed," I say.

"I could tell you let the outside sounds get to you," Paul says. "You gotta use those ears of yours to drown them out."

"What're you talking about?" I say.

"Focus on something else to listen to," Paul says. "It's…. It's like aiming a gun. You ever done that?"

"No… I can't say that I have," I respond.

"Now this is just difficult to explain," Paul says.

Paul pauses, trying to pick his words.

"Okay, I'm going to walk you through this," Paul says.

"All right." I nod.

"First things first, focus on the target," he says.

I look at the target, the grass next to it still smoldering.

"Just the target, don't focus on the grass," Paul says.

I shift my gaze to the target alone.

"You see it?" Paul asks.

"Yes," I respond.

"All right, now, hold your hands out and visualize your electricity."

I hold my hands out and close my eyes, starting to visualize where the electricity is going to go.

"Don't close your eyes," Paul says.

"All right," I respond, opening my eyes.

"Now, look past your hands and focus on the target like that. Visualize your electricity hitting it."

I focus on the target, my hands, and the world around me starts to grow blurry, as the only clear thing in my vision is the target.

"What're you thinking about?" Paul asks.

"The target," I respond.

"What are you visualizing?" Paul asks.

"My electricity hitting the target."

"Now, drown everything out, like you're… on your phone, and shoot."

I stop, keeping my eyes on the target, the sounds around me slowly starting to fade away as my pure attention is on the target. I'm trapped in a bubble where the only thing I can see and hear is the target.

I reel my hands back and shoot them forward once more. Electricity jettisons out of my hands, arcing through the air with a hiss and a crackle, as it connects onto the chicken wire, electrifying the target.

"I did it… I did it!" I exclaim.

"Again," Paul says.

"Again?" I ask.

"Yup, do it again," Paul responds.

"Okay," I respond, readying myself once more.

I walk through the setup Paul walked me through, stare at the target until everything becomes blurry, drown out all the sound, visualize the electricity. I reel my hands back and push forward once more.

The electricity arcs out of my hands again and whizzes past the target, fizzling out only a few feet after.

"I… missed?" I say.

"You went too fast," Paul responds. "You did a good job the first time, but you got too excited that you did it once you went back to the start."

"Oh," I say.

"Again, you did good," Paul adds. "But do it again, and do it slow, like we did the first time."

I nod. Okay, slow… Got it. Focus on the target… Then… visualize the electricity. Just like the first time, the world grows blurry. Okay, now, drown out all the sound.

And… go.

I push my hands forward, and the electricity hisses through the air once more, hitting the target.

A voice cracks through my focus. "Again."

I push my hands forward again, nailing the target.

"Again."

I do it a third time, hitting the target once more.

"Try…. your Left hand."

I drop my right hand and throw electricity with my left hand, just nicking the target on the left side.

"Now, your right hand."

I drop my left hand and throw electricity with my other hand. I'm more accurate this time, not nicking the side of the target but not hitting dead-on like I did prior.

"Good," Paul says, pulling me out of my focus.

"You think so?" I ask.

"Well, you're not perfect, but you did hit the target each time. Granted, it's all about practice from here on out. Just honing it in so you can do that on the fly."

"How come I did it when I was at the facility but not until now?" I ask.

"Don't know. Could be something along the lines of you just being hopped up on adrenaline. People do crazy stuff on it," Paul says.

"But what about me not being able to do it after the fact?" I say.

"You expelled all your energy," Paul says.

"What do you mean?" I ask.

"You got tired," Paul replies. "Nobody can run forever, nobody can lift heavy things forever, and sooner or later, you get tired. I'm assuming that's how it works."

"You don't know?" I ask.

"I got tired when I was running from the facility, my abilities stopped working, and then I slept, woke up, and could use them again." Paul continues, "You'll just have to know when to use it, and not get tuckered out when it matters most."

"Gotcha," I say.

"Now, you can keep practicing if you want, but I'm going to—"

Paul's sentence is cut off, as the sound of a honking car is heard.

"What's that?" I ask.

"A car," Paul says. "But that's coming from down the driveway."

We both look to the driveway as three dark vans barrel down the path. All of them sporting a logo we all know too well.

"Go, get Lynn and Penelope inside," Paul says. "Then, come out here. Hopefully we can resolve this peacefully."

CHAPTER 26

James

THERE'S SOMETHING SO calming about being outside. Granted, it's been a very long time since I've taken a break from anything. I spent so much time running around, working, doing errands, and watching my family that I don't remember the last time I've really had an off day. Even just being in the facility, planning the escape with Lyla and Kellie, still felt like work.

Well, I guess also almost getting shot would fit into that category, wouldn't it? Still gives me shivers.

As I pull myself out of my daydream, a football rolls to me feet. Looking up, I see Kellie with a big grin on her face.

"How'd I do?" she asks, grinning.

"You could be doing better." I chuckle. I pick up the football and ready a throw.

"Look where my hands are at," I say, showing her the ball. "Then, it's all about spinning the ball when you throw it."

I throw the ball, and as it spirals through the air, Kellie holds her hands out to catch the ball. It bounces out of her hands, but she manages to recover and actually catch it.

"I did it!" she exclaims, jumping in the air.

"Nice!" I say. "Now, try throwing it back."

Kellie looks at the ball and attempts to emulate the way that I held the ball in my hands. She holds the ball behind her and attempts to throw it to me. The ball leaves her hand and spirals through the air, landing closer to me but not making the distance.

"That was pretty good!" I say.

"Awesome! I'm getting good at this!" she exclaims again.

I pick up the ball and walk over to where she is, setting the ball back on the ground.

"We're done?" she asks.

"For now, yeah," I say, sitting down on the ground.

"What do you want to do now?" Kellie asks.

"Right now? Nothing," I say.

"Nothing?" Kellie asks.

"Yep," I respond.

"All righty," she says, sitting down next to me.

We both sit in silence, staring off into the distance.

"So, when do you think we'll be leaving?" Kellie asks.

"I dunno, I was gonna ask Lyla if we should leave tomorrow. But I think she might want to stay another day," I say, pointing to the large tree, where Lyla and Paul are standing. Paul seems to be explaining something to her. She holds her hands out, and we see a flash of electricity erupt from her hands. The blast of electricity doesn't reach the square-looking object in front of her.

"What do you think of Lyla's… powers?" Kellie asks.

"What do you mean?" I say in return.

"I dunno, she seemed so… scary with them when we were at the facility," Kellie responds. "Like she was someone else."

I think back to that moment, sitting on the top of the wall, watching Lyla run from guard to guard, electrocuting them with each blow from her hands. I also remember the scream Thorn let out when she enveloped him in electricity.

"Yeah, I know what you're saying. It was uncomfortable to watch,"

I reply. "But that's what Lyla and I thought about Paul when we first met him."

We both look back to the tree and see Paul nod in a fatherly manner as Lyla attempts to use her powers again, coming up short once more.

"Paul turned out to be a nice guy," I say. "I mean, look at his family." I gesture to Lynn and her daughter, who are now playing with one of those very large bubble wands. "They're good people."

"I guess," Kellie responds. "They've been so kind to us."

"Yep," I say. "I don't want to overstay our welcome. But I think if anything, Paul helping Lyla with these… powers she has might be good for her."

"You're right," Kellie replies.

I lie down on the ground, facing the sky. The clouds above me morph from shape to shape as the wind blows them by. Kellie manages to speak up again.

"Can't help but be kinda jealous," she says.

"Of?" I ask.

"Lyla, I mean she's got super cool powers," she says.

"You're jealous of her 'cause she can shoot lightning out of her hands?" I ask.

"I feel like that's a given," Kellie says. "You ever wanted superpowers?" Kellie says.

"I mean, when I was a kid, sure. But now, I don't even know what I want anymore. So much about us has… changed," I reply.

"Sure, I understand that, but, like, come on, wouldn't you think it'd be super cool to have powers like that?" Kellie continues, "To be able to shoot lightning out of your hands? Or fly?"

"I think we'd have to be birds if we wanted to fly," I say.

"That's the craziest part," Kellie says. "We could've."

"I know what you mean." I laugh.

"So, back to the point," Kellie says. "Are you scared of her?"

Thorn's scream plays through my head again.

"Oh yeah, I'm scared. But she's our friend. We've been through a lot, the three of us. We've gotta have faith in her," I reply.

"I can agree with that," Kellie replies.

We both sit in silence again until Kellie speaks up one more time.

"What about everything?" she asks.

"What do you mean?" I respond.

"Just in general, how are you so… calm through all this?" Kellie asks.

"I'm not," I say.

"You're… not?" Kellie says.

"Nope," I reply. "Ever since I came to that facility, I've been constantly on edge. But I can't just walk around showing everyone I'm terrified."

"You could've fooled me," Kellie says.

"Lyla's seen it firsthand," I say. "Before we met you, we got into a fight with Paul, you know that."

"I heard," Kellie says. "But what about it?"

"We could've totally avoided the whole thing, but… we didn't." I continue, "I tried running away. I mean, you've seen Paul. He's massive. He's an actual honest-to-god grizzly."

"I don't really blame you for attempting to sneak off like that," Kellie says.

"Yeah, but I left Lyla, the person I befriended, someone who needed my help," I say. "Because I got cold feet."

"But you two were in over your heads, picking a fight with Paul," Kellie says.

"Yeah, but look at us now: we escaped the facility. I think we're way over our heads now. This whole situation is a bunch of bad things after another," I say. "But that seems like the nature of how our lives have changed."

"I guess," Kellie responds. "So, what're you going to do about it?"

"I don't know. Once we get out of here, we should avoid confrontation. Just make it back to my house, and my adventure will be over," I reply.

"You're not coming with us to Lyla's?" Kellie asks.

"I don't plan on it," I say. "I already told her as much."

Kellie gives me a look. It's almost disappointed, but it also has a hint of understanding.

"I don't blame you for not wanting to go with us," Kellie says. "But I feel like you should."

"I probably should," I reply, "But remember, we have lives we left behind when we changed. I can't just abandon my sister. I need to get back and help her."

"With what?" Kellie says.

"Keeping things going," I reply.

"I guess," Kellie responds. "But you don't think for the few weeks you've been gone, she's been doing fine herself?"

"I don't know." I say. "I don't know how she's doing, and that's what's so terrifying. It's always been the two of us. I can't have her by herself. She probably thinks I've abandoned her."

"What do you think will happen when you come back?" Kellie asks.

"I don't know," I say. "And that's what terrifying."

"Well, you'll have to find out," Kellie responds. "I didn't think that my dad would be so on board with me being a raccoon."

"That's your family, isn't it?" I retort.

"Not the point, dude," Kellie says. "The point is, we don't know what's going to happen, and you've been worrying all this time about every little thing."

"I guess," I say. "I'm just not sure what I'm supposed to do about it all. It's stressful."

"That's life, isn't it?" Kellie says. "Especially now, we need to work together and stay on our toes."

I nod, as she's got a point. Regardless, I can't think of what's going to happen to me when I make it home. I want to think that things are going to be okay, but I've managed to push all these thoughts into the back of my mind and not think about them. Camouflaging myself behind a veneer of calm and collected. Now, it feels like the closer I get to home, the more I want this adventure to end, and the more I want to go back to the way things were.

I don't respond to Kellie, as our attention returns to the day we've been having. Being outside, sitting in the grass, watching the others play in the grass. It's nice.

I turn my attention towards Lyla, who's now running up to us.

"James, Kellie!" Lyla says. She seems visibly disturbed.

Kellie jolts up, and I follow.

"What's going on?" Kellie says.

"Grab Lynn and Penelope. They've found us!" she yells.

"F-found us?" I say.

"You're talking about the RCC, right?" Kellie asks.

"Yes. Grab Paul's family, and head inside. Paul and I are going to handle this," she says.

Kellie runs over to Lynn and Penelope and guides them to the garage.

They found us? How? Did they track us? Did they know we were coming to Paul's? Is this a coincidence? This can't be happening. I don't want to go back. I don't want to return to that place. If they catch us, are they going to take us to the facility all the way out on the East Coast? I don't understand what's happening.

"James!" I hear a muffled voice call out to me.

"JAMES! ARE YOU LISTENING?" I snap back from my thoughts and see Lyla staring at me.

"Go!" she says.

I nod quickly and turn towards the garage, but the sound of screeching tires stops me in my tracks.

I turn back to the driveway, as Paul's now caught up with us, as well as the cars. The doors open, and many men in SWAT uniforms holding rifles step out into the driveway. They surround our front. I glance back to the garage and see Kellie leading Lynn and Penelope inside.

The front car door opens, and a man steps out. Wearing a lab coat. It's… Oh god, it's him. Still seeming well put together, despite the fact that his face has been adorned with a large bandage over the left eye and the side of his face. He's sporting a Kevlar vest underneath the lab coat. This… This can't be good.

"You people… are so predictable," Thorn says, with a sneer.

"What do you want?" Paul responds.

"Well, obviously I'm here for you," Thorn says. "I'm not here for small talk, Paul."

"We're not going anywhere," Paul says. "I've made it to my family. I'm not coming back with you."

"There's no home base rules in rehab, Paul," Thorn says. "You're a danger to society. The injuries sustained by my employees the past few days proves this."

"That's self-defense," Paul says. "You know you were going to keep me there forever."

"Because of this exact reason," Thorn snaps back. "You're a danger to your family, and yourself, because of that godforsaken instinct of yours. And your… newfound abilities. We don't understand them, and this further proves that you don't belong in society until you have that under control."

Thorn turns to Lyla.

"I expected to see you here too." Thorn glares at Lyla. "After your little stunt… and my injury. You also need to go with me."

"I'm not doing that," Lyla says.

"Here's the thing." Thorn chuckles.

The guards all raise their guns at us.

"I'm not asking," Thorn says.

"We're not going," Paul says. "Can't you leave us alone?"

Thorn takes a deep breath. "Jesus Christ, have you people not been paying attention to what I've been saying this whole time? You are a danger to yourself, and others. I'd like to solve this diplomatically, without the need for violence, and you're seriously testing my patience."

"Goes the same for us," Lyla says.

"Why're you so worked up about this?" Thorn says. "You could've gone out to the East Coast and enjoyed a nice little relaxing vacation, and I would've shipped you back in two weeks. But no. You had to plan some stupid little escape."

Thorn points at his face. "And look where this got you. I'm not even upset that you did this, seriously. That's just impressive. Bravo. Now, though, the damage is done, and you're as much of a threat as Paul is."

Thorn then turns to me.

"And you, I don't even know what you're doing here. I expected you to slink back home. Why're you hitchhiking with these people?"

"I… I… uh—" I start to respond, but I'm cut off.

"I already know that the raccoon is in the garage. Just go back there and wait for this to all blow over. I'll come get you two after all this, and then, you can all come with me to the East. Sound like fun? Go," Thorn says, brushing me off.

I look to Lyla, and she nods. I take that as my opportunity to run back to the garage.

As I'm running, I hear Thorn say one more thing… before all hell breaks loose.

"If you're not coming with me, then I have no choice. Just… make it quick."

The sound of gunfire erupts through the front yard, followed by the sound of crackling electricity.

CHAPTER 27

James

As I RUN into the garage, I turn back and see Paul use his abilities to shift the ground up, flipping one of the vans in front of him. Lyla follows suit, by using her powers to electrocute one of the guards, holding a weapon, shooting it sporadically in random directions. The other guards drop to the ground to avoid fire, followed by Thorn.

I make it into the garage. Hiding in the corner, my heart racing, I can barely breathe. My surroundings are starting to fade away as I re-capture my breath.

The only thing I can hear is the fire of weapons and the sound of crumbling rock and crackling electricity.

As well as the pitter-patter of footsteps coming towards me.

"James, you okay?" I hear a whisper call out to me.

I turn to the left and see Kellie. She's looking me up and down. I glance down to my hands and realize that I'm now the color of the wall behind me. The only part of me that doesn't blend in is my clothes.

"What're you doing?" she asks.

"I don't know… I guess… I did it subconsciously…" I reply, watching my skin return to its original green sheen. This is exactly what happened the first time Lyla fought Paul…

"Look, we need to get out of here," Kellie says. "This went south really bad."

We both hear a massive crash, followed by the sound of someone screaming, their voice shaking like a broken record.

"I know that..." I say. "Let's just get your car and go."

"No, we need Lyla! And Paul, and his family!" Kellie says, slinking over to the opening of the garage.

"We can't! They're fighting those... guys out there! We need to leave on our own! We can take Lynn and Penelope, but they're distracting them long enough to escape."

"I'm not arguing about this. We need to help them," Kellie says, peering out of the garage.

We both look out of the garage... it's like a war zone out there. Men in SWAT uniforms rushing towards both Paul and Lyla. A man charges at Paul, who grips the ground and pulls it up, tossing him away like a sack of flour.

Another man rounds the group to flank the two of them. Lyla turns her attention to this man, holding her hands out. Electricity erupts from her palms, arcing through the air like a confused hummingbird.

One bolt misses, connecting to the ground, singeing the grass, while the other connects to the man's weapon, causing him to jitter, firing the weapon haphazardly. As he collapses onto the ground, a stray bullet whizzes past us, hitting the bumper of the van in the garage.

We unanimously agree that we shouldn't be staring and pull ourselves back into the garage.

"If we give them enough time, maybe they'll take them all out..." I say.

"Don't count on it," Thorn says, appearing around the wall of the garage in front of us.

Kellie yelps as we both jump back into the garage.

"Do you know how hard it is to keep morale up in a rundown school full of crazed animal people after four of them escape?" Thorn says, approaching us. "It's near impossible. We've had tons of problems thanks to you four, but we can't do anything about it. We have to be calm; we have to make sure they're taken care of. It's frustrating, borderline infuriating. I've stopped taking appointments thanks to you four. Because I've spent every waking moment since you four escaped trying to find you."

Thorn steps closer, pulling a pneumatic tranquilizer gun from his coat.

"They don't even give me a real means to defend myself," he scoffs, pointing it as us. "Thing is, it works great on animals. Just like you… creatures. Now, I may not be able to help the boys out there take out our mutual friends, but once they're… down for the count, I'll be able to take you two in and prevent all of this from happening again. Granted, we'll have to think of a new story for you, Kellie, going and talking to your parents like that, after we made the perfect reason you can't come back."

"You… did that?" Kellie asks.

"Who do you think runs this whole operation?" Thorn says. "I don't just run the stupid facility you four got out of. I was out here for normal business. I go from place to place every few weeks to keep tabs on them. Of course, some people get out, but we always find them. This is the first time we've had someone develop… abilities… before we eliminate them."

"You… do… what?" Kellie says.

Thorn doesn't respond, as he turns his weapon to Kellie and pulls the trigger, hitting her in the leg.

"Stop. I'm not going to continue this game," he says, as Kellie slinks to the floor.

"Kellie!" I yell.

"She's not waking up for a while, James. Now, we can talk like men… Well… man and chameleon." He chuckles.

"I know you won't put up much of a fight," he continues. "Always the brains, never the brawn, and never willing to stand up when it matters."

Thorn steps closer, reaching into his pocket. "Thing is, I could definitely use someone like you. Someone who listens, doesn't ask many questions, a little smart. You'd make a good success story, maybe even help out at the facilities."

Thorn takes out another tranquilizer dart and starts to load it into his gun.

"But what am I saying? You'd never agree to something like that, even after all you've seen, so… maybe if you're good."

He aims the gun at me.

"Maybe I won't keep you forever," he says.

Before I know it, I feel my body move without me thinking, directly at him.

My hand reels back behind me and forms into a fist. As I twist my upper half towards him, all my weight conglomerates into a single punch, hitting him in between the eyes.

Thorn drops the tranquilizer gun and stumbles back. Gripping his head, he looks up at me, his expression one of determination.

"Perhaps I was wrong."

He looks down at the gun in between us. I look down too.

We both dive for the gun. I manage to knock it out of the way. Thorn grabs on to me and socks me in the face before attempting to get up.

I manage to use his momentum to pull myself up instead, keeping him on the ground. I dart towards the gun.

I feel a tug on my backside, as I belly flop onto the floor. Turning around, I see Thorn's managed to grab my tail and pull me back.

"You're just like the rest, aren't you…." he says, stepping on my arm as he walks to retrieve his weapon.

"I'll make sure to put in my report that you're prone to….

un-animalistic outbursts for your subspecies. Changes theories about this whole instinct thing, doesn't it?" he asks, to no one.

"You're making this company look like a total sham with our little skirmish. Good thing we're in the middle of nowhere. People probably think Paul's out here shooting guns for fun. Good for us; not for your friends, though," Thorn says, picking up the gun.

"Now, why don't you be a good boy, and take a nice na—" Thorn's comment is cut off as the *CLANG* of metal is heard. Thorn collapses on the floor, unconscious. Lynn steps out from behind the van in the garage, wielding a cookie sheet.

"That'll give you enough time," Lynn says, obviously shaken up.

"I'm so, so, so sorry, Lynn," I say, standing up, grabbing the tranquilizer gun Thorn left on the floor.

"No, it's not your fault. If you weren't here, they still would've come for Paul. I didn't know it was this bad," she says.

"I still feel like we're to blame," I respond.

"Save your apologies for someone else. I don't want to hear them," Lynn says sternly. "Right now, the most important thing for you is that you get Kellie and Lyla out of here."

I turn to Kellie's car, which has been riddled with bullet holes.

"Yeah," I say. "It's up to me, isn't it?"

Lynn nods.

I run over to Kellie and sift through her pockets, grabbing her car keys.

"I'll be back for you," I say.

I run to Kellie's car and hop into the front seat, putting the keys in the ignition. I turn the keys.

rrrrrRRRR CHUN CHUN CHUN.

It's not starting…

I try again.

REEEEEE CHUN CHUN CHUN.

I take the keys out and run back to Lynn.

"The car's not starting," I say.

Lynn hands me another set of car keys.

"Take my van," she says.

"I can't," I respond. "You guys need to get out of here too."

"Take the mini-van, James. You and your friends get out of here. We'll be fine," Lynn says.

"I can't—"

"I'm not asking," Lynn says, glaring at me.

I sigh. "Thank you, Lynn. I'll repay you somehow."

"I know you'll find a way." She gives a quick smile. "Now go!"

I nod and run to the other side of the van and pick up Kellie, laying her in the back seat.

Now, it's time to go get Lyla.

I step out of the garage again and see several guards surrounding Paul. He's clearly bruised, and Lynn's handiwork fixing him up has been undone, as his shirt is stained with red from reopening his injuries.

Two men approach Lyla. She readies her hands, casting a bolt of lightning at the one who's trained his gun on her. The second ducks out of the way, running around to face her in the back. As the electricity hits the first man, the second raises his rifle to hit her from the back. She's completely unaware of her attacker. Without thinking, I call out to her.

"LOOK OUT!" I shout.

Lyla turns to me, before spinning to the man behind her. But it's too late. He hits her in the side of the head with the butt of his rifle. Lyla collapses onto the ground like ragdoll.

I start sprinting to Lyla. The guard aiming their weapon at her looks up at me and trains their weapon on me. I slow down, bracing myself to be riddled with lead, but right as they're about to fire, the ground beneath them raises into the air, tossing them aside. I look to Paul, who nods in understanding as multiple guards jump onto him.

He's slowly being taken down by the guards, one at a time. They're holding his hands down, preventing him from using his abilities. Paul growls in anger. He's running out of steam, and I'm running out of time.

Looking down in my hand, I completely forgot I'm still holding Thorn's tranquilizer gun. I know I can use this, and I know I need to do it now. Raising the weapon up to fire… But I've never done this before… I've shot weapons once before, but those were on a range… This is a real situation, and I only have one shot. I can't miss… My hands shake as I desperately try to find something to shoot, something that can help turn the tide of this battle.

As I scan the battle ground, inching closer towards Lyla, I try to keep myself alert. I could sneak over. If I think hard enough, I could try to blend in with the ground. But that's useless. It's… it's cowardly.

I need to do something to actually help. As I look over to Paul, I see several men jumping on top of him to contain him. I can tell he's getting worse for wear… Then, it clicks in my head. I can do something!

I change course and start to start to close in to the dogpile on Paul. I ready myself and look for an opening. As I look to the man holding down Paul's hand, I can see the nape of his neck exposed to the air.

Holding the weapon up, I take a deep breath, waiting for an opening to shoot. As I hold my breath, I look past my weapon and train the sights on my target…

Now? No, wait, I'll miss… Now? Not yet. I just missed my window…

Now.

I shoot the tranquilizer dart. It flies through the air with a whistle, directly on target to the guard.

The dart… reaches the guard….

And dings off his helmet.

Oh god. *I missed.*

The guard turns his attention to where the dart came from, but that was his final mistake, as Paul frees one of his hands. Paul digs his hands into the ground, as the earth around him shakes. The earth shoots up one by one, knocking each guy off their feet, and away from Paul. Each man shouts as they're flung back, toppling in a ring around Paul, who's surrounded by pillars of earth.

As they're all reeling on the ground, Paul gets up. Gripping his re-opened wound, he stumbles towards me, clearly out of energy.

"Nice shooting, kid," Paul says, out of breath.

"T-Thanks…" I respond.

"Now, get Lyla! And get out of here!" Paul exclaims.

I nod and run to Lyla, dropping the tranquilizer gun in the process. I manage to pick up Lyla with what strength I have and start hauling her unconscious body to the van. The men knocked down by Paul manage to get up, pulling out their weapons to open fire on us.

Paul is following me, As the men start firing, a wall of earth emerges at my side, every bullet hitting the rising walls with a distinct *shuup* sound as we sprint back to the garage.

We work our way slowly to the garage. Paul pauses from holding up walls for us and turns defense into offense by hurling large dirt rocks at the men, knocking a couple of them over, but in the condition he's in right now, he's missing more than he's landing his hits.

"You need to go now," Paul says in between throws.

"What about you and Lynn? And Penelope?" I ask.

"We'll be fine. They're going to keep hunting us," Paul says. "If you split, they're not going to come at full force like this. It's better this way."

"Are you sure?" I ask.

Paul nods solemnly. "This is goodbye, James."

I nod. "Thank you, Paul, for everything."

"You'd do the same, yer good people," he says.

We hear the sound of squealing tires once more.

"There's more people. Get in the van and go!" he says. "I'll take it from here."

"But—" I try to say.

"GO!" Paul roars.

I open the back and put Lyla in the seat next to Kellie. I scramble around the car and hop in the front seat. The car starts like a dream. I move the shifter into reverse and start backing out of the driveway, narrowly missing Kellie's car, and Paul.

As I switch the car into drive, I see more vans approaching down the driveway, each one being flipped onto its side by Paul, using whatever strength he has left in his abilities to pave the way for our escape.

I hit the gas, as the van's engine begins to redline, and we start speeding down the driveway. I see in the rearview mirror guards getting out of the van and running towards Paul. By the time they're out of my sight, the only sounds I hear are gunfire, the rumble of the earth, and the roar of a lone bear.

Without thinking, I drive back onto the highway, my foot still glued to the floor.

The roads start to blur together. I can't tell how long it's been. I keep checking the clock. Ten minutes… Twenty minutes… Fifty minutes… I finally begin to come to my senses when I start to feel the sucker punch Thorn laid into the side of my head.

I start to slow the car down to the speed limit and catch my breath. If this is what's going to happen to me if I make it back to the house… it's not safe there for me either. But… I need to find my sister, even if it's the last thing I do… My adventure… doesn't end here.

Just then, I hear rustling in the back.

"Paul!" Lyla springs to life. "Wha—Where?"

"We left," I say solemnly.

"What about Paul?" she says, frantically climbing into the back seat to look out the back window.

"I… I don't know, Lyla… He told us to leave, and the last thing I saw was… guards surrounding him."

"You… You can't be serious… We have to go back!" she screams.

"We can't!" I yell. "They sent more people! You've been out… for… over an hour… They would have killed you."

"But… But…" Lyla says.

"I'm sorry, Lyla," I respond. "Paul said… we need to keep moving forward."

I don't hear anything from Lyla, but looking into the rearview mirror, I see her slink down in the back seat, disappearing from my view. The only way I know she's still there is the sporadic breathing and the sound of her whimpers.

CHAPTER 28

James

THE CAR RIDE is silent. I keep checking the rearview mirror to see if Lyla's okay. I can barely see her; she's staring out the window. I can't see her face, but she's there.

"Lyla." I attempt to talk to her. But I receive no response from her. I can't help but think to myself that I'm somewhat to blame for how she's feeling. But, then again, I did what I was asked to. By Lynn, and by Paul.

I keep my eyes trained on the road. Staying inside of the slow lane, letting cars pass us, but keeping my eyes out for any vans that have that godforsaken logo on them.

I hear movement in the back seat. I look up to the rearview mirror once again but don't see anything. Lyla's still staring out the window, watching the landscape slide by. I feel something brush up against my shoulder. And for a moment, I draw my attention to the passenger seat. It's Kellie, sitting down and buckling herself up.

"Hey," I say.

"Hey," she replies.

"How long have you been awake?" I ask.

"A while," she says. "You don't look so good."

"I could be better," I reply. "Lynn saved us from Thorn."

"And this is…." she asks.

"Their car," I reply.

"Oh," she responds.

"It wasn't good, Kellie," I continue. "Lyla almost got… taken or killed by one of those SWAT guys. I ran out there to save her. Paul helped."

"Where are they?" Kellie asks.

"I don't know," I respond. "The last I saw, more cars were coming, and Paul told us to go. Said he'd be fine."

"And you… believed that?" Lyla finally speaks up.

"He wasn't giving me a choice," I respond. "I tried to tell him we wouldn't leave him, but he was adamant we needed to leave."

Lyla doesn't respond.

"You think they're okay?" Kellie asks.

"I hope so," I respond. "But there were… a lot of them."

"I see," Kellie responds. "I'm… I'm not sure what to say."

"We hope they're fine," Lyla says. "That's all we can do."

"Are you… okay?" Kellie asks.

"No," Lyla says.

"We were all there," Kellie says.

"I know," Lyla responds.

"Do you want to—" Kellie continues.

"I get it. I understand what you did, James. I understand that Paul basically forced us to leave," Lyla says.

"Yeah, but—" I try to continue.

"I'm not done," Lyla says, now moving to the middle of the car. "But we could've done more. Couldn't we?"

I shake my head. "I don't know. I don't think we could have. You were… unconscious, and Kellie was shot by Thorn."

"Shot?" Lyla asks, turning to Kellie.

"Not with a gun," Kellie says. "It was one of those… tranquilizer things?"

"Yeah," I reply. "I was next. If it wasn't for Lynn… it would've been over for all of us. I think Paul realized that when I ran out there to save you."

Lyla sits back in her seat. "I just thought that… maybe we still had it in us."

"I think we overestimated ourselves," Kellie says. "We're not like you. We can't defend ourselves like you and Paul can. We were backed into a corner with Thorn while both you and Paul fought off all those guards."

"And," I continue, "you two might've fought a whole group of them… But they were sending a second one in."

"I still can't shake the feeling that we didn't do enough," she says.

"The truth is, we did all we could. The only thing we can do is…" I say.

"Keep going," Kellie chimes in.

Silence fills the car.

"Do you think they made it out?" Lyla asks.

"I… I don't know," I respond. "I hope that they did, and knowing how Paul managed to get shot and somehow still make it home, I'd like to think he's stronger than we all realize."

Silence again.

"It's okay to be upset," I continue.

"I… I know," Lyla says. She shifts in her seat. I can tell that we're all thinking the same thing. Paul might not have made it. But none of us really want to say it. He was strong, but he was also worn out, and more people were coming. I'm the only one who saw with my own eyes. Should I have lied? Told them everything was fine? And left it as that? No, that would've only come back to bite me.

But… all we can do is keep going. We can't stop the car and turn around; that'll get us captured, or even worse, killed. I'm the one driving, and we need to keep pushing forward.

"So…" Kellie says, breaking the silence. "Where are we going now?"

"We're going to my house," I reply.

"We're still going?" Lyla says. "You're still going home?"

"I have to," I say. "Though, I know I can't stay. That'd be stupid. That'd only put me in the sights of the RCC. And on top of that… it'd put my sister in their sights too."

"So… you're coming with us?" Kellie says.

"It's the only choice I have," I respond. "I'd like to stay home and hope everything turns back to normal. But I know it won't. Not until the RCC isn't in the picture anymore."

"Are you saying we should do something about it?" Lyla asks.

"No, are you serious?" I say. "I'm saying we need to get as far away from them as possible. We'll still go to my house, check up on my sister, and then it's to your place, right?" I ask Lyla.

Her expression shifts from one of surprise and then to one of embarrassment.

"I… I don't know," she replies.

Kellie turns around to face her.

"What do you mean, you don't know?" she asks.

"I don't know if I want to go back anymore," she says.

"You said you were going to," I say.

"I know… It's just… things are… different now," Lyla continues.

"What makes them different?" I ask. "It can't be all of this that's the only reason."

Lyla doesn't say anything. I can tell she's thinking about what she's going to say next.

"No, it's not that. I think we've all kinda realized we can't change anything about us. It's more or less… about…" she stammers.

"Just say it," Kellie says.

"It's about a phone call I had with my aunt," she finally opens up.

"What about it?" I ask. "Was it about you being changed?"

"Maybe?" Lyla continues. "She sounded off. Like something else was up, and I don't know what's going to happen when I go back."

"Do you think she… changed too?" Kellie chimes in.

Lyla stops entirely, her expression changing from embarrassment to shock.

"I… I don't know if I can even picture that," she says.

"It's entirely possible," Kellie says. "It didn't just happen to us."

"I get that…" Lyla says. "There's just… something unsettling about thinking about my aunt like that."

"I mean, I guess?" Kellie says. "I guess I can't picture my dad as a raccoon."

Kellie gives a little smirk.

"I don't think that's what happened," Lyla says. "I'm just worried her reaction to me is going to be… bad."

"Well, you're going to have to deal with it," I respond. "I don't know what my sister is going to think when I come home looking like this."

"I mean, she's still your sister, right?" Kellie adds. "She might not freak out."

I try to picture a situation where I open the door and my sister actually is excited to see me. But, for the life of me, all I can think of is her screaming in horror. Phrases like "What happened to you?" and "You're not my brother anymore!" are the only things that ring out in my head.

"I don't know," I say. "I'm probably not going to think about it until we get there."

"How much farther, anyways?" Kellie asks.

"Soon… I think," I respond. "It's been a while since I left town. I do remember this exit coming up."

"Can… Can we stop?" Lyla says.

"Why?" I ask.

"I'd like to just go to the store. Or something. My head hurts, and I need something to eat," she squeaks out.

"Do any of us have money?" I ask.

I see Kellie reach into her pockets and pull out her phone.

"I've got one of those digital phone wallets. If I've got money on my phone, I could use that," she says, opening her phone.

"Good thinking," I say.

"The money should be saved, and I can use it without service," she says. "I had to once when I was in a dead zone."

"Wait… No, oh god, no," I hear Lyla say from the back.

"What's wrong?" I ask, looking through the mirror into the back of the van.

"I don't… I don't have my phone," Lyla says.

"What?" Kellie asks, turning around.

"I left my phone on the counter at Paul's," Lyla says, clearly distraught.

"That's fine," Kellie says. "We didn't have service, remember?"

Lyla calms down a little. But I can tell she's still on edge. "I know, but it's still my phone."

"Do you need it for anything?" I ask.

"No," Lyla says.

"Then you're fine," Kellie responds. "It's not the end of the world."

"I get that," Lyla says. "I just used it a lot, and it's got my aunt's number on it. I don't remember it."

"You know how to get home, right?" I ask.

"Yeah, I know how to get home," she says.

"Then we'll have to do it the old-fashioned way," I say, turning the car into the oncoming exit.

"Now, I'm just going to pull into the nearest supermarket, and we'll get the stuff we need. You do have money, right, Kellie?" I ask.

"Yeah, I've got thirty-four bucks," she says.

"More than enough," I say.

"Are you… nervous about going in?" Lyla asks.

"I mean, a little," I say. "If anything, we might not see any people like us in there."

"I don't know if I want to go in," Lyla says.

"You want the pain medication, right?" Kellie says.

"Yes," Lyla says.

"Then don't you think you should come in with us?" Kellie snaps back. "We'll only be a bit if you come with and help us look."

"I mean, I guess that's fine," Lyla sneers. "I just don't want to draw too much attention."

"We've been drawing attention since we got out of that facility," I say. "There's no going back. We gotta suck it up for this one thing. We'll have to do it eventually, so better to rip the band-aid off now."

Lyla sighs as I pull the car into the parking lot for the supermarket. I slide into a parking spot in the middle of the lot and put the car in park.

"All right, so what're we getting?" Kellie says, looking at us both.

"Pain meds," Lyla says.

"Some kind of food?" I say.

"What kind?" Kellie asks.

We all stop to think. We're close to the house, but we've still got about an hour from where we're currently at, to when we get to my house.

"Probably something small," I say.

"Small?" Kellie asks.

"Well, yeah, something small, we're close. But we've got a way, and if you're hungry, we can't waste all our money on food. I'm sure that we'll probably have something back at my house," I reply.

"All right," Kellie says. "Let's just go inside then."

I nod, and I look to Lyla. "You coming?"

"Yeah," she replies.

The three of us swing the doors open on the car and step out into the parking lot. The supermarket looms over all of us. It's been a long time since we've been in a supermarket. Not like any of us haven't been in one before. I guess it's just how many things have happened these past few weeks that makes it feel like it's been years since I've ever been in a supermarket.

We all start walking down to the front doors.

"Do we have any idea what we're getting?" Lyla asks.

"Aside from the pain pills? Not sure…" Kellie says, skipping across the asphalt.

"What are you doing?" I ask.

"The ground, it's hot," she says. "I don't have shoes."

"Let's just keep going," Lyla says, picking up the pace.

We all walk up to the front doors, and once Kellie steps from the black tarmac to the grey concrete, she lets out a sigh of relief. The sliding doors open, giving us a blast of cool air as we walk inside.

Inside the vast, white, and surprisingly sterile supermarket, we see plenty of people roaming the aisles. Actual human people. Granted, we've seen plenty of humans on our journey, like the ones in the facility, and even Paul's wife. But we haven't seen so many in one place. It's weird, like we've travelled back in time to before this even happened. It's normal, but we're not.

"I don't know if I want to stay here," Lyla says.

"Nervous?" I ask.

"Yeah," she replies.

"Me too," I say, "but you wanted the pain meds, so let's get them and go."

"I'm sticking with you," Kellie says, following Lyla.

I watch as they disappear into the back of the store. I guess… I'm on my own now. I start making my way down the aisles, keeping to myself.

Avoiding the glances of the other people trying to get their shopping done, I can see eyes staring at me, each aisle I go down. Families stepping to the side to let me pass, watching me as a walk through the halls. I feel socially naked, like I'm being gawked at every step I take. The supermarket feels like it's became a zoo, and I'm the attraction. I see children pointing at me, with concerned parents stepping to the side. With Kellie and Lyla gone, I'm on my own.

Why am I even here? Snacks, that's right. I'm supposed to get food for the group. What aisle is it? I've always been able to figure these places out, but my mind is blank. What aisle has food in it?

It feels like I've lost all sense of direction. I look around. I can't tell if people are still staring, but I sense it, like they all look back to what they're doing as soon as I make notice of it.

I look up to see the aisle in front of me has snack foods in it. Okay, this one. I don't even care what's down there. I just need to get something to tide us over till we make it back to my house. I turn down the aisle and start walking to the end. I see lines of single serving bags of chips—barbeque, salt and vinegar, regular—and beef jerky, candy, etc.

These will do. I try to look at the prices, but the numbers are a blur. I can read fine, I've been able to read fine this entire time, but I can't tell what these prices are. It doesn't matter. I need to find Lyla and Kellie. I can't stand this anymore.

I grab a few bags of chips and snacks and turn towards the middle of the store. But just then, I see someone step down this alleyway, cracking a smile and wearing…

A blue polo.

Oh no. It's an RCC person. They're not one of those guards who tried to capture us. But they're someone who works for the company. I start backing up, trying to not make eye contact with the person. If I turn around, I can just walk away and go find Lyla and Kellie.

I start walking to the end of the hallway.

"Excuse me!" the voice calls out.

I don't have time for this. I need to leave. But I can't; my legs won't move. I can't get away from them. It's like they've locked me in a trance and are keeping me here until they get a closer look.

"Excuse me, sir?" the person says. Their voice calls out to me.

I force myself to turn in their direction, "Y…yes?" I ask.

"Are you okay?" they ask. The person, now in front of me, is a woman in her late twenties. Dark hair, and a smile that tows the line of being an act and genuine.

"I…I'm fine," I say, trying to step back once more.

"Well, you don't seem fine," the woman retorts. "I was just nearby, and someone who saw a…" She scans me up and down. "Chameleon acting strange was walking down this aisle."

"Sorry," I respond quickly. "Just a little anxiety stricken today."

"Is it because of the people staring?" the lady pries.

"No, no," I respond. "No, it's just been… one of those days." Does this lady not know me? Does she not know about the other facility, where Lyla, Kellie, and I broke out?

"It sounds like you've got some underlying problems, don't you?" the lady asks. "I'm with a company called the RCC. It stands for—"

"Reform Corporation for the Changed, I know," I say.

"Oh, you're familiar with us?" she asks.

"…Yes," I respond. This lady doesn't know who I am. Maybe… maybe I can get out of here without causing any trouble.

"So, you know about our mission? To help people like you?" she says.

"Yes," I respond. I gotta think up something to end this conversation, and quick. "Your… people came to my door a few days ago."

"I see," she replies. "I haven't heard of any chameleons in this area."

"I live farther north. I'm just on my way home from a friend of mine," I reply. Ah! I shouldn't've said that.

"Oh, I see," the lady says. "Are you sure you're not interested in what we have to offer?" She hands me a pamphlet, the same pamphlet they gave all of us when we first got here.

"No, I'm not… I'm not interested," I say. "I'm perfectly fine with my life right now, and I have things I need to do," I say, stepping around her.

"You're one hundred percent sure?" The woman keeps prying. "You seem like you could use some counseling."

"Listen, I really do appreciate you looking out for me, but it really does feel like you're patronizing me. I told you once, and I'll tell you again. I'm not interested," I say, backing up.

"I… I understand," she says. "But if you change your mind—"

"I gotcha, I know where to look!" I say, turning around and walking down the hallway.

I'm not going to be changing my mind. I start making my way to the pharmacy. I… I think I really did just get out of that, didn't I?

Jeez. I need to consider myself lucky. The adrenaline I feel propels me to the other side of the store where I remember seeing Lyla and Kellie walk down. The feeling of people staring at me is still there, but it doesn't bother me as much. Probably because I'm still a little fired up from that conversation.

I make my way to the pharmacy, scanning the aisles for Kellie and Lyla. Eventually, from behind me, I hear a "Hey."

I turn around and see Lyla and Kellie. Lyla's got a bottle of water and some Ibuprofen in her hand, and Kellie looks shook.

"You okay?" Lyla asks.

"Sort of," I say. "Let's leave."

"What happened?" Kellie asks.

"I saw an RCC person here. They… they didn't recognize me, though. I'd like to not stick around," I reply.

"Woman, right?" Lyla asks.

"Yeah," I respond.

"We saw her too," Kellie says. "She's been wandering this place since we walked in. We've been avoiding her like the plague."

"Well, let's keep doing that and get out of here," I say.

Kellie and Lyla nod, and we all start walking to the self-checkout aisle. Thanks to our immense amount of luck, the self-checkout is relatively empty. The three of us approach a terminal.

The machine's automated voice activates. "Please scan your items now, and then place them into the bagging area."

I've heard these lines hundreds of times; all supermarkets have the same stupid voice. Kellie starts bagging our items, as Lyla scans them.

"2.99, 7.99," the voice says.

I look around for that woman again, wondering if she knows where I am. I don't see her, though. We're in the clear.

The automated voice chimes again, and Kellie mumbles in sync with it, "Thank you for shopping with us today."

She grabs the bags, and the three of us start walking out of the store. We head out into the parking lot and start moving towards the car. I turn around to see the doors open, and the lady step out.

"Hey! Wait!" she calls out.

"Go faster," I say to Kellie and Lyla. Both of them pick up the pace.

I turn around briefly and yell out to her. "I told you, I'm not interested!"

"You can't avoid us forever!" she says. "You have a problem! You need treatment!"

"And this is supposed to sell us on it?" Lyla shouts.

"You're dangerous individuals!" the woman yells.

The three of us jump into the car, I put the key into the ignition, and start the car, putting it into reverse.

We pull out and get back onto the road, pulling out from the supermarket.

"We're dangerous?" Kellie asks.

"They'll say anything," I respond. "It's what they did to me."

"We're not dangerous," Lyla adds. "It's them who are the dangerous ones."

Chapter 29

James

I take a turn out of the parking lot and back onto the highway. I watch as the speedometer rises from 45, to 60, to 70. Placing the van on cruise control, I finally feel like I have a chance to relax again.

"How're we doing?" I ask Kellie and Lyla.

"Better, now that I have something," Lyla says, cracking open her water bottle and taking some of the pain medicine.

"Still a little weirded out by the person who was following us around," Kellie remarks. "Felt like everyone in there was staring at us."

"Yeah," I reply. "I had that same feeling too. Felt like everyone was gawking at us."

"I mean, we're not exactly normal looking," Lyla replies.

"Well, yeah," I say. "But it's been, what? A few weeks now? You'd think people wouldn't stare… right?"

"I get where you're coming from," Kellie says. "But this is also a massive thing that's happened to the world. It may have been a few weeks, but it's going to take a long time before people start… I don't know, treating us normally."

"I guess," I say. "I guess we can't help but still think about it too."

"It's always hanging on in the back of my mind," Lyla says. "Thought about it when I woke up in the facility, thought about it when I saw myself, thought about it when I saw you guys. Heck, I'm still thinking about it as we're heading back to my home."

Lyla scoffs to herself. "I don't think we'll ever get used to it. Every time one of us says how long it's been, it just feels further and further away, like a dream. Every day that goes by feels like the normal things that we used to do drift further away."

Silence in the car.

Kellie chimes in next. "You think... we'll get to a point where we don't even remember what it was like to be human?"

"I... I don't know," I say.

"It feels like a blur now," Kellie says. "Like, I remember bits and pieces of being normal, doing normal things, going places, and not getting stared at."

"Me too," Lyla says.

"Yeah," I add.

"But now, it feels like those are just vague memories, ya know?" Kellie continues, "Like, am I missing out on something important being like this?"

"I don't know," I reply. "Seems like it sometimes. Being in that place, the facility. It feels like years."

Nobody says anything as we continue to cruise down the road, signs passing over our heads.

"It does," Lyla says.

"Yeah," Kellie replies.

Silence again. I don't even know how to continue this conversation. What do I say to them? Do I tell them that everything is going to be fine, and we'll all live happily ever after? Or do I tell them that things are only going to get more difficult from here on out?

We're in desperate need of some good news. Every time we think that things are going to get better, they always somehow manage to get worse. The most horrific part is that I don't know if they're going to get better. I don't even know if I can tell them that with a straight face. We don't know if going to my house is going to result in disaster or disappointment.

Worst part is, I don't know which is worse.

All these thoughts flow through my head, as I'm watching the exits pass by, keeping my eyes peeled for one that I know I need to take.

Exit 190… 4 miles.

Exit 186… 6 miles.

Exit 174… 12 miles.

Exit 162… 4 miles.

Exit 140. That's the one.

I flip the blinker on and turn into the exit. The highways of the open road slowly turn into the suburbs of a small town. One I know all too familiar. We start driving down the side roads, passing small businesses. As we approach a red light, the car stops, and I spot a place on the corner.

It's a small pizza place, red bricked walls, and a plastic sign that's lit up with florescent lights. The logo beams green and red, with the name "Giovanni's" on it.

I can't help but bring myself back to a time when my sister and I were at the beginning of being on our own. Sitting outside where the metal tables line the sidewalk. Pizza was always cheap there, three bucks a slice, and they were big slices too. We'd eat there maybe twice a week if we didn't want to cook, and with us just starting out on our own, three bucks for what could have equated to a quarter of a whole pizza was more than enough for us.

Eventually, after things started getting better for the two of us, and she got her first job, we'd only go back for nostalgia.

Still fixated on the pizza place, I hear Kellie break through my concentration.

"James, go. The light's green," she says.

"Huh? Oh, okay, sorry," I say, continuing our drive through my little town.

Other small businesses pass by on the road as we make our way down the street. Lucky's, the consignment shop my sister and I bought her desk at when she started going to college. The corner store, where my sister had her first job. The Sweets Emporium, where I did a painting job and got a ten-pound bag of candy as a gift. I don't think my sister and I ever ate candy again after that…

It all feels like it was ages ago… like I'm seeing these memories as a spectator out of my own body. Not myself, but sharing the memories of someone who doesn't… exist anymore.

Out of pure muscle memory, I make a turn down a small road, trees lining the sidewalks, nearly blocking out the sky. The closed-off suburban street becomes a jungle of colored siding and different hues of green. Continuing down the road, I hear Kellie speak up.

"Man, this place reminds me of home. It's cozy," she replies.

"I've never lived in a place like this," Lyla says. "It's always been apartments for me."

"It's a nice place," I reply. "But I had to work for it."

"Work for it?" Kellie says.

"Yep," I reply. "I gave up a lot to support my sister after my mom left us. We both eventually paid off the place. I didn't think I'd ever move either. But now… I don't know."

The car falls silent.

As I round the bend, I see it. Right at the end of the road, sitting promptly on the corner of a 90-degree turn. My home. A white, two-story house, fit for what was once a family of four. Now reduced to a family of two.

"There it is," I say, slowing the car down and pulling into the driveway.

I put the car into park. Turning off the ignition and unbuckling myself from the seat, I open the door. There's something different about being home; the air is different, the sounds are different. Everything's different. But, even throughout all that, I'm back, and nothing seems to have changed.

I look at the lawn. It's slightly overgrown, but I can tell that someone's been mowing it every week. That used to be my job. Maybe my sister hired someone to do it? Or she started to do it herself...

I walk up to the garage door opener and flip open the lid to reveal the keypad. Out of pure instinct, I type in the code. One of the things I'll never forget.

1605.

The door hums to life, and the garage door opens. Kellie and Lyla hop out of the car and close the doors as the garage door finishes its journey onto the rack in the ceiling.

The garage is empty. My sister... isn't home.

"Nobody home?" Lyla asks, peering into the garage.

"She's probably at work," I reply, stepping into the garage. "Come on."

I walk into the garage and wait until Kellie and Lyla are inside with me, before closing the garage door from the inside and opening the door into my house.

Kellie and Lyla follow me inside as we walk through a small hallway into the kitchen. The kitchen is a little unkempt. My sister, she's always been one of those people who absent-mindedly forgets to put stuff away when she's done with a task, and it shows. Empty boxes sit on the counter, pots and pans in the sink, and trash that's almost full.

I sigh, and head into the kitchen. I start picking up the boxes and putting them into the trash can. Once the counter has been cleared off, I tie the trash bag together and set it on the floor.

Kellie and Lyla peer into the kitchen.

"What're you doing?" Lyla asks.

"Cleaning up," I say.

"Why?" Lyla asks.

"'Cause it's the right thing to do," I say. "I just got back, and I'm sure my sister will be home from work soon. I think it'd be a good start to have everything cleaned up before she gets back. You can help if you want," I reply.

Lyla pauses for a few seconds; Kellie however, responds.

"Sure, what do you need me to do?" she asks.

"Go into the living room and see if anything needs picked up," I say.

"Sure thing," Kellie says, walking over to the living room.

"Thank you," I reply.

"No problem!" Kellie says, her tone optimistic.

"What do you need me to do?" Lyla asks.

"Take the trash out," I say.

"Sure," she replies, grabbing the bag. "Where do I go?"

"Out the garage and through the small back door on the wall; the cans should be out there," I say.

"All right," she says, walking the bag to the door.

"Thank you, Lyla," I say with a grin.

"'Course, dude," she says, smiling back.

As Lyla disappears out into the garage, I turn my attention to the dishes in the sink. These need to be washed, but before I start attacking these by hand, I could check the dishwasher. Opening the door under the counter and to the right of the sink, I look inside the dishwasher. It's empty. At least she's taking care of those. I can't remember how many times we'd argue about whose turn it was to take care of the dishes.

It got to the point where we had to set up a schedule for who's going to do them. I chuckle to myself as I grab the pots and pans and neatly stack them in the dishwasher. Once the pots and pans are in, I close the door. Turning on the dishwasher, I hear the door open. I turn around to see Lyla coming back in.

"Hey, do you know where the, uh… bathroom is?" she asks.

"Yeah, it's right next to the stairs," I say, pointing to the living room.

"All right, thanks," she says, walking to the living room, where Kellie is.

I now move to the sink, turning on the tap. I put soap on my hands and clean them of any food stuff I got on them, moving them from the dishwasher. I've always hated doing the dishes; it made me feel ill, nauseous even. But I've done them so many times now that it doesn't even matter anymore.

Turning the tap off, I hear the sound of the garage door opening again.

I freeze.

My sister's back. I haven't seen her in how long? And I just walked into my own house after being gone for three weeks like I own the place.

Panic sets in. What do I do? Do I meet her at the door? Do I surprise her? I don't want to have the cops called on me, let alone tell them where I've been. They could be working for the RCC, or at least… believe in their lies.

I need to deescalate the situation. I need to talk to my sister as soon as possible.

Slowly, I start moving to the garage door, hoping I can make it there before my sister does. This isn't the kind of reunion I wanted…

I make it to the door, and I put my hand on it to turn the knob. I slowly start to turn the knob, expecting some resistance. But it's not moving… I know she's… she's on the other side.

I pause. I can't keep the door closed. I need to say something…

"Riley?" I manage to croak out.

Silence on the other side of the door. Then the knob starts violently jiggling.

"James? Is that you?" the voice on the other side of the door calls out. It's her; it's my sister. "Please, let me in! Where have you been?"

"I can… I can explain everything… I just. I just don't want you to freak out…"

"What're you talking about?" she calls out again. "Open the door!"

"Okay," I say. "Just… please don't make a scene."

I let go of the door and step back. The door flings open, and my sister almost falls into the door. She stops, pulling her blonde hair back to see. As she looks up to meet me eye to eye, she freezes.

"Please, don't freak out," I say.

What I would have expected her to do is step back and take a breath, remain calm. Like she normally does. But she doesn't. She stands there frozen. Not looking me up and down, not yelling, not attacking me.

Just… standing.

CHAPTER 30

James

"RILEY?" I ASK, trying to get her attention.

She doesn't respond.

"I'm… I'm sorry you had to go so long without me," I try to say, but she holds her hand up, stopping me from continuing.

She instead doesn't reply, but she walks past me. Peering into the kitchen as she walks down the hallway, I can't tell what's going on with her. I've never seen her act like this before.

She continues past the kitchen into the foyer. She stops again. As I slowly follow from behind, I can tell what she's looking at.

Kellie and Lyla are stopped in their tracks, looking at her.

"Uh, hello," Lyla says.

Riley raises her hand and gives a halfhearted wave and then makes a sharp turn to the stairs, walking up.

"Riley," I say, following her upstairs.

She doesn't respond. Instead, she turns directly into her room at the top and closes the door.

I stop my ascent. I don't even know what to think. This isn't what I thought was going to go through my head when I thought about coming back. I thought that she might be a little taken back by my appearance, but I thought she'd be happy to see me.

I thought that maybe she'd be mad that I was gone, and maybe she'd understand my reasoning that I left. I thought that maybe things would be a little rough to start, but they'd eventually get better. That's how they've always gone, and I've been so used to it. I guess I was wrong.

I hear Lyla and Kellie approach from behind.

"Is everything…. okay?" Kellie asks.

"I don't know," I respond. "She just went… to her room."

"Shouldn't you try talking to her?" Lyla asks.

"I… I guess," I say.

"Then go," Kellie says. "Go talk to her."

I pause, before continuing up the stairs and towards her room at the top. As I make it to the top of the stairs, the hardwood stairs turn to carpet. I stop at the entrance to the hallway, leading to my sister's room at the end of the hall. The door's closed. I know she's in there. But every step I take towards the end of the hallway, the more I feel like I'm not going to like the conversation coming up. I don't know what to expect, and I don't know what's going to happen. I just know that whatever it is, it's not going to be good.

I dread it. I don't want to do it. But I know that it's something I'm going to have to do.

Every time I get closer to the door, it just feels farther away.

Finally, I make it to the door. Raising my hand, I take a breath.

I can do this.

I knock on the door, lightly.

"Riley?" I say.

Silence from the other side of the door.

"You… there?" I ask.

Silence again, but for a moment, I hear her voice on the other side.

"What happened to you?" she asks, her voice cracking.

"I… I don't know," I respond.

"Is this why you left all of a sudden?" she asks.

I pause.

"Y-yeah," I respond.

"Why did you leave?" she asks. "I wake up, and you're… you're gone. You leave some vague note and say you're going to be back in a week, and then you don't show up until three weeks later and act like nothing's wrong."

"I just… I thought…" I continue.

"You thought what?" she asks. "That you were going to scare me? Freak me out?"

"Y-yeah," I say.

"Well… yeah, I'm definitely a little freaked out." She continues, "One day you're here, the next you're gone. I went out trying to look for you. I went to all of our spots, trying to find you. Instead, I see all these… people, running around, freaking out. Saying that they're monsters, they're changed, they're… animals. But… that wasn't what was scary."

I don't respond.

"What was really scary… was seeing you vanish out of nowhere. Just like Dad. Just like Mom. I thought I had to start all over again. After that first week… when you didn't come back… I thought I lost you."

"I didn't… I didn't mean for you to… think that," I say.

"I know you. I know you don't do things without any kind of reason. But it didn't feel like that," she says.

"I… I know," I continue. "I just thought you… wouldn't… like what you saw."

"We're family," she says. "You're my brother. You didn't do this to yourself."

A slight pause.

"We've worked through so much together. This was… a big thing, you know? Not for me, but for you. It's different, it's weird, yeah, I know. But we should have worked through it together."

"I know," I say.

"You remember… Jasmine, from work, right?" she asks.

"The girl in the shoe department?" I ask.

"Yeah, her." Riley continues, "I came into work the day after you left. She was there, and she was like you. Didn't even recognize her, She's a fox now… I think. But it didn't seem to bother her at all. We talked about it. Told her I thought this happened to you too and asked why you'd run away."

"Oh," I say.

"She said the same thing you did. Said that her family wasn't super thrilled about her being one of those people. Said that they basically cut all contact with her. She didn't want it, she didn't ask for it. But she got it. She understood that this was all new, and we needed time to get used to it."

I can't bring myself to say anything.

"I just… I wish you would've given me that chance." Her voice trembles.

"I made… a mistake," I say. "I know I shouldn't have left. We could've worked through it together. Like we always did."

"We could've…" Riley continues. "And… I'd like to think… we still can."

"I'd… I'd like that too. But… I don't know if I can," I say.

No response from my sister. Instead, the door flings open.

"Why not?" she says, staring at me. "Why can't we work through this together?" Why can't we just… try and make things work? Try and make things go back to the way they were?"

"I've been… caught up with some bad people," I say.

"What, those people downstairs? The one's you just *let into our house?*" she exclaims.

"No… not them!" I say. "Just give me time to explain."

Riley stops and takes a deep breath.

"Okay," she says. "I'm listening. Tell me, why we can't go back, why we can't go back to the way things were and try to live normally."

I pause before continuing.

"When… when I left," I start, trying to formulate a sentence that she'd not get upset at. "When I left… I did intend on coming back in a week. I don't know if you know about them, but there's this… group. They're called the RCC."

"The people who rehabilitate people like you?" she asks. "That's where you went? That place is for people who've been turned into wolves and lions and shit, James! You're a chameleon for crying out loud!"

"I know, I know," I continue. "But the thing is, they claimed that they'd help me figure out how to get used to it all."

"That's supposed to be my job, as your sister, your *family*. Not some jerks in lab coats!" she says.

"I'm… I'm sorry Riley, I wasn't thinking. The whole idea… it backfired," I say.

"It…backfired?" she asks.

"They… they never wanted us to leave," I say. "I had to… escape, with my friends."

"The… people downstairs," she says.

"Yeah, the people downstairs." I continue, "We've been… on the run from these people. They're relentless. They brought guns, the guy running the facility is a nutcase… and… I don't even know if they've followed us here."

"What… What did you do?" Riley asks, her expression changing from anger to worry.

"All I did was try to leave; they wouldn't let us. They said that it's got something to do with… instinct."

Riley averts her eyes, and I can see the gears turning in her head.

"Like, you're not entirely human?" she asks.

"I don't know. That's what they're telling us, but nothing's happened to me. Maybe to one of my friends downstairs. But I don't know if they're even telling the truth. They've kept me this whole time. I wouldn't be here if it wasn't for them."

Riley looks back at me. "Then… why can't you stay here?" she says. "Just… just you? We can still work through this together. And we can deal with these people if they do show up."

"It's not that simple," I say. "If they come back, whether it's just me or it's all of us… I don't know if they're going to be keen on talking things out."

I pause.

"And… and I made a promise to my friends. A promise I'd help them get home."

Riley doesn't respond.

"Do you… have a choice in this?" she asks.

"At this point," I say, "I don't know if I do."

"I just. I can't let you go," Riley says, turning to me, tears welling up in her eyes.

"I… know," I respond. "I don't want to go either. But I can't… I can't put you in danger."

"I get that," she says. "But there's got to be something I can do."

"I don't know if there is," I respond.

"Can't we… take your friends to their destination, and then come back?" she asks.

"What're you talking about?" I ask.

"We take your friends home, and then we split off and go back to the way things are. We move forward, just like we always do," she says.

"I… I don't know," I say.

"We could do that," she continues. "Then, you can keep your promise, and then I can take you back home. We're family; we're supposed to stick together."

"I know," I say. "I can… I can ask them."

"Just… ask," she says.

I nod. "Wait here."

I walk to the stairs and head down. Stepping to the bottom of the stairs, I look into the living room where Kellie and Lyla are sitting, waiting for me.

"So… what happened?" Lyla asks.

"She's not happy I left," I say.

"I mean, I would be upset too in her situation," Kellie adds.

"Yeah, I know," I continue. "She doesn't want me to leave."

"The RCC is probably following us," Kellie says. "You can't stick around and risk your sister getting hurt."

"She's right," Lyla adds. "I don't want anyone else to get caught in the crossfire… not after what happened at Paul's."

"I know," I said. "So… she wants to go with us."

"To my house?" Lyla asks.

"Yeah," I say.

"Why?" Kellie asks.

"Because she doesn't want to lose me," I say. "After you get home, I'd come back here."

"And what about the RCC?" Lyla asks. "They'll eventually turn up."

"I know," I reply. "But I just don't wanna burn the only bridge I have left in my family."

"I get it," Kellie says. "'It was… easier for me to let go."

Lyla pauses. "So… we go our separate ways when I get home?" Lyla says.

"I guess so," I reply. "If the RCC shows up… I'm sure I can think of something."

"I don't like it," Lyla says.

Silence.

"But if she wants to come with us, and that's where we part ways, I guess it's okay."

"I'm fine with it," Kellie says.

"I just have a bad feeling about letting her tag along. I don't want her to get hurt," Lyla continues. "Let's just hope the RCC isn't already here when we leave."

"Thank you," I say, before heading upstairs.

By the time I get upstairs, I see Riley at the top, switched out of her work clothes into a shirt and pants, waiting for me.

"I heard," she says. "We do this one thing, and then it's back to normal... right?"

"Right," I say.

Riley approaches me and hugs me. Instinctively, I do the same.

"I missed you," she says.

"I missed you too," I reply.

"Let's go," she says. "I don't know how long the drive is. But if what you're telling me is true, then we need to leave now."

I nod. "It's true."

"I've got an open mind," she says. "At this point... anything can happen, I guess."

She heads downstairs, and I follow. By the time we make it to the bottom, Kellie and Lyla are already in the foyer.

"Come on," I say. "Let's take you home."

Lyla nods. "All right."

The four of us walk out of the house through the garage, the door opening slowly. I have this gut feeling in my chest that once I can see the outside, there's going to be vans of RCC men in armor with rifles pointed at us.

The door opens up, and the cool evening air rushes in, taking over the trapped heat inside of the garage. Once the door reaches its final resting place at the top of the garage once more, I see...

Nobody.

The roads are silent, empty, and nobody's waiting for us on the lawn.

My sister's car we kept from our dad is parked neatly behind the van we took from Paul's.

"Should we take my car?" Riley asks.

"It'd probably be a good idea," Kellie says. "They remember the van. They saw us leave in it."

Lyla nods. "Probably a good idea to stay low anyhow."

Riley nods. "I guess… We can keep the van in the garage."

"I don't know if that's a good idea," I say.

"We can't leave it in the driveway, James," Riley says. "If these people are looking for you, they'll be looking for the van."

"I guess," I respond, taking the keys out of my pocket.

I get into the van, turn on the ignition, and pull it into the garage. Turning off the car, for what feels like the final time, I step out.

"All right," I say. "Ready?"

"Ready as I'll ever be," Riley responds.

She unlocks the car, and Kellie and Lyla pile into the back.

I follow, stepping into the passenger seat.

"So," Riley says, closing the garage door and starting the car, "where are we going?"

"My place," Lyla says.

"Okay…" Riley says.

"Lyla," she responds.

"Lyla… got it…" Riley says, pulling out her phone. "Put your address in."

"All right," she says, taking the phone.

"Oh, James," Riley says, turning to me and opening the console in between our seats. "Here."

Riley places my phone in my hand. Surprisingly enough, it springs to life the moment I tap the screen.

"Please," she says. "Keep it on you at all times."

I nod. "Okay."

"Here you go…" Lyla says.

"Thanks," Riley responds, plugging her phone into the car.

I look at the screen. Lyla's address is placed on the GPS. The time of arrival says four hours.

"Quite a drive," I say.

"Yep," Lyla says. "Didn't realize how far from home I actually was."

"We'll do it," Riley says.

"You need someone to stay up?" I say. "It's late already."

"Yeah, you can stay up if you want. I'd appreciate the company," Riley says.

I nod.

"I don't know about you," Lyla says, "but I'm beat. I'll try to stay up, but no promises."

I chuckle. "Try your best," I say.

Riley puts the car into reverse, and we pull out of the driveway.

Staring at my house, it feels like I'm still leaving a piece of me behind, despite the fact I'm taking a piece of home with me to somewhere I've never been, and I'm worried.

Not because I don't think I'm going to see home again, but because I'm bringing my home into the unknown. These past three weeks have shown me things I didn't expect, things I didn't think I could handle. Now that I've overcome them, now that I feel like I'm someone new on the inside, and not just the outside, this feels like a final test. Either… I'm going to pass with flying colors, or I'm going to flunk. The thought of flunking is drastically worse than I could possibly imagine.

CHAPTER 31

Lyla

Homecoming

I'm standing in the middle of a forest. I don't know where I am, but I can tell in the back of my mind that it's the one at the cabin. Where this all began. I can't see the cabin; I can't see anything. A veil of darkness closes in on me. As the cold embrace of the black sky draws closer to me, I feel that freezing feeling creeping up on me again.

I try to move my legs, but they're unresponsive. I feel the presence of someone in the trees obscuring my vision. I can't tell who it is, but I know they're there.

"H-hello?" I manage to squeak out.

The rustling of leaves and cracking of branches circle around me. Like a predator closing in on its prey. I don't know who or what it is.

Soon, a figure emerges through the brush. A figure I didn't think I'd see ever again.

Myself.

A blurred image of what I used to look like stands before me. The only defining features of myself I can see clearly are my hands, my figure, and my hair.

This blurred mirror image of myself stares me down. I can't tell its expression, but I can tell it's analyzing me.

"Wh…what do you want?" I ask.

Silence. The sound of the rolling wind and the rustling trees are the only sounds between the two of us.

"You…" the figure speaks, its voice a whisper, coming from all directions.

"You did this to me," it cries, pointing a finger at me.

"W-what?" I ask back.

"It's all your fault!" the voice cries out, echoing around me.

Other voices chime in, ones I can't make out, all chanting, "Your fault, your fault, your fault."

My mirror image lunges at me, grabbing me by the neck, pinning me to the ground. Its hands dig into my neck.

I try to fight back, pushing at my mirror image, yet, as I start gasping for breath, my hands pass through its body. With each swipe at this figure, I start to lose more and more energy.

The voices continue chanting all around the two of us. "Your fault, your fault, your fault."

The more I stare into this figure's blurry visage, the more I can see rage seeping from its body.

"S…s…stop," I wheeze.

The figure doesn't respond.

I see two pairs of feet step forward from the darkness, obscured by the figure inches from my face, hands on my throat. I can't make out who they are.

But a distinct voice calls out to me…or rather, the figure starving me of oxygen.

"Sweetie, be nice to the animals."

It's my mother.

"M-mom," I attempt to call out, but the figure presses its hands tighter around my neck in response.

"Don't hurt them, honey. They're friendly," another voice calls out, my dad's.

"Please…" I plead to the figure.

I try even harder to stand up, fighting off the figure attacking me. With every swipe, every move, I can't budge. It's pinned me down, sitting on my waist and pushing my head into the dirt below.

I try to move again, do anything. But right as I'm starting to move enough to push the figure off, the ground beneath me gives way, plunging me into an abyss of black below.

The only light coming in as I fall comes from the soft light of the hole I fell through.

My stomach sinks into my body as I plummet into the inky abyss. The figure watches me from where my descent began.

I can't tell when I'm supposed to hit the bottom, but the chanting has subsided, leaving me alone for a moment. I close my eyes, only to feel the jolt of solid land. I spring awake.

Opening my eyes, everything's a haze. I immediately start gasping for air, only to realize that the seatbelt is choking me.

I pull the seatbelt away from my neck and unbuckle it. But, instead of being released from my asphyxiation, I fly upwards, hitting my head on the roof.

Regaining my bearings, I realize that I didn't fly up. I fell… down.

I'm upside down… The car's upside down… We… We crashed…

I frantically start looking around for anyone else in the car. Kellie, James, Riley… Where are they?

Nobody is in the seats. I'm alone. Oh god, what happened?

I start crawling along the roof of the car, looking for any exit.

The window is broken open on the other side of the car, leading onto the road. Frantically, I crawl out of the car and onto the grass.

Standing up, I feel something wet underneath my feet. Looking down onto the grass, I notice something I hoped I wouldn't see…

Blood.

I frantically start patting myself down to see if I'm the one injured. But… I don't find anything. I'm untouched.

I don't know what's happening, but someone's hurt, and I need to find them.

I start climbing out of the ditch and onto the road, following the trail of blood through the grass. As I get to the top of the ditch, the night sky gives a clear view of the wreckage I ended up in.

Fire litters the side of the roads, vans and cars knocked over on their sides, smoking or engulfed in flames. Broken glass litters the asphalt as one figure shambles down the middle of the road, illuminated by the red-orange light of the flames.

I start moving down the road towards the figure.

"H-Hello?" I yell. "Are you okay?"

As I continue down the road approaching the figure, I can finally make out who it is.

Tattered lab coat, blackened and burnt at the ends, a torn sleeve, broken glasses, a stare of pure rage, and half a head of singed hair.

It's… him.

Before I can think, he raises his hand, and the sound of exploding gunpowder is heard. A whizzing sound jets past my head, making a loud ding in the wreckage behind me.

I turn around and start running.

Pure survival is the only thing in my mind as I run down the street, past the burning wreckage and crashed cars. I need to find a means of escape. I can't die, not now. As I run through the wreckage, I manage to see someone facedown on the side of the road. As I approach them, I start to realize who it is. Red hoodie, dark hair, striped tail…

Kellie…

I reach down and start shaking her.

"Kellie, get up! We need to go! Now! He's coming!" I yell.

But there's no response from her.

"Kellie, come on, get up! Please! We need to leave!" I scream.

Still no response.

I grab her shoulders and start pushing her over, and as I do that, I realize something.

The trail... of blood... from the car...

Leads to her...

As I roll her over, gravity takes hold... Her torso splits from her hips, sending the only identifying part of my friend sliding into the ditch below, unraveling a pink and red ribbon of entrails as its only connection to her lower half.

"Kellie?" I ask... to no one, already knowing the answer.

I stand up... start stepping back... "No..."

No.... This... this can't be real...

As I step back, attempting to process what... what I just saw... I back right into.... him.

I spin around again, falling onto the road.

He doesn't say anything to me, just staring me down.

I can't bring myself to say anything. The only thing I can do is let tears run down my face. I gasp for breath again, inhaling burning air and the smell of fresh, spilled blood.

Finally, he speaks.

"You did all this," he says, raising his weapon towards me.

"People like you..."

"Things... like you."

"Shouldn't exist."

Right as the front of his weapon illuminates the immediate area, everything goes black.

"Lyla?" a voice calls out.

The bright shine of light obscures my vision as I jolt forward, being stopped by the seatbelt of the car.

I gasp for air once more, only to feel someone grab my hand.

I quickly look to my left, to see Kellie… a concerned expression on her face.

"You… you okay?"

I let out a massive sigh as I relax in my seat.

"Oh god… Yeah. I am now," I reply.

James looks into the back of the car from the passenger seat in front of me.

"You were shaking while you slept. We almost stopped the car for you," he says.

"I wish you did," I reply.

"Was it some kind of nightmare?" Kellie asks.

"Yeah," I reply. "Thankfully it's… it's over now."

"You wanna talk about it?" Kellie asks.

"Not… not really," I say. "Maybe… later."

"I've had some pretty messed-up nightmares," Riley chimes in from the driver's seat. "I know how it is."

I nod. "Yeah, I'll… I'll be fine," I reply, turning my attention to the window.

Jesus… What even was that dream I had? Was it some kind of pre-monition? What did… what did he mean when he said I did that? Was it… because of my abilities? Or… was it because of us escaping? Like we caused all that damage in our escape? And… Kellie. Seeing what… what happened to her in my dream? What about even before that? Why did I see… me? Why did I do that to myself?

I think I get it. But… I don't want to dwell on it. It was too much, and I'm ready to get out of this car, before something actually happens to us. I'm just… I'm just glad it's over.

The GPS starts talking. "Turn left in .01 miles, and your destination will be on your left."

Finally, we're almost here. I fidget in my seat. I'm ready to get out of here, but… I'm not sure if I'm ready to see my aunt… not after every-thing that's happened with all of us.

The GPS chimes again. "You've reached your destination."

"Welp," Riley says. "We're here."

"Yep," I say, unbuckling my seat. I go to reach for the handle to open the door, but I stop. James and Riley get out of the car. I hear Kellie's door open behind me.

"You coming?" Kellie asks.

"Yeah," I say. "I'm getting out." I force myself to open the door, the crisp air hitting my face. I can tell just by the smell, it's home... I'm home. But am I ready to be here?

I don't have much time to think about it as I step out of the car. In front of a building I know all too well. The grey brick apartment complex. It's nothing special, but it's where my aunt lives. Where I spent a lot of my time when I turned sixteen and I left my parents' house to live with my aunt.

Not that I didn't like my parents, but I spent so much time alone, I thought I could do it by myself. My mom told me that she had no qualms about me moving out, but if I was going to learn any kind of self-discipline, I had to live with my aunt.

Of course, I agreed, and I roomed with my aunt. Until college, then... I moved out. I remember saying my goodbyes to her; we were less aunt and niece and more sisters. It was heartbreaking. No more sitting on the couch late on a Friday with pizza, watching shitty soap operas. No more going out just for kicks.

But, after college, I had to come back. But I guess we were busier; things didn't completely return to normal... Those moments we had, they were fewer and farther in between. Then I started making friends my own age. Spent more time with them. Years went by after college, and those moments were gone, I guess.

Then, the cabin.

Now, I'm back, and I wish they were under better circumstances. I wish that I didn't take that time for granted. Now, I don't even know if things will remain the same.

I feel a hand on my shoulder. I look to my side, and it's James.

"You ready?" he asks.

"I don't know," I say. "I'm scared of what's going to happen."

"You can't stand out here, though," he says. "You've gotta face it, one way or another."

"I know," I say. "Still…" I think back to that conversation I had with Jessie at Paul's. What she said to me…

"That….. that *thing* happened to you… didn't it?"

I still don't understand what she meant by that. Or anything after that question. It bothers me. The one person I've held so close to me. Someone who knows me better than my own mother. Someone I trusted every fiber of my being with. She couldn't let something like this change her perception on me….

Could she?

I sigh. James is right. Me standing here on the sidewalk staring at the apartment complex isn't going to help me figure this out. I need to face it myself. I need to get these answers for myself. Even if it's going to hurt. Even if something bad happens when I walk through the door. I need to do this myself.

I start walking forward. Heading towards the apartment complex. Everything feels unchanged, the cracked stairs, the splintered banister. The posters on the walls from music tours long past. The slight dinginess of the apartment hiding the truth of the well-kept apartments inside. Nothing changed since I left. The only thing that's changed… is me.

Reaching the third floor of the apartments, I recognize the tacky welcome mat in front of my aunt's apartment. The text, "We're not buying, get lost!" emblazoned on the mat in bold black letters.

I can't help but chuckle to myself, remembering seeing it every time I came home, and hearing people ask about it when they came over. It was stupid, but it was funny regardless. I think that we lost a package or two because the delivery guy had to get a signature but didn't want to cause a fuss, which then turned into just that when my aunt caught him trying to leave a note saying he missed us.

These memories, they were of a better time. Now, I don't know what's going to happen when I knock. Standing in front of the door, on the tacky welcome mat. I don't know if I can do it, and like the delivery man, I turn around to head back downstairs. But when I turn around, I see James, standing on the stairs, blocking my path.

"What're you doing?" I ask.

"Preventing you from leaving," he says.

"I don't know if I can do it," I say.

"You have to," he says.

"You don't understand," I say. "I called her before this, and her response…"

"It doesn't matter," he says. "You came here for a reason. To see your aunt, to see your family. We went back to my house, and I talked to my sister. I thought she was going to hate me…. but she didn't," he says. "You have to do this, not for your family's sake, but for your own."

I… I don't know what to say to him, but he's right. I need to do this. But….

"I'm scared," I whimper.

"We all were," James says. "Kellie was scared, I was scared. But you're going to keep being scared, and it's going to follow you your whole life until you actually do something about it. So, do it now."

I shakily nod.

I turn around and raise my hand to knock on the door.

I close my eyes, my heart pounding, that… that freezing feeling creeping up on me again… preventing me from moving. But… I've got to break through it. I've got to do this… no matter what happens.

I.

Need.

To.

Knock.

Tap.

Tap.

Tap.

The sound of my knocks on the door feels like I've broken through something. The feeling I've had, the freezing feeling, subsides quicker than before.

It's like... I broke some kind of habit. Like I've overcome a hurdle.

I feel... free. For a moment.

I can hear footsteps coming to the door.

I know who's on the other side; I'm just... worried of what's going to happen when this barrier is broken between us.

Suddenly, the *click-clunk* of the lock vibrates through the door.

The door creaks open. All I can see is a figure on the other side.

"J-Jessie?" I ask.

The door flings open, and before I can think, I'm caught in an embrace from my aunt, her dark curly hair caught in my face.

"Ohmigod, it's so good to see you!" she exclaims.

I hug her back.

"Y-yeah," I say... "I'm... I'm sorry I was gone." This... this wasn't what I was expecting. Her tone over the phone was something completely different to the person embracing me now. But I... I don't mind this change of tune. Something in the back of my mind, though, something tells me it's a farce. Like she's making it up, like I'm just imagining her being excited to see me. I try to shake it, since for now, things are okay...

She finally lets go, giving me enough room to breathe.

"Please, you were... god knows where," she says, stepping back.

"Dang, you rock the whole..."

"Look?" I say... still taken aback from the past few minutes.

"Yeah! I can still totally tell it's you. Even if you're, uhhh…"

"A possum," I say.

Jessie snaps her fingers. "Yep! Should've known that. Come on in!"

Jessie looks to James on the stairs. "Who's that?" she asks.

"Hello," James says. "I'm James."

"You two the only people here?" she asks.

"No," I say. "We've got two more people by the car."

"Bring them in too," she says. "I've gotta talk to you, Lyla."

CHAPTER 32

Lyla

Homecoming Part 2

It's weird, being home, sitting on the old couch, leather tearing at the seams, exposing the cushion underneath. Bright wallpaper, the flowery pillows, the stupid doily on the coffee table Jessie refused to get rid of from Grandma's. But regardless, there's a comfort to it.

My aunt comes out, setting down a bottle of water on the table.

"Take this," she says.

"Thanks," I reply.

"It's nothing. We're still sisters, aren't we?" She laughs, sitting down in a chair across from me.

"Yeah," I say, smiling.

"Granted, we didn't have a lot of time like we used to, now did we?" She laughs again. "But that's what happens when we get older."

I nod. "Yeah. And… and I'm sorry about that."

Jessie looks at me with a concerned expression.

"You don't have to be sorry," she says.

"I feel like I should be," I respond. "I spent too much time out do-ing things for myself. I didn't make time for you. It's been the one thing on my mind for the past few weeks, how excited I was to move out, to go to college, to live with you. I feel like I've lived my life too fast. And now, everything is different, and I feel like I wasted my life. I wasted my connections with my family."

Jessie shakes her head. "You're young," she says. "It's not like your parents are faultless either."

"I understand why they did it," I say. "I get it."

"And the fact that you're making the choice to come back, even when you had a perfect excuse to not come back," she says, gesturing at me. "You could've started a whole new life. Been someone else." She continues, "But you didn't. You know that, I know that. Your parents know that."

My parents… I need to ask Jessie about my parents. Before I can say something, the door opens again, and James, Kellie, and Riley walk through.

"Oh, these are my friends," I say.

"Hello," Riley says. "I'm James's sister, Riley."

"I'm Kellie," Kellie introduces herself.

"Hello! I'm Jessie," Jessie says.

"Nice to meet you," Kellie says.

"Well, it's nice to meet you too, Kellie. Thank you for taking care of Lyla for me," she says with a big smile.

"I'm glad you all made it here in one piece," Jessie says before standing up. "Lyla, can you come with me?"

"Uh… sure," I say, standing up.

Jessie gestures to the hallway behind her. I look to my friends and give a nod before following her down the hall.

Jessie walks into the door just before the end of the hall, hanging a right. Oh lord, I know where she's going. As I turn the corner, the purple paint of the walls brings back a feeling I didn't think I'd feel in a long time. Looking onto the walls, old band posters curl on the edges, the white dresser mocking the rest of the slightly edgy décor. This is my room. It feels like I haven't been in here in ages, even though I've spent every night in this room up until the cabin trip.

Surprisingly, the room is cleaner than I remember leaving it. My clothes don't litter the floor, and my bed is made as if nobody ever lived in here.

Jessie closes the door behind me, before turning to face me.

"I don't want to talk about this in front of your friends. But we've gotta talk about your parents," Jessie says, her tone more serious than it was when we were out in the living room.

"Are… are they okay?" I ask.

"Yes, they're fine," Jessie replies. "I called them, after you called me a couple days ago."

"You said you were going to," I reply. "Do they know… do they know about this?" I say, gesturing to myself.

"I had to tell them." Jessie continues, "It was the first thing your mom thought of when you went missing."

"You've been talking to her?" I ask.

"You went missing," Jessie says. "It's not like I wasn't going to tell your mom about it."

"I mean… I guess," I say. "I kinda wish I could've told them about… what happened."

"I know, and if you didn't disappear, that's probably how it would have gone," Jessie says. "But your mom found out pretty quickly. So I was backed into a corner… I'm… sorry."

"It's fine. I get it," I say. I am disappointed, but I know my aunt, and I know she wouldn't lie about it.

"So… are they coming here?" I ask.

"No." Jessie continues, "You'll have to go to them."

"Go to them?" I ask. "Where are they?"

"You know…" Jessie says, her tone shifting from serious to consoling.

"They're at the restaurant, aren't they?" I ask.

"Yep. I know you hate that place."

"Of course I hate that place," I say. "Why wouldn't I? I feel bad I stopped them from having their dream, and now they're having it. But they don't have time for me. Jessie, I've been out of school for two years now. And they just... moved on like that?"

Jessie sighs.

"They never moved on. Your mom asked you to come work with them, didn't she?" Jessie says. "You told her no. We had this exact conversation that night. I said it was a good idea, and you couldn't give me a reason for you not wanting to. You said you didn't want your parents' help. You didn't want to burden them with your own bills and problems. You even said you didn't want your parents as bosses."

"And I stand by that," I say. "I wanted to spend time with my parents now that I was back. But it was always about the restaurant with them. It was always about working, about following their dream. They never had time for me when I was a kid."

"Because they were doing it for you," Jessie says.

"Because I was the problem, the mistake," I say. "You know damn well they didn't plan me," I say. "But they got lucky, they had stuff going, so it was fine that they had to work a little extra to support me. But that meant that I didn't see a lot of them. And now when they want to spend time with me, it's only when they're working. It's not like we could do things like me and you both did."

I sigh.

"We did fun things. We did pizza at night, we went out, we went to the movies, we went mini-golfing, bowling. We even went to amusement parks and town fairs. Sure, I might've hated some of that when you babysat me when I was a kid. But it felt like more of a childhood than only seeing my parents right before bed. I couldn't get them to do anything. And then they try to connect to me by involving me in the one thing that prevented them from seeing me in the first place? We wouldn't be spending time with one another;

we'd be working, co-existing. I didn't want to mix work and family like that."

Jessie sighs and sits down on my bed, patting the side for me to join her. I begrudgingly sit on the bed next to her.

"You know they still care about you," Jessie says.

"Maybe they do. But they never decided to reach out, especially now," I reply.

"Maybe they feel the same way," Jessie adds.

"Not true," I say. "I tried. They didn't."

"Until when?" Jessie continues. "You tried a few years ago, and then what? You gave up?"

"They didn't have time," I say.

"They're your family. They would've made time eventually," Jessie interjects. "Why do you think they want to see you now?"

"Because they want to see what happened to me. They want to see me. Maybe it's like closure for them. Oh, look at what our kid has become, thank god we have everything we have now," I continue.

"That's wrong," Jessie says.

"How is that wrong?" I ask.

"'Cause the moment I called your mom, she didn't even say hello. She knew why I was calling. Your dad nearly ran through a group of people to come to the phone. They wanted to know where you were, they wanted to know what happened to you. They never gave up on you. They never even gave up hope you were going to come back," Jessie replies, her voice stern.

Jessie stands up, facing me.

"I… I never told you this. To be frank, I probably shouldn't, but I know the moment you walk out of this apartment, you're going to get into that car with your friends and run off again. I'm sure it took you forever to walk up those stairs and knock on the door."

"That's not true," I say.

"Nonsense. I know you. We're sisters. I've lived with you for how long? I know you," Jessie says. "When you moved in, almost every week, when you went to school or work, your mom called. Always asking me how you were. Always apologizing, always saying how she felt like she failed. Always saying how she thought you were going to do great things, how you were going to be better than her."

"Why'd she always call you? Why would she never call me?" I ask.

"That's not for me to answer. That's something you need to ask her," Jessie says.

I... I didn't know that Jessie was talking to my mom behind my back like this. How come she didn't contact me? Even back then? I would've answered the phone. I would've picked up immediately. I still feel like I would've done the same. I... I don't know what to say.

"Are you going to go see them?" Jessie asks.

.

.

.

"Yes," I say. "I told myself when this all started, I would. I guess... I guess I'm scared is all."

"You've got every right to be scared." Jessie continues, "I don't know what you're feeling. Heck, I never did. But I know you'll feel a lot better if you go. I know it's been scary, but like you said. You said you'd go before coming here. You're here now, so you've gotta follow through with it... right?"

I nod.

"I do... don't I?"

Jessie nods in reply.

I stand up from the bed, take a deep breath, and walk up to my aunt.

"Thank you," I say, giving her a hug.

"Of course, Lyla," she replies. "That's what… that's what I'm here for."

I open the door out of my room and start walking down the hallway, making my way to the front door.

I pass James, Kellie, and Riley, who are all sitting on the couch, talking amongst themselves.

"Come on, guys," I say, opening the front door.

"Oh! Okay!" Kellie says, jumping off of the couch and heading for the door.

"Thanks for having us," James says to my aunt, who followed me out to the living room.

"Of course. Again, thank you for taking care of Lyla," she says with a warm smile, looking at me as I hold the front door open for everyone.

"You remember how to get to the restaurant, right?" Jessie asks me as my friends exit the apartment.

"Yep," I say. "Hard to miss it when it's so close."

Jessie nods.

"Come back soon, okay?" she says.

"I will," I reply.

I walk out the door and close it behind me.

I take a deep breath and start walking down the stairs.

"Where are we going?" James asks, following me down the stairs.

"Remember how I told you about the dream my parents had?" I say.

"Yeah," he replies. "What about it?"

"I didn't mention it before. But they did eventually open a restaurant. I've always…. always hated the place… But if we want to see them… we're going to have to go there."

"Oh," Kellie says. "Are you… gonna be okay going there?"

I reach the bottom of the steps and step out to the sidewalk. The afternoon sun is blinding… Not a single cloud in the sky.

I reach for the top of my head and grab the sunglasses I've had on me. Holding them in my hand, I think back to that horrible nightmare I had.

Whatever happened in that dream wasn't real. But I can't help but feel like it's an omen, an omen of something I'm capable of doing.

Or was it a metaphor of what I'm going through now?

Whatever it was, I won't let that happen to me. I won't let myself run from my problems, and I won't let myself become whatever I saw in that dream.

"I don't know. But I did make a promise to myself to come back. And despite everything inside me telling me to not go… I'm not going to listen," I reply, putting on the sunglasses.

"Sounds like you're making the right choice," Riley says.

I nod.

"Well, let's go. We're walking," I say, heading down the sidewalk.

"Walking?" James asks, catching up to me. "We're not taking the car?"

"Don't want to," I say. "It's just a… a gut feeling that I need to walk."

"Oh… okay," James says. "You're not… worried about people see-ing us?"

I'm super worried. Heck, I want to take the car too… But there's this feeling inside of me, this feeling that if I take the car, and we get there, I can leave easier, run farther, turn my back and never return. But at this point in time, every little part of me wants to have every meticu-lous detail make it harder for me to get out of this situation. Prevent me from doing the same thing I've done so many times.

Jessie's words keep ringing through my head.

"That's something you need to ask her."

She's right. She's always been right. And I can't hide from it any lon-ger. This stupid issue that's been plaguing me from the very beginning, even before all the changed stuff, the stuff with Dr. Thorn. The stuff with Paul, meeting James and Kellie. Even Carter.

This is the one thing from my past that won't go away, that won't change overnight. This… this is something I need to take care of myself, the one thing that keeps me connected… to before. The one thing…

The one thing I can fix.

We reach the crosswalk at the end of the block. Nobody's coming, so I just start walking across the street, keeping my eyes out for cars as I pass.

James, Kellie, and Riley follow behind me, James taking extra care to check for vehicles.

"Do you know where you're going?" Riley asks, as we make a left turn at the end of the crosswalk.

"Yeah. I remember. It's the one thing about my parents that I won't ever forget," I say.

"Gotcha," Riley says.

"How far is it from here?" Kellie asks.

I point to the end of the next block coming up.

"We turn right at this intersection, and it'll be at the end of the road. It's a three-way stop right there. Super hard to miss," I say.

"Oh. Okay," Kellie says.

We start making our way to the end of the block, and as I'm ready to turn right, I can't help but wonder what's going to happen when I get there. Are my parents expecting me? Are there going to be people inside? Am I going to walk through the door and cause a scene just by the way I look?

The problem is, I can't think about these things. I can't let my mind wander like that. The more I think about it, the more I want to turn around and go back to my aunt's. Pretend like nothing happened and try to live that normal life I felt when I was at Paul's.

I don't want to think about that either…

I turn the corner, and I can see it. Right at the end of the road, stopping cars, forcing them to turn either right or left… or to come in.

Hagen's Hot Spot Bar & Grill.

I remember my dad describing it to me as "prime real estate" when he called me about it after Jessie told me. He was so proud of it… said he even came up with the name himself.

My response was to complain about the parking.

Maybe Jessie was more right than I realize. Maybe I wasn't the problem for them in the end, but I was the problem for myself.

I continue down the sidewalk, passing parked cars and cafés. People watching me from the windows.

I can hear James and Kellie talk behind me.

"Are they staring at us?" Kellie says.

"Probably," James replies. "But we're almost there. Best to not let it bother you."

"Maybe I'm helping?" Riley chimes in.

"Doubt it," Kellie says. "I can't tell what they're thinking. I think that's the worst part."

As we reach the final crosswalk leading to the front of the restaurant, that little feeling comes back. The one that's telling me to turn and run. It's like a mutated version of the freezing feeling that I've felt time and time again.

The light turns red, forcing me to stop, the feeling making it easier to prevent me from jaywalking a second time.

The time between the light turning from red to green feels like it's taking forever. Seconds feel like minutes. That urge to turn and run back creeps up on me. Like a voice telling me: it's okay to give up, it's okay to run, it's okay that you don't have the answers—you haven't had them for so long. What's the problem if you never get them?

But I can't listen to that voice. I'm so close.

I know I can do this.

I'm done pushing it away any longer.

The light turns green.

Like I've never been held back before, I take a step. For the first time in a long time, I feel free.

Each step is lighter than the rest. Each line in the crosswalk like a finish line I've refused to cross before.

I reach the other side of the road, the neon sign glistening in its orange and white hues.

I'm here. The front door is right here.

I reach out to open the door, my hand gripping the cold steel handle.

"What're you waiting for?" Kellie says.

"I don't know," I say.

"Open it," James says.

I open the door. The ring of bells emanates through the restaurant, and as I take off my sunglasses, I see multiple heads turn to our group.

"What the..." Kellie says.

As my eyes adjust to the interior of the restaurant, I start to form a clear view of the building.

The slightly dim lights, the wooden finish on every booth, the red carpet, the several flatscreens playing the news. And each person at a table.

All of them...

Changed... like me, like James, like Kellie.

I can't help but stand in awe. What... what're all these people doing here? What're all these people doing in my parents' restaurant?

One of them, a bird, calls out into the back.

"Hey! I think Lyla's here!"

How do these people.... How do these people know my name? How do they know... I'm here?

I hear rummaging in the back... the whoosh of the loose kitchen doors open.

And someone steps out.

It... it can't be.

The person standing at the other end of the room has peppered dark curly hair tied up in a ponytail, white apron, blue plaid shirt pulled up at the sleeves.

But….

She…. She looks just like me. Grey fur, white face, black hands. There's no mistaking it.

She's a possum too.

"L-Lyla?" she asks, in a voice I remember too well…

That's…. that's my mom…

Someone else steps out from the door as well…

Taller than the other person at the door, he wears the same apron, grey hoodie, short dark hair… and the same furred complexion as me and the other person.

No… you've got to be messing with me… That's not….

"Well, I'll be…" The voice adds, "She's back."

Not my dad too…

I take a step back… then another…

James's voice echoes throughout the building.

"Are you… are you okay?"

The world blurs.

Then… nothing.

CHAPTER 33

Lyla

As soon as the world vanishes, I hear the voices of people calling out to me.

"Is she okay?"

"Lyla! You good?"

"Over here, right here."

I can feel myself being lifted up, as I start to drift away again.

Silence, for a moment. I'm alone with my thoughts again. I can't decipher them…

For these few moments, I feel at peace, like I don't remember why I even crumpled to the floor in the first place.

It feels good.

But I feel the world reemerging: colors coming back, pale whites, and the distinct smell of chemicals. As the world around me forms from blurred shapes to actual images, I find myself sitting in a room on a rolling chair. I'm behind a desk… A computer is sitting in front of me. I start looking around to take in my surroundings.

A filing cabinet under the desk, notes plastered on the walls. "Pay Louis by Friday." "Call Insurance Company about Fire Hoods."

As I shift to my left, I see someone sitting in a chair next to me.

"Lyla, you there?" the voice says. "Your friends, James, Kellie, and that Riley girl helped move you in here."

Finally, everything comes into view, the other person looking at me with concern only someone like me could understand.

It's my mom. And she's still changed… Just like me.

Now I remember why I crumpled.

I slide back a bit in the rolling chair.

"…Yeah, I'm… I'm here," I say.

My mom breathes a sigh of relief.

"Well, that's good. You gave me and your dad quite a scare when you collapsed like that," she says with a grin. "I'm glad you're here." She reaches a hand out to touch mine.

I slide back a bit more, just out of reach of my mom. This is… this is too weird for me. Like, I can imagine other people being changed. It happened to me; I'm over that… but… I couldn't imagine it happening to my own parents.

My mom sees me pull away from her, and her demeanor changes from relief back to concern.

"Is there… something wrong?" she asks.

I don't know how to respond. I start stammering.

"I… uh… you're…" are the only words I manage to get out.

My mom seems to make the connection, looking at her own hand.

"Oh! Oh…." she says in realization.

I shake my head.

"I… I didn't think…" I stammer out.

"Neither did we," my mom says. "Me and your dad…" She chuckles. "Gave each other quite a fright that morning." She starts laughing. "Your dad was insistent for a few hours that we were both some kind of werewolves!" She starts laughing more.

I can't help but start to laugh about it as well… My mom's always had this contagious laugh.

"That does sound like dad," I say between giggles.

"Right?" My mom continues, "By the time we turned on the TV in the morning, we noticed it happened to more people than just us."

She takes a breath. "First thing we thought about was you, though."

"Me?" I ask. They were thinking about me? It doesn't sound right. Like the version of my parents I had in my head was different from the one sitting in front of me. But, after talking to Aunt Jessie, it seems a little more realistic.

"Of course, we called my sister, Aunt Jessie. She called you as soon as we got a hold of her, but you didn't pick up. You know your dad, though, always worrying about you. He thought something bad happened, but your aunt said she'd take care of it. You were with friends, after all," my mom says.

"Yeah... The night before," I say.

"But now you're here, and that's what matters," my mom says with a smile before continuing her story.

"Not soon after we turned on the news and heard about what happened to everyone... This advertisement for this company came up..." my mom says.

"The RCC," I reply.

"Yep! That's the one," my mom says, pointing in agreement. "I don't remember everything they said, but we watched the ad, me and your dad. Said all sorts of malarky about instinct and stuff. Real silly stuff. Me and your dad. We didn't want to just give up the restaurant 'cause some company told us we were different. We felt like we could make it work. And since... well, since you weren't picking up, we thought you'd eventually come back here," my mom says.

"Granted, at first I was expecting you to come back not as a possum! But after you called Aunt Jessie yesterday, your dad called it."

Right on cue, my dad stops at the front of the door.

"Oh yeah, I one hundred percent knew you were gonna be a possum." He chuckles. "You're our kid!"

They both laugh.

It's so weird… seeing them like this, like me.

"How're you guys… fine with this?" I ask. "I woke up, and I was… freaking out the whole time."

"Well…" my dad says. "We're still us, right?"

"I guess," I respond.

"That's the thing," my mom says. "Sure, it was strange at first… It's not every day you wake up like one of those fairy tales I told you as a girl. But… after a while, you get used to it. The more people you meet, too… We've been like this for… well, it's been about a month now since we've been altered… I think that's enough time to get the hang of everything."

"Don't forget all the people here. They've been great as well," my dad adds.

"Oh yeah, and all the other people here," my mom says.

The other people… all those people out there… they knew me.

"One of those people out in the dining area," I say. "They knew I was coming?"

"Oh yeah," my dad says. "Once you left your aunt's, she called us right up and told us you were coming. We told everyone to keep an eye out for someone who looks just like us."

"Aunt Jessie knew you guys were changed?" I ask.

"Not at first," my mom says. "She knew we were worried about you after all of us became altered. But she didn't know we were altered until she came to visit the house."

"She was very… very surprised to see us," my dad said. "But hang on a second… Did you say changed?"

"Yeah?" I say. "Isn't that what it's called?"

"Only if you've been to…. Wait, is that where you've been?" he asks.

"The RCC?" I ask. "Someone working for them found me on the side of the road and took me there."

"Wow," my dad says. "And they… let you out?" he asks.

"No," I say. "I…. I escaped."

My dad comes into the room from the doorway and closes the door behind him.

"Now, sweetie, I don't mean to alarm you…" my dad says. "But… were you followed here by chance?"

"N-no," I say.

He sighs heavily.

"Oh, thank god."

"What's going on?" I ask.

"This place…" my mom says… "It's not just a restaurant anymore."

James

I fumble through the menu for Hagen's Hot Spot Bar & Grill. Menu items litter the page. Each one fitting right in next to another, like puzzle pieces constructing a stereotypical sports bar buffet. My sister is sitting on her phone across from me, distracted, yet surprisingly attentive.

Kellie sits next to me, staring off into space. I can tell something is on her mind.

"You think Lyla's gonna be okay?" Kellie asks.

"I'm sure she'll be fine," I say. "She's done this before, remember?"

"Yeah, I know… It's just, can't help but worry about our friend, ya know?" Kellie continues.

"I gotcha," I say.

Kellie fidgets in her seat, trying to get comfortable, coming close but never making it.

"I'm getting antsy," she says. "You think it'll be okay if I walk outside and get some air?"

I shrug. "You could always ask someone."

"I'll just… go out the back," she says, getting up from the booth and heading to the doors leading to the kitchen.

I turn my attention back to the menu. Until my sister says something, pulling me from my nutritional reading.

"I can't remember the last time I've been in a booth like this," Riley says from across the table.

"Yeah, it's been a while hasn't it," I reply.

She is right. The last time we sat in a booth like this was when she got the job at the department store. We went out to some bar and grill like this. Hung out for a few hours, celebrating her new job. Talking about all the money she was going to make, and how that would help our bills.

"You're thinking about when I got the job, aren't you?" Riley asks.

"You know me too well." I chuckle.

"It's weird," she adds.

"What is?" I turn my attention to my sister.

"Just, sitting here. Driving out here, all the way for your friend," she says.

"I mean, I think the past month has been nothing but weird," I reply.

"I'm not going to lie," Riley continues. "I'm still miffed about that. You up and left."

I sigh. "I know. It… it wasn't right of me to do that," I say. "But I did make some friends along the way, and after everything we've been through."

Riley shakes her head.

"I've been thinking about it too," she adds. "The whole drive out here, when we weren't talking. I was thinking about all the stuff you told me about. It sounds… unreal. Like I wouldn't have believed you if you told me before all this. But now, I don't know what to think. I guess… I'm just glad you're back. I'm glad you didn't abandon me."

"It was never my intention. When I wrote a week on that note, I did mean it," I say.

"It's hard to believe that when it's been more than one," Riley adds.

I nod.

"I know. But after this, we can go back," I say.

"Yeah, that is the plan, isn't it?" she replies.

"Mhm," I agree.

Riley looks around, and then back at me, leaning in and dropping her voice.

"Have you seen this many people like this before?" she whispers in my ear.

I glance around. From where I'm sitting, Riley is really the only human in here. Everyone else is changed, like me.

"Not since the facility," I say.

"What do you think everyone is doing here?" she asks.

"I don't know. We could always ask them," I say.

"Should we?" she replies. "I don't know if I want to."

"I thought you were okay with all of this?" I ask.

"Well… yeah, I am," she says. "I just feel like I'm… out of place is all."

I nod. "So you think *I* should ask, that's what you're saying."

"I'm not saying that at all!" She crosses her arms. "But if you want to… be my guest."

I shrug. "Okay," I say, getting up from the booth.

Looking around the room, I keep my eyes peeled, trying to find someone who at least looks like they know what this place is.

I could go try to find Lyla and her parents… But, after she passed out, I don't know if she's awake or talking to them. Plus, she hasn't seen them in a while, so it feels… wrong to intrude like that.

Scanning the room, I see a mountain lion who's in high spirits, talking to another person, a rabbit. Seems like they both might know something about what's going on.

I walk up to the table. The rabbit catches me approaching and gets the attention of the mountain lion.

"What's up, Chameleon?" The mountain lion chuckles.

"Hey, guys," I say, approaching the table. "Am I intruding?"

"Not at all!" the mountain lion continues. "I just found out this guy used to go to high school with me! Small world, right?"

He taps the rabbit on the shoulder playfully.

"Yeah, we used to have the same bio class," the rabbit says, sheepishly. "This guy here was quite a whiz with the books."

The mountain lion gives a hearty laugh. "This guy kept asking me for notes all class, when he wasn't stuffing me in lockers!" he says with another laugh, heavier than the first.

"Funny… how life works out like that." The rabbit chuckles. "Seems like the shoe's on the other foot, isn't it?"

"Water under the bridge. We're all in this situation together. No time for stupid rivalries now," the mountain lion says. "Now's the time to make friends. And speaking of friends, what can we do for ya?"

I take a seat at the table.

"I'm wondering what this whole place is about," I ask.

"You don't know?" the rabbit answers.

"No, I came here 'cause my friend's parents run this place," I say.

"Oh! You're talking about Connie and Clark's kid," the mountain lion says.

"She's here?" the rabbit asks.

"Yeah, she's here. She passed out right in the front door. To be fair, I probably would have too if I didn't know my parents were altered like that," the lion says.

"Oh. I hope she's okay. They came out and told us to keep an eye out. Can't believe I missed her showing up," the rabbit adds.

"The three of us didn't even know you'd all be here," I say. "I thought this place was just some restaurant."

"It kinda is," the rabbit says. "It used to be. And they still give out food. But it's not open for the public anymore."

"Yep," the mountain lion continues. "I don't know the whole story, mind you. But after Connie and Clark woke up altered, they started letting people like us come in. Eventually, so many people showed up with stories of... them that this place is almost like a truck stop for altered. Keeps us out of the public eye until we know where we're going next."

"Who's... them?" I ask.

"He's talking about the RCC," the rabbit says.

"You guys are also hiding from the RCC?" I ask.

"Yep," the rabbit says.

"Mhm," the mountain lion responds. "You know about them?"

"More than my fair share," I say. "The three of us used to be at one of their facilities down south."

"How're you here?" the rabbit asks. "They don't let anyone leave."

"We... escaped," I say.

"You're one of the lucky few," the rabbit says. "Some people who've escaped have come here."

"What'd they say?" I ask.

"All sorts of things." The rabbit continues, "The inside is depressing, people don't get along. Mandatory psych evaluations from therapists, telling you stuff about how you have instincts like an animal. And worse."

"Worse?" I ask.

"Mhm." The mountain lion adds, "Someone who came in just a few days before you said that there's facilities where people who show up disappear. I don't know how valid those claims are. But they came to my door so many times in a week, I had to leave. Something's bound to be going on."

The rabbit chimes in again.

"Oh, also, someone who also escaped told us something else."

"What'd they say?" I ask.

"They said that if you do manage to escape, they'll hunt you down and bring you back. We... we don't know what happens after that," the rabbit says.

"Is that why the windows have all the blinds down?" I ask.

"Yep, Connie and Clark are a little worried that the more escapees come, the more the RCC is going to notice. So, we gotta keep a low profile," the mountain lion adds.

"Say, you said there were three of you, didn't you?" the rabbit asks.

Kellie

As I open the back door to the restaurant and step outside, I feel like a weight's been lifted off of me. It felt a little too crowded in there, and sitting inside waiting for Lyla to come back was getting boring.

I reach into my pocket and pull my phone out. Of course, my battery is dead. I don't even think I charged my phone this whole time. I was hoping to at least have something to do while I stood outside. But I guess not. The small alleyway I'm in is fine for standing outside. But without someone to talk to or something to do... it quickly becomes stale.

I walk to the end of the alleyway and peer out into the parking lot. Just like the alleyway, there's not much going on.

I see a yellow car drive by, but it doesn't slow down or stop or anything.

This place feels dead, almost eerily quiet.

I walk to the other end of the alleyway and peer out into the street. I don't really see anything either on this end. No cars, no people.

Nothing.

That's... weird. I feel like there should be more people around...

I start to walk to the edge of the alleyway, looking out onto the street but remaining in the shadows.

I peer down the sidewalk. I actually see some people walking down the road on the right, rounding the corner as the small town transitions into the suburbs. Looking to the left, I see something that I didn't see when we walked to the restaurant.

A park.

The green of the grass and the trees calls out to me. I look around the dank alleyway. Even though the sun beats down on me, the crisp air and the light breeze make that park all the more alluring.

Before I know it, I've stepped out onto the sidewalk and am moving to the park on my own.

Man, I can't remember the last time I've been to a park. I remember going out with my dad once when I was younger. All it had was just a single metal set of swings, and one of those half-dome jungle gyms. It wasn't much, but to me as a kid, it was everything. Now that I think about it, being older, all of that stuff feels so small.

I pass building after building, walking to the park. Each one feeling more squished together than the last. As I continue down the road, I look behind me, the restaurant moving farther from where I'm standing. It feels like I've cut a line from me to safety.

I can't tell if it's me being paranoid... but I feel like someone's watching me. But I've been with James and Lyla for how long? I'm just paranoid...

Right?

.

.

.

.

.

Wrong.

As I turn towards the park again, I feel someone's hand cover my mouth as I'm lifted off the ground.

I try to scream, but they've got a grip on me. I can barely breathe, let alone open my mouth. I try to kick and pull at the person who's grabbing me, but with my legs dangling, I can't do anything about it.

I'm dragged into a small alleyway in between buildings.

Thrown onto the ground, I try to stand up and yell, but the sharp *click-clack* of a rifle keeps me on the ground.

Two men are situated behind me in SWAT gear, pointing rifles at me, and two more are standing in front of me, pointing rifles as well.

From the two men in front of me, I see….

Him.

Thorn pushes through the two men. His expression lacks empathy or remorse. He glares at me, and whatever he's thinking about… it… can't be good.

"Kellie," he says.

"Wha—" I start to say, until he puts a hand up.

"What am I doing here? How did I find you? Is that what you're asking?" he says.

"Y-yes?" I say.

"Thought so," he says, tossing a phone in front of me.

I look at the phone on the ground. One thing sticks out to me.

The grey floral case.

"Your friend's stupid," Thorn says, putting a hand to his head. "How do you just *leave your phone* at a stranger's?"

He crouches down to my level.

"Even more… she's just so damn predictable too." He continues, "Going to see her family? Everyone does that. I'm sure you did it, and James did it too." He stands back up, towering over me.

"…So?" I try to retort.

"So? You're kidding, right?" He laughs. "It makes it too easy to track you down. To find you. Dress up like you're on a Sunday stroll, ask a couple questions, find out that for some reason… a lot of changed have been showing up and going to that one restaurant…"

Thorn snickers. "Plus, all the people who don't have the… fortitude to keep their snouts shut like to talk. A little info here, a little rumor there in exchange for… some amenities, or false promises of short stays. It all comes down to here."

"What's your point?" I ask.

"Are you just playing stupid? Or do you not get it yet?" Thorn sneers. "If I opened the door to that restaurant, how many changed would I find in there? Ten? Twenty? Fifty? It's a treasure trove of… dangerous people. People who run, people who want to fight… Like your friend Lyla."

Thorn reaches under his coat and pulls a pistol out. Twisting something on the end of it.

"Granted," he says, "I would've liked for it to be Lyla in your position, but you'll do fine."

He finishes adjusting the weapon and trains it on me, nodding to the others to do the same.

"As soon as they find out you're gone, the plan is that it'll hurt morale. People will think the restaurant is compromised. They'll all scatter, of course we'll lose some of you, but the cowardly ones are easy to catch, plus, I'll have a few hours to gather more than just a few men and a single van. Then, when I march into this town with a small army tonight, they'll all be so disorganized and focused on their survival that we can just… mop up."

Thorn presses the gun against my face. Everything around me starts to blur. I lose sight of the men with their trained rifles on me. The only thing I hear is my increasing heartbeat.

"'Cause that's the difference between us and you. All of you, you're focused on survival, you're focused on making it to the next day. It's the one thing that I've seen throughout talking to everyone in these godforsaken facilities. It's an animalistic instinct that we all share, but you, your kind, have it turned up to eleven. Comradery and friendship, it doesn't mean anything to you when your whole physical image has been thrown out of balance. What you're used to, it's not there anymore. So you latch on to what you do know. You're not human anymore, so you don't act like it."

Thorn chuckles; it's clear he's enjoying this.

"Is it in your head? Or is it something built into you? Something that changed when you did? Even I don't know. But I've seen people bark, meow, run on all fours, etcetera, etcetera. You get the picture. Maybe it's real, maybe it isn't. But I can't find out if you people are running out of the facilities in droves."

I can feel my whole body shaking, as I hear Thorn pull the hammer on the back of his weapon. The cold steel pushes against my head.

This…. This is it, isn't it?

I never should have left the restaurant… I should've stayed where it was safe. Maybe he's… maybe he's right… The only thing I can think about right now… is somehow… making it through this. But no matter how many times I try to think of a way out of this… it always ends up with me….

Dying.

I can't help myself. As I feel the gun push against my head, tears run down my face. I close my eyes, waiting for the inevitable.

Thorn's voice rings out in the darkness.

"So… Raccoons can cry… Interesting."

Then…

Nothing…

I wait for what's coming to me… But I don't hear anything… I just want him to get it over with… I'm done…

Until…

"Oh SH—"

RATA-TATA-RATA-TATA!

RATA-TATA-RATA-TATA!

RATA-TATA-RATA-TATA!

RATA-TATA-RATA-TATA!

I open my eyes and attempt to scramble backwards, brushing past two pairs of legs… The sound of slightly muted gunfire is the only thing I can hear. As I back up onto the street, I hit my back against a van parked in the alleyway, blocking my exit.

I turn to face the alleyway. And I see the two soldiers that were behind me, the people I crawled behind… shooting the two men behind Thorn. I watch as Thorn dives behind a nearby dumpster to avoid the enemy fire.

"What're you doing?" Thorn's voice calls out to the two men who've stopped shooting their weapons, as the rest of the situation comes into clear view, the other side of the alleyway riddled with bullet holes. The two men backing up Thorn at the end lie motionless on the ground.

Neither man responds to Thorn; they stare at the motionless bodies on the ground.

I hear the first thought that comes to my head, spoken in unison out of the men in front of me.

"What have they… done?"

W-why did they… say that?

Both of the men turn to me, their expressions of bewilderment and fear matching mine, eyes wide, mouths agape, like paintings of horror frozen in time.

"G-go away!" I shout. "Stay back!"

The men mimic my voice, still holding the same expression as me.

"Go away! Stay back!" they both yell, turning to one another, drawing their weapons.

I go to yell once more, as I watch the two men, frozen in time, riddle one another with gunfire.

As soon as the first shot rings out, I turn around, averting my eyes from what happens. I duck under the van and squirm to the other side. Pulling myself up from the asphalt, I start running back to the restaurant.

The only thing I can think about is what I've witnessed. Why did they do that? Why did those people save me from Thorn? But... then again, why did they…. Why did they mimic me? Why did they stare at me with those…. those expressions?

I didn't make them… do that…. did I?

No, that can't be right. I can't do anything like that. I can't do those things. I'm not like Lyla. That's impossible.

But I… I saw them. I saw myself in them. I saw my horror… I…

I don't know what I saw. I don't like what I saw.

Picking up speed down the sidewalk, I keep running. The distance to the restaurant feels farther and farther the more I run.

I feel like I'm running down that hallway once more. Back in the facility. Thorn's words ring through my head, about me.

I can feel myself losing balance again, just like last time.

But… The more I think about running back to the restaurant, to tell everyone about what happened, to tell someone… about what I saw… I regain my balance… Thorn's words ring out in my head.

"Even I don't know."

Finally, the alleyway I left comes into view. I grab on to the corner of the building beside it and pull myself into the alleyway, running to the door in the back. Flinging it open, I rush inside. Slamming the door behind me, someone in the kitchen staring down at their phone looks in my direction.

"Whoa? You okay?" they ask.

"They're… They're coming!" I yell in between breaths, hands on my knees, staring at the floor.

"Who's coming?" they question.

As I stand up to face them, we lock eyes.

Their expression changes from concern to abject horror. As this happens, I can feel something inside me ache, something I haven't quite felt before… like someone's grabbing the core of my body and gripping it.

"Oh… OH GOD!" they scream, backing into a wall.

Chapter 34

Kellie

Awakening

"Don't look at me like that!" they scream, putting a hand over their eyes.

"L-look at you like what?" I say, still strained from my sprint back to the restaurant. "I'm… I'm trying to tell you something important! We need to tell everyone!"

The person attempts to move their hand to face me once more. But as soon as they make eye contact with me again, they recoil in fear.

"STOP IT!" they yelp, turning around and making a run for the door. "I… I can't!"

I… I don't understand what's going on… I need to tell someone… about what I saw. But… that person… what did they mean by "stop looking at me." Is there something… wrong with me now?

No… no, it can't be me. Lyla and James have been my friends this entire time, and I remember plenty of times I've talked to them perfectly fine without them freaking out like that guy…

But… What about those… those people, in the alleyway… the way they repeated what I said… the way they…

My thoughts trail off as the door opens from the front of the restaurant and into the kitchen. Lyla and her parents… James too… and a small crowd form around the door.

If that guy in the kitchen told me to stop looking at him, I don't know if I should look at anyone else… at least until… I know what's happening.

As the door opens, and everyone enters the room. I turn around and look at the wall. The only thing I can rely on now is my hearing.

"Who is that?" a voice calls out. If I'm remembering correctly, that's Lyla's mom. My suspicions are proven correct when Lyla answers her.

"It's one of my friends. Kellie," Lyla says. "Kellie, you okay?" she calls out to me.

Am I okay? No, of course not. I'm not okay… I… I know what I saw… And I want to tell them about it. I want to break down. I feel a flurry of emotions that I can't quite explain. I have so many things I want to say. But… as I open my mouth to respond, all I can muster out is:

"I'm… I'm fine."

That's not what I wanted to say… That's not what I wanted to say at all. But… I need to tell Lyla and everyone about what I saw. Or at least… what I was told.

I hear Lyla's footsteps coming closer to me.

"Why're you facing away from us?" she asks. "Someone came running out of the door… What… what did you do?" she asks.

"I didn't do anything…" I stammer out under my breath. "I… I didn't mean to do anything."

Lyla's steps get closer.

"Kellie… I can't hear you," she says, her voice more stern. "What did you do?"

"I didn't do anything," I speak up. "It… it doesn't matter. I need to tell you something."

I can sense Lyla's right behind me.

"Can you turn around and face me?" she asks. I hear James in the back speak up too.

"Where did you go?" he asks.

"I don't know if I can," I say. I'm stumbling over my words in my head. How do I explain to her about what happened when I came in here? What if it happens to her? What did I do to that person? I need to find the words to explain it to her. I can tell... I can sense... her feelings...

I can sense her... feelings?

It's like a cold breeze, crisp, but it's also smooth, like a blanket. It's radiating from her...

The more I focus on it... the more I feel that gripping feeling inside of me tighten.

It hurts... in a way I can't fully describe. It feels like someone told me the worst news imaginable, and I'm devastated. The more I focus on this... this radiating energy from Lyla behind me, the more that gripping feeling feels like a knife through my heart. An invisible stab through my core. I feel it underneath my skin, underneath my bones. Underneath everything that I am physically.

Then... tears... again.

Lyla's voice brings me back from my thoughts.

"Kellie? Kellie. Talk to me," she says, grabbing my shoulder. I try to pull away, but... she's stronger. She spins me around.

And... just like with the guy who saw me come back inside...

We lock eyes.

Lyla's worried expression drains from her face. The crisp and comforting feeling radiating from her changes into something else. It feels shaky, sickly, but it feels small and timid...

It feels like what I felt... in the alleyway.

I... I think I've figured out what I did to that person...

Pulling away from Lyla, I turn to the side, breaking eye contact from her. As I do that... that radiation she emanates dissipates into a new one. Warmth.

I can't tell what's she's thinking… but… somehow, I can tell what she's feeling.

I hear her voice. It's shaky, but there's understanding in it.

"I… I get it," she says.

All I can respond with is…

"I'm sorry."

I can hear Lyla's footsteps move to face everyone.

"I'm… I'm going to talk to her," she says.

"What… what happened?" James asks.

"You look like you saw a ghost," a voice adds; I think it's Lyla's dad.

"I'm… I'm fine," Lyla says.

"Are you sure?" Lyla's mom asks.

"Yes… I'm sure. I think… I just need to talk to her alone," Lyla says. "We'll be in the back alley."

"I'm coming with," James says.

"It's fine, James," Lyla replies. "I've got this."

Lyla pushes past me, refraining from making eye contact with me. I see her feet step around me and push open the door to the back alley.

"Come on," she says.

Keeping my sight off of everyone, I step out into the alleyway as the sun starts to properly set in the sky. While I can't see the sun itself, the reddish pink sky is proof enough. Taking a seat on the back porch steps, the door shuts with a loud thud, and I can hear Lyla taking a seat next to me.

I still don't know what's going on, but I think I'm starting to get the picture. Before I can say anything to forward the conversation, Lyla speaks up.

"I know what you did," she says.

I don't know how to respond. But I know what she's talking about. Whatever I did to that person in the kitchen… it happened to her when she looked at me.

"When you looked at me. I felt something. Something awful," she continues, pausing for a moment, trying to form the words.

"That feeling... it was something I've felt before... Something I didn't think I'd ever feel again. But... it was coming from you. You gave me that feeling... as if you took something from yourself and planted it in my head."

I think I know what she means... but I don't know if I should say anything, I need to hear it from her.

"What feeling was it?" I ask.

"It was the feeling I felt back at the facility. Hopelessness, like you were about to... die," she says, taking a breath. "I felt that... while all of us were attacked by those guards. But... right as I felt that..."

She stops.

"You know the rest," she says.

I nod. That was what I thought she was going to say. And part of me knew that this is what happened to me. I said it before: I did think it'd be cool if I could do something special, like Lyla... But... now, it's clear that I've gotten that wish.

But it doesn't feel like how I thought it would. It doesn't feel like I deserve this. After everything I saw in that alley, this is... my reward? I don't even understand how this works. I don't understand what I do with this...

"What happened?" Lyla asks.

"What... what do you mean?" I respond.

"Kellie, you made me feel the same way I did before I got my abilities. Like you were about to die." She continues, "What happened to you?"

She turns to face me, but I turn away. I still don't understand how this works. I don't want to look at her and force her to feel what I'm feeling again.

"I walked outside," I say.

"By yourself?" she asks.

"Yeah," I say.

"Where'd you go?" she asks.

"I saw a park down the road." I continue, "I tried walking down there... and... I was grabbed."

"By who?" she asks.

I scoff. "Who do you think?"

"They're... they're here, aren't they?" she questions.

I shake my head.

"Was... Was he..." she asks.

"Yes," I respond.

"Oh," she says.

The two of us sit in silence, as the cool breeze blows through the alleyway. I still can't bring myself to face her. Unless I want her to go through what I'm feeling right now.

Lyla finally speaks up.

"What... what was he doing here?" she asks.

His words play through my head again. His sneer, his face. His intent to make sure this conversation isn't happening again. But... against all odds, it is.

"He's coming," I say.

"What?" she asks.

"He's coming to take us all to some facility. Tonight. He implied that... anyone who stands up isn't going to come with them, He's bringing people, a lot of them," I clarify.

I can feel the radiant emotions coming from Lyla change again. It feels like an ice-cold gust of wind. Something that you'd only feel standing in a cemetery at night.

"Oh..." she says. "We've gotta tell people." She goes to stand up, but I grab her hand, pulling her back down.

"Wait.... That's...that's all he said before...." I trail off. Right now, the most important thing to me is making sure that Lyla knows about what's going to happen to us if we don't do anything to stop him. But… I can still see those people, the gunfire. The four guards who didn't make it home tonight….

Because of me.

"Before what?" Lyla asks.

I take a deep breath. Should I tell her? Should I bring what happened into this conversation? Everything in my body tells me that I should. If I don't, I'm going to be fighting it alone. That's not something I want. That's not something I can do alone. Not this time. I need to tell her.

But there's something inside me, holding me back, like a single thread keeping me from breaking free and opening up. I know I need to talk to someone about it. I know what happened shouldn't be seen by anyone out there. But some feeling inside of me, some feeling I can't describe, keeps me from saying it.

Somehow, I manage to squeak out something.

"Something happened to me," I say. "I need to… tell someone about it."

"What happened?" Lyla asks.

I pause, trying to formulate words about what I saw. Trying to tell her what happened in that alleyway. I can't get the image of those men out of my head, staring at me. Yelling the things I said back to me like some demented broken record.

Only to…

Only to…

Shoot each other.

I try to find the words.

"They were… they were pointing guns at me, Lyla," I say. "Thorn was mocking me. Telling me that he was going to round everyone up. Saying that I was the weakest link. Killing me would ruin morale for you and the rest of everyone at the restaurant."

I pause, trying to choke the rest of the words out of me.

"Before he could… shoot me… Something happened."

Lyla pauses.

"I think I know," she says.

I nod.

"I think I know what happened too," I say. "I got… an ability. I don't know what it is. But the two people behind me…"

The memory intrudes my thoughts once more. The gunfire. The screaming. The voices.

"They killed everyone, Lyla… and then they turned to me… and started speaking my words…" I say. "I made them do that…"

"Kellie, no, no, you didn't," Lyla comforts.

"Lyla, I did," I say. "They repeated me word for word. They looked like they had no control over their own bodies. They moved like puppets, and I was scared of them. And they… they…"

I finally turn around. Facing Lyla, tears stream down my face.

"They both attacked each other," I whimper.

Lyla's expression doesn't change. She doesn't reel back like she did in the kitchen. Instead, she just grabs me, pulling me close to her.

"Kellie, that… that wasn't your fault. You didn't do that on purpose. You hear me?" she says, her voice airing concern. Her emotions radiate warmth again.

"I did…" I whimper. "I made them do those things. It's my fault they… they shot one another."

"No, it's not. You didn't know what's going on. You didn't know that you were doing that until it was too late. You can't blame yourself for that. If you do that… it can eat you alive. It'll ruin you, and James and me. We can't let that happen to you."

My breathing falters as I choke in breath after breath. I finally said what I was going to say. I finally got to tell Lyla what happened to me. I don't even know what I expected from her. But something about this, about feeling her emotions flow out of her body like a space heater, hearing her tell me these things, it feels more genuine. Less empty.

But it feels like cheating. Like I have forbidden knowledge I shouldn't have. The price I paid was the lives of others.

"Kellie, you need to listen to me," Lyla says. "What you saw. It wasn't your fault. You did this in self-defense. You didn't know what you were doing. It's not your fault. What matters is that you're safe. Those people, they weren't good people."

"I… I know…" I choke. "I just… I just worry it's going to happen again."

"If James and I are here, we'll make sure it doesn't happen again," she says.

Her radiant warmth doesn't shift. I know she's telling the truth.

"I know you will," I respond. "I just… I feel like I don't understand what's going on with me now… I did those things, Lyla. I made those people do those things, and now I don't even know what's going on with me. What's… what's going to happen if I do something again…"

"It's something that we have to work through together," Lyla says. "I know how you feel."

I pull away from Lyla's hug.

"How? You didn't see what I saw," I say.

"But I could have," Lyla says. "Remember when we were back at the facility?"

I try to think back to that. Seeing Lyla awaken her abilities. Seeing her shock Thorn, cementing his complete hatred for us. Seeing him at Paul's. Seeing the repercussions of Lyla's abilities.

"I… I could have killed him," Lyla says. "I keep kicking myself, seeing him show up. Thinking about if I should've that night…."

Lyla pauses, and for a moment, I feel her emotions shift. To something more dark.

"But I had a dream on the way to my aunt's. It felt like a vision, a premonition of what would've happened if I did. I don't know what it meant. But I saw all of you… dead. Thorn… the only one alive, telling me that all this damage was caused by me, by my abilities."

She pauses again. Her emotions turn back to warmth.

"I told myself that I can't let that happen," Lyla says. "That I can't let myself go that far. Even if I don't understand my abilities fully."

Lyla turns to me, still not affected by my gaze.

"Kellie, I didn't get that much training at Paul's. I'm still winging it. I still don't know how any of this works. I just know that I can't use my abilities all the time because it makes me… cold… physically. And somehow, sleeping makes it come back. I'm like a living battery," Lyla continues.

I think to the gripping feeling inside of me. The more I try to focus on Lyla's emotions, the more it hurts the very core of my being.

"But now… we can work through this together. We can figure out what exactly happened to us. We're not alone. You've got me… and I've… got you," she adds.

I nod.

"We'll… we'll work through this together. We have to. I can't… I can't help but feel remorse for what happened in the alley, Lyla…."

"It's natural. But… I know I'm not good for advice. But you can turn that remorse into something else… helping other people. Stopping Thorn," she says.

Her words echo in my head. I can't help but have the alleyway play on loop in my head like a song you can't get to stop playing. But in a sense, she's more right than I thought. What's happened… has happened… Things aren't going to be the same, and I can't do anything to save those people, no matter how bad they were. No matter if they were going to kill me. But what I can do… is I can help save everyone else by stopping Thorn and making sure that he doesn't lay a finger on this place.

"You're… you're right," I say.

Lyla nods.

"You have the capability to control your abilities. You're doing it now," she says.

I... I am. Lyla hasn't been affected by looking at me this whole time. I was so focused on telling someone about what happened in the alleyway... but I couldn't find the words... so... I used my ability. Now... now that I've gotten it off my chest... we can face one another.

"We can do this together." Lyla continues, "Me, you, and anyone else in our situation, powers or not. We can do this together. We might not be perfect, Kellie."

She hugs me again, tighter than the last time.

"But we can do our best to make sure that anyone else who needs us can be helped by us," she says.

I shudder. Her words and her warmth radiating out of her solidify her promise to me. I wrap my arms around her.

"It's... it's all we can do. Isn't it?" I ask.

"It's better than nothing," she says, letting go.

I sit back on my own once more. I still have many racing thoughts in my head. But I feel better. Not great, but better.

"We do need to tell everyone about Thorn," Lyla says. "If you escaped him... we... we don't have much time."

"No," I say. "We don't..."

"Do you... want to head inside?" she asks.

I nod.

"I don't think I want to be outside alone..." I say.

She nods.

"I understand. Come on. We need to tell everyone," she says, standing up and opening the door for us to walk inside.

I stand up and brush off my hoodie. Wet spots, marking my tears, start to dry.

"We can do this, right?" I ask. "Stopping Thorn?"

"I... I don't know," Lyla responds. "But... we have to try."

CHAPTER 35

Lyla

STEPPING BACK INTO the kitchen of the restaurant, Kellie and I slowly make our way to the doors leading into the front area. Peeking my head through the door, I can see everyone talking amongst themselves, as if nothing is wrong.

It's a quaint sight. Something that I wish I could keep, but with what I know, it's not going to stay like that for long.

Kellie peers through the slightly open door as well.

"So, are you just going to go out there and tell everyone?" she asks.

"I'm… I'm not sure. We need to tell them… But I'm worried that they won't listen to us," I reply.

"Should we tell someone we trust first?" Kellie questions.

She's right. Maybe if we tell the people we trust first, we could use them to help us wrangle the rest of the building.

"Good idea," I say. "Grab James, and I'll get my parents, meet us in the office, and we'll talk to them then."

Kellie steps out from the kitchen and into the open front of the area. James and his sister sit at a bar, talking to some other changed like old friends who haven't seen one another in a while.

Now, it's my turn. I've got to find my parents and wait for everyone to reconvene.

I turn around and start heading to the office situated on the side of the kitchen. Seeing that the door is closed, I knock.

I can hear my mom on the other side.

"Hello?" she says.

"Can I come in?" I ask.

"Of course, sweetie. Come on in," my mom answers.

I open the door and step inside, where my mom and my dad are in the middle of a conversation.

"We've gotta do something about the food," my dad says. "It's been a week now, and the next shipment isn't coming in."

"I know," my mom replies. "I've tried calling, but they're not picking up. We'll have to find another means of food if we want to keep feeding everyone. How much do we have left?"

"I don't know," my dad continues, putting a hand onto his head. "Maybe two weeks? Maybe one? It depends if people keep coming in."

"We'll figure it out," my mom says before turning to me.

"So, is your friend going to be okay?" she asks.

"Yeah, she'll be fine. But she saw something else we need to talk about," I add.

"What is it?" my dad asks.

"We need at least my friends here," I say. "We need to talk to people we trust first."

My mom nods. "All right, is your friend coming?"

I open the door and try to look through the window leading into the main area. I see James stand out of his chair and start walking towards us.

"Yeah, they're coming," I say.

The door to the kitchen opens up, and Kellie, James, and Riley all walk towards us into the office.

Once everyone's inside, Kellie shuts the door behind us, keeping us shielded from everyone else outside.

"So," James says. "What's going on? Are you okay, Kellie?"

"Not really..." Kellie replies. "But what I'm feeling isn't important. We've got something worse to worry about."

"What is it?" Riley asks.

Kellie looks towards me and nods. "You tell them," she says.

I take a deep breath. And prepare myself for what I'm about to say.

"The RCC knows we're here…. They're coming to take us all, to-night," I say.

Silence consumes the room, and for a moment, it feels like it's pulling the walls closer towards us.

"What do you mean they're coming?" my mom asks.

Kellie steps forward and adds on to what I said.

"I was approached by the one who runs the facilities in an alleyway outside of the restaurant. They know we've been here for a while now, even before the three of us came here. They're planning on taking all of us to facilities, and anyone who doesn't comply…"

Kellie trails off…

"I see," my dad says.

"So… what are we supposed to do?" Riley asks.

"We could… fight them," I say.

"You want to fight them?" my mom asks, reeling back at the thought. "Sure, maybe we could take on a few of them… but this sounds like it's going to be bigger than that… I don't think we're going to survive something that… that big."

"Maybe…" James adds. "But some of us can do more than throw a punch."

"What're you talking about?" my dad asks.

"Has nobody ever brought it up?" I ask.

"Brought what up?" my dad asks again.

I open the door to the kitchen and step out, gesturing for everyone to follow me.

"This," I say, holding my hand out.

I try to remember what Paul told me, about focusing on what I want to do with my abilities. I stare at my hand, imagining forming a small arc of electricity in my hand.

As I drown out the other sounds from inside of my head, I watch as a ball of arcing electricity emerges from my hand. I stop focusing and let it fizzle out. Looking up, I see my parents' looks of both concern and amazement.

Nobody says anything, leaving me to continue the conversation.

"I know I'm not the only one with a gift like this," I say.

"How did you…" My mom trails off.

"I don't know," I say. "It just happened when we were escaping, and now, I have this ability to control electricity."

James chimes in.

"One of our other friends has an ability like this too… but…." He trails off.

"We don't know what happened to him," Kellie adds.

"But, if anyone else in this building has abilities like us," I say, "we might just stand a chance."

"So, what do we do then?" my dad asks.

"We could try to rally the people in the front," James says.

"Do you think they'll listen to us?" Kellie says. "We told you guys first 'cause we trust you."

"Kellie's right," I add. "We need to know that we can count on every one of you."

"You know I'll stand by you guys no matter what," James says.

Riley doesn't say anything. Her expression makes it feel like she's lost in thought.

"If we… do fight…" Riley says. "Are we going to be okay? What about you?" Riley turns to James.

James puts a hand on his sister's shoulder. "This is more important than just me, Riley. This is everyone here. People who have lives. We can't just let the RCC come in and snatch everyone up."

"But…" Riley says. "You could get hurt… or even worse. I don't know anything about fighting. Who's to say all those people out there know?"

James shakes his head.

"You're right, but what're we going to do? Run? Like we've been doing this entire time since we left the facility?" James says.

"If it wasn't for us escaping together," Kellie says, "I don't think I would've ever seen my dad again."

"I don't think I'd ever see my parents again," I say.

"We can't run anymore," James says. "And if anyone out there has some kind of ability like Lyla… Then… we've got more of a chance than we think."

"And what about the people who don't?" Riley says.

Silence falls throughout the room.

"We'll still have to fight," I say. "Throwing, swinging, kicking, whatever it takes."

"Everyone in this building has been hunted down by the RCC at least once," my mom adds. "They've attempted to come for us, and we moved here, pretended like we left town. They've hunted you down too, haven't they?" My mom turns to me.

I nod.

"They've been following us since we left," I say. "If we run again, they'll just keep looking for us. Right now, we've got more people than we've ever had before. If we want to make a stand, now is the best time."

My parents turn to one another, as if they're having a conversation only they can hear. James looks to Riley, and by the look of her face, she's weighing the options in her head.

I look to Kellie, who turns to me and nods.

Everyone breaks from their silence, with my mom speaking first.

"So, are we just going to go out there and convince everyone to fight?" she says.

"We could," Kellie says. "If we could find out how many people have abilities, maybe that'll help convince others that this isn't a suicide mission."

"It's a good plan," James says. "But will people be willing to expose themselves like that if we ask the whole restaurant?"

"There's really only one way to find out," Kellie replies.

"So, do we want to go out there and try to rally everyone?" I ask.

Everyone nods in agreement.

"So then. Who's going to do the talking?" I ask.

"We can," my mom says. "It's our restaurant; people will be more likely to listen to us."

"Then let's do it," Kellie says.

All of us walk out of the kitchen, with our group leaving at once. Conversation in the restaurant slowly dies down as my parents walk to the front of the building, situating themselves in front of the bar, where everyone can see.

Soft murmurs of people asking what's happening fill the dead air while my parents find it in themselves to inform everyone about what's going to happen.

"Hello, everyone," my dad says. "I'm glad all of you are here. And we're touched at how many people we've helped over the past month."

"But," my mom says, "there's been something that's been brought to our attention."

"What is it?" a voice calls out from the back.

"I'm not going to sugar coat it," my dad says. "The RCC knows we're here."

The room starts picking up in volume as conversations start rising.

"Hang on," my dad continues, causing everyone to return their attention to my parents.

"They're not coming… yet," my dad says. "But we've came to a conclusion that requires all of your help."

"What's that?" a voice calls out from the back. "I'm not going to go back to one of their stupid facilities!"

"We know. So," my mom says, "we're asking you to help us fight them off when they come."

The conversational murmurs pick up again. People talking to one another. A feminine voice calls out from the crowd this time.

"You want us to fight?" the voice asks.

"Yes!" my mom says. "If we don't stand up now, they'll take all of us in. Me, my husband, our kid!"

"But what about us? What about our families?" another voice croaks.

"If they take you too, then you won't be able to see yours!" my dad says.

"But if we fight, don't they have weapons? They won't hesitate to shoot us!" the voice croaks again.

"That's a possibility," my mom says. "But you'll have to be prepared for that. We can plan this out, we can work together!"

"Why don't we just leave now?" Someone steps out from the crowd, a dog. Her voice is concerned and scared. "They're not coming for us now. We can get out of here while we still can, walk, run, take our cars, take buses. Leave for home, leave for wherever we're going while we still can!"

The voices pick up louder, phrases like "good idea" and "I'll go now" passing from mouth to mouth, like a communal vocabulary.

"No! If we leave now, we'll lose what we have here. We have enough people to really make an impact!" my mom calls out to the crowd.

But her voice is drowned out by the group, who continue to talk amongst themselves about who's going where and when they're leaving.

"We've got people who can fight!" my dad yells. "Talented fighters, people who can do things nobody thought was possible!"

Someone calls out from the crowd once more, "If we fight back, they'll go from taking us in to surely killing us! I don't care if this place goes down. I just don't wanna be in it when it does!"

*Yeah*s and words of agreement rise throughout the restaurant, drowning out my parents' pleas.

People start standing up and make their way to the front door, as the door opens and a gust of cool night air flows through. People start making their way outside.

The crowd's murmurs turn from words of agreement into condolences as they flow out of the restaurant like a funeral procession on their way to the cemetery.

"You won't stand up for us? You won't make sure that we're not hiding in shadows anymore?" my dad calls out to the crowd shambling into the streets.

"COWARDS! YOUR'RE MAKING A MISTAKE! THEY'LL FIND YOU! THEY ALWAYS HAVE!" he yells at the crowd as they continue to pool out into the cold.

As the final set of feet exit the restaurant, only two other people remain inside of the building.

"Hey..." James says. "I know those guys."

The two people who haven't left yet are a mountain lion and a rabbit, both sitting at a high top in the back of the restaurant.

"Everyone left, huh," the mountain lion says.

"Can't blame 'em," the rabbit adds. "If I was in their position, I would leave too."

"Why didn't you?" my mom asks.

The mountain lion shrugs. "I kinda like this place. Plus, if we're going up against the RCC, I feel like I could take a couple of them on. I have a bone to pick with them anyway."

The rabbit adds on to it. "Plus, seeing this place get taken over by those pricks isn't worth it. You said you've got good fighters, and I believe you."

"What can you bring to the table?" my dad asks.

Both the rabbit and the lion look at one another, and then back at us. Like they're hyping up to tell us that they can't bring anything to the table.

"You're not going to believe us," the rabbit says.

"But we've got… superpowers… We think?" the lion says with a nervous grin.

Chapter 36

Lyla

"No, we believe you," I say, stepping forward.

"You do?" the rabbit asks.

"Yep," Kellie says. "She and I have powers too."

"What can you two do?" the lion asks.

"I can control lightning," I say.

"I can…" Kellie adds, "see people's emotions?"

"I'm able to control air," the rabbit says.

"I'm able to control water," the lion adds.

James speaks up.

"Oh, we never really got your names," James says. "If you're going to be fighting alongside us, we should know your names at least."

The rabbit and the lion look at one another, before the rabbit speaks up.

"Oh yeah, I guess we never really did give out our names. Whoops."

"I'll start. I'm Wayne," the lion says.

"Hutch," the rabbit responds.

"His name isn't Hutch." Wayne snickers. "It's actually Lionel."

Hutch jabs Wayne in the shoulder. "My last name is Hutcheson; it's a nickname. Nobody back home calls me Lionel, jackass. You know this."

Wayne puts his hands in the air. "Sorry, sorry! Just setting the record straight is all. We aren't back home anymore."

"Just use Hutch. It's… easier that way," Hutch says, obviously embarrassed.

"All right…" James says. "Nice to properly meet you both. Now, we need to focus on what to do when the RCC comes. Do we know how much time we have?" James turns to both Kellie and me.

All eyes in the room move to Kellie, who just realized that James is talking to her. She takes a step back, overwhelmed by the amount of attention she's receiving. Even more, I think she knows she's going to have to recall some of the things she was told in the alleyway. I know that it's important, but I can't help but be a little worried that she doesn't want to talk about it in front of everyone.

"Uh…" Kellie stammers. "I'm… I'm not sure."

"Not sure about what?" James asks. "How long we have?"

"Yeah… they didn't say a specific time, he just said 'tonight.' But I'm assuming we at least have more than a few hours," Kellie continues.

"How do you know that?" my dad asks.

"The number of people who attacked me…." Kellie continues, holding back something inside of her, keeping her from going into full detail like she told me outside.

"There were only four people. Including…. including him," she says, forcing out the words.

"Who's… him?" Riley questions.

"She's talking about Dr. Thorn," I say.

"The guy who runs the RCC?" my mom asks.

"Oh, I've heard about him." Wayne adds, "He's this psychologist guy, right?"

James nods. "Yeah, that's him. We've run into him a few times."

"Each time…" I say.

"He's gotten more desperate," Kellie finishes our sentence. "It's like he's not the same person from the facility anymore. He's hell-bent on taking us in. Or killing us. I don't know which he prefers now…"

"So, he's dangerous?" Hutch asks. "I've heard stories from people here about him. But nobody said anything about him being dangerous… He just seemed like a really nosy shrink."

"Not after what happened when we escaped," I say. "But that's not important. If he's leading the charge on the restaurant, he's going to come with friends."

"Like… 'friends with guns' friends?" Wayne asks.

"Most likely," James says. "He's brought them in before, men in SWAT outfits, armed."

"So, what do you suggest we do?" my mom asks.

"Well…" I say. "We could try to disarm them?"

"What do you mean?" Wayne asks. "Disarm them? Then what?"

"Beat them up, knock them out, whatever we need to do," I continue.

"You think that just beating them up is going to deter them? What if we have to do worse?" Hutch asks. "I don't think we want them coming back."

"I'd prefer if we didn't do anything worse than that," Kellie says.

"She's right," James adds. "If… God forbid we actually kill one of these guys, who knows what'll happen. It'll just give them more of a reason to use force on us, and others. We're doing this not for us, but for the sake of the other people out there like us, we need to take caution. We'll have to fight, that's inevitable, but if we can do it in a way where we win without killing, don't you think that's the better option?"

Hutch puts a hand on his chin, the gears turning inside of his head. "I guess that makes sense. But we'll be holding back."

"I've been giving it my best," I say. "I'm not killing anyone."

"I haven't used my powers in a fight before," Wayne says. "I just know I can use them. How do we know that I won't mess it up, or kill someone?"

"I can try to teach you both." I continue, "I was taught, a little bit. I know the basics, but that's about it."

"Anything helps." My dad adds, "If you can teach these guys, then it's better than them not knowing."

"But what about us?" my mom says.

"We can still help," James says. "While Lyla's helping Wayne and Hutch, the rest of us can help set up barricades to slow down the RCC."

"What do you mean by barricades?" my dad asks.

"Well, how many cars are in the parking lot?" James asks.

"Maybe two, three tops." My dad continues, "Our cars, and the company food truck."

"What do you want to do with the trucks?" my mom asks.

"We can set up barriers around the restaurant," James says.

"And what if they get past them?" Hutch asks.

"That's where the tables come in," James says.

"You want to uproot every table in this place and turn those into barricades too?" my mom asks. "That's a big ask."

"You want to win this or not?" I say.

My mom lets out a sigh. "Yes, but I'd prefer if we don't lose everything in the process, our cars, the food truck, the tables we sit customers in."

"We'll have to. We're going to need all the help we can get." James continues, "So, do you have tools?"

My dad pauses, thinking about what's going to happen to the restaurant.

"Yeah," he says with a disappointed tone. "There's tools for small-time repairs in the back."

"Are they good tools?" James asks.

"It's a power drill and some other various tools, mostly stuff for fastening." My dad continues, "If you're trying to ditch the tables and stick 'em in the street, they'll do it."

"All right, then that's what we'll do," James says definitively. "We move the tables, the cars, and the trucks to block out the street. If you've got a dumpster in the back, that could help close up any gaps that one car can't. Assuming that they're coming tomorrow, we do it all now while there's still light out and take watch during the night."

"Can we do that?" Hutch says.

"We have to. We need to do everything now," Kellie says. "He mentioned coming after everyone is scattered. If he's planning on coming now, it'd be when we're at our weakest."

"Tonight," I say. "So we need to start moving then."

"We're really doing this, huh?" Riley asks.

"We know they're coming. The quicker we do this now, the more we'll be prepared when the time does come," Kellie says.

"It's really only us…" Wayne starts counting heads. "Us eight then," he says.

"It'll have to be," my dad says. "We can take our chances. Best case scenario, we drive them off."

"Worst case?" my mom asks.

"We run, or they take us in," my dad says.

"We'll make sure that doesn't happen," James says. "I know it's a lot, and to be honest, I'm freaking out a little bit, but even if we don't have abilities like Kellie, or Lyla, or Wayne and Hutch… we can help by making sure this place is protected."

"And we'll do it together," I say.

My mom walks over to me, putting a hand on my shoulder. For a brief second, I feel something I hadn't felt in a long time.

"We will, and whatever happens, I'm glad you're here," my mom says.

It's hope.

"So, let's get to it," James says.

James starts walking to the exit. "Grab the car keys, Mr. Hagen, we've gotta start moving cars."

"You can just call me Clark," my dad says, grabbing something from behind the bar and following James outside. "You don't gotta be so formal."

My mom steps back and takes a breath. "I have to admit, I'm kind of scared," she says with a worried grin.

"I think we all are," I respond.

"Well… this is something we have to do. So, we should do our best, right?" she asks.

"Yep, but even though there's a little bit of us, these gifts, powers, whatever, they'll be a big help. I'll… I'll make you proud, Mom," I say, trying my hardest to not get choked up.

"I know you will. You always have," my mom responds.

She looks around and gives me a quick hug to my shock, before heading to the front door. "I'm gonna help James and your dad. Get busy, all right?" she says.

I nod, still frozen from the hug my mom gave me. I can't remember the last time that's happened. It's… strange. Almost as strange as everything we've been through.

Finally recovering from… that, I turn to Wayne, Hutch, and Kellie.

"You guys ready to learn?" I ask.

Wayne and Hutch shake their heads in agreement.

"You bet!" Hutch says.

"'Course, we gotta be ready, right?" Wayne laughs.

Kellie just gives a slight nod.

"All right, I'll meet you guys in the parking lot. Should be open now that the cars are being moved," I say.

Wayne and Hutch both make for the front door, but Kellie sticks behind.

"Hey… you sure you can teach me?" Kellie asks.

"I don't see why not," I respond. "You've got abilities. Maybe we can learn something new about them."

"But…" Kellie continues. "I'm not moving air or shooting electricity like you." She continues, "My abilities… they're more…. personal."

"I'm sure we can figure it out," I say. "You've gotta be ready for anything. I'm sure these guys will help us too."

"I'm just worried about what's going to happen," Kellie says, looking around, trying to find something tangible to hang on to. "I know we kinda have to do this, but can we?" she asks.

"Only one way to find out," I say. "But we'll be there to protect everyone."

Kellie takes a deep breath and nods. "All right, I trust you," she says. "We've made it this far, haven't we?"

I nod. "'Course, and I'll be damned if we don't make it farther. You're with us now, and you did the right thing by telling me what happened. And I know everyone here will make sure it doesn't happen again," I say.

"All right, I'll meet you outside… I guess," she says.

"I'm coming with you," I say.

"Not yet," Kellie says, pointing to Riley, behind me. "She wants to talk. I can see it."

Kellie starts making her way to the parking lot, as I turn around to face Riley.

"She's right," Riley pipes up. "I do wanna talk."

"What's going on?" I ask.

"It's about James," she says.

"What about him?" I question.

"I don't know about you, but I'm worried about him," she says.

"'Course I'm worried about him," I say. "We're all going to be in danger. And I'm gonna make sure nothing happens to all of us."

"I get that," Riley says. "It's just… I haven't seen him in a while, and now we're supposed to be fighting these people. It's dangerous, and now, I don't even know what I'm supposed to be doing! James is running around making…. barricades, and you're about to teach some people how to use superpowers? And I'm here… doing what? Standing around twiddling my thumbs."

"You can always help him," I say.

"And I will. But what if he gets hurt? What if I get hurt? What about your parents, or Kellie? Those people who left, they're right: it would be so much easier to just run. This isn't my fight. I don't think it's James's either."

"You may be right. It's not your fight," I say. "But for James, it is. I can't tell you that and have you believe me, and I'm not trying to be… rude or anything, Riley…" I say.

"But in all honesty, James has to do this. He knows as much as I do, as much as Kellie does, as much as my own parents do, that if we want to live a life like yours, we need to stand up. These RCC people, they're not going to stop until Kellie and I, and most importantly, your brother, are in one of their facilities. But if we stand up, maybe we can get some other people like us, and if you stick around, some other people like you, to help stand up for us too."

I sigh.

"Then, maybe we can go back to the way things were. But at this current point in time, it's not like that. While some people will accept us, some people won't. The RCC is trying to make sure that the ones that won't are the ones in control, and we can do something about it. And just like I told Kellie, I will do *everything* in my power to make sure that everyone here lives through this. Including you and including James."

I pause. In my mind, I think if I just stop talking for a minute, maybe something I say will settle in on Riley.

"I get it," she says. "I'm… I'm not one of you guys. But you're right. I've got friends, and now I've got family who are like this. Maybe this isn't a hundred percent my fight, but maybe I can do something. I don't want to die, or get hurt, or lose James again. That's what I'm worried about the most. But maybe, if we do something about these RCC people who keep chasing you guys around, maybe we can go back to how it was before all this."

"So," I say, "you trust me?"

Riley pauses, thinking about her answer.

"Yeah, I have to," she says.

"Then let's get ready for what's coming," I say.

Chapter 37

Kellie

"What the hell is taking her so long?" Hutch asks, his foot tapping the ground.

"Not sure," I say. "She shouldn't be much longer. Maybe she's talking to someone?"

"Just don't wanna wait is all," Hutch continues. "She's supposed to teach us something about our superpowers. You'd think she wouldn't take her sweet time. Not like we have much anyways."

"Chill out, dude," Wayne adds. "We've got time."

"Do we?" Hutch glares at Wayne.

Wayne glares back at Hutch. Whatever issues they've had in the past, they're certainly coming back for a moment. Both of them look at one another like old rivals. I can feel these emotions radiating off of them. It's prickly, like those burrs you'd get caught on your pants when hiking.

I don't know if the situation is going to escalate, but if it is, I should try stopping it.

"Guys, chill out. Wayne's right. We've got time," I say.

Hutch shifts his impatient stare to me now.

"Sure, we do," he says.

"Look, man, she'll be out here in a second," I say. "She knows how important this is."

Just as I say that, the jingle jangle of bells rings out. We all shift our view to the door and see Lyla step out with Riley.

"See?" I remark. "She's coming over now."

Hutch scoffs.

As Lyla jogs up to us, I can feel the auras of both Wayne and Hutch shift again, returning from prickly to a calm hum.

"Sorry, guys," Lyla says, stopping in front of the three of us. "Got caught up talking to Riley."

"It's fine," Wayne replies.

"Yeah," Hutch concedes on his impatience. "It's chill. So, what do ya have planned for us?"

"Well," Lyla says, "I mean, I'll teach you guys how to, I guess, properly use your abilities."

"We can use them," Wayne says. "What do you mean by *properly*?"

"I mean like use them correctly." Lyla continues, "Sure, you can use your abilities. Anyone can. When I first got mine, I used them right off the bat."

"So, what're you saying?" Hutch asks.

"What I'm leading to is this," Lyla continues. "I was inaccurate. I wasn't able to use them for a while. I used up all my power, and I got tired out."

"Tired out? What're you talking about?" Hutch says, continuing his line of questioning.

"It's just that," Lyla says, "I got tired out. I learned it from a friend; we get tired, like mentally. Lethargic and slow, and we can't be as effective with our abilities."

"So, you're going to show us how to be efficient and accurate," Wayne says.

"That's about all I know right now," Lyla says. "I can't really do much more than that."

"Well, that'll help us regardless," I say.

"Then let's get started," Hutch says. "What do you want me to do first?'

Lyla looks around, like she's trying to find something for Hutch to test his powers on.

Again, her aura catches my attention. It's like a song you can't get out of your head. It just worms its way in; it's obtrusive. But I do notice something about her. It's misshapen, feels like gelatin almost… she's confused.

Maybe I can do something to help her.

I start looking around the area, trying to find something for Hutch to focus in on. Just paper, cans, and other assorted junk strewn about the parking lot.

The only other things here are myself, Hutch, Lyla, and…

Wayne.

Hmmm…

"Hey, Lyla," I say.

"Yeah, what's up?" Lyla says, poking around the cars in the parking lot.

"What if Hutch just used his powers on Wayne?" I ask.

"What?" Wayne says. "Why me?"

"I don't mind it," Hutch says with a smirk.

"It's just air, right?" I say. "As long as we're not hurting one another, we could just try that out."

"You cool with that?" I say to Wayne.

"I mean… I'm not sure," Wayne says, running a hand over his head.

"I'm not gonna hurt you, dude," Hutch says. "Think of it like sparring."

"Sparring?" Wayne says. "You've used that one before, dude. You aren't fooling me."

"Oh, please." Hutch chuckles. "This time I really mean it."

"How do I still not believe you," Wayne says.

"You're way bigger than me now. I think I know when I'm not supposed to kid around," Hutch continues.

"I'm holding you to it," Wayne says.

Lyla reenters the conversation. "If you guys are cool with that, I guess we can do it."

"Awesome," Hutch says.

"So, here's what I'm going to have you do," Lyla continues. "Push him."

"Push me?" Wayne says.

"Yeah, push him with your powers," Lyla says.

"Sounds good to me," Hutch says, shaking his hands and hopping up and down.

Hutch continues to psych himself up before he takes a breath and sticks his hands out. A gust of air blows past all of us and at Wayne, who holds his arms up for impact. As the gust of air hits him, he doesn't move.

"Well…" Wayne says, "that wasn't so bad."

"What gives?" Hutch says, looking at his hands. "I gave that a lot."

"Yeah, but you didn't focus," Lyla says. "You didn't channel it into one area."

"What're you talking about?" Hutch asks.

"Try this. I want you to visualize what you want to happen," Lyla continues.

"Like, imagine myself pushing Wayne over with my powers?" Hutch asks.

"Exactly," Lyla says. "Anyone can just use their powers. Watch."

Lyla holds her hands out as the air crackles with the sound of sparks. Electricity erupts from her palms and zigzags out in a wayward direction, fizzling out on the ground.

"But watch that stop sign right there," Lyla says, pointing to the stop sign right at the three-way intersection.

Lyla takes a breath and aims her hand at the stop sign. The air crackles again, and electricity fires from her palm once more. But, instead of zigzagging aimlessly through the air, it flies right to the stop sign, the electricity's impact onto the metal causing sparks to fly every which way.

"Okay. Impressive," Wayne says.

"Sure, sure," Hutch scoffs. "Let me give it a shot."

Hutch takes a breath and holds his hands out once more. Hutch's aura changes with this new advice from Lyla. It's light, floaty, but also powerful, like a toy car on top of a ramp, ready to race down.

Hutch takes a step forward, and while the air by me slides by softly, a *WHOOSH* of air ripples around Hutch.

Wayne braces himself as the air rushes towards him, planting his feet on the ground. The gust of wind races past him, sliding him back but not knocking him over.

"That was great!" Lyla says. "But you still didn't knock him over."

"Well, ya know… maybe I was holding back," Hutch says with a smirk before stopping and putting his hands on his knees, taking a breath.

"I call BS," Wayne retorts with a chuckle. "You did move me, though."

"Still impressive," I say.

"Thank you. But… dang, I didn't expect it to take so much out of me. You're right, though, I feel tired. Like, sleep tired, not workout tired," Hutch says. "Why? I'm just moving air." He turns to Lyla.

"It's 'cause you're using energy," Lyla says.

"What're you talking about?" Wayne asks.

"I guess I could explain it like… you're using a muscle, right? But the one you're using is your mind. You're moving stuff with thought. The energy has to come from somewhere—it comes from up here." Lyla taps her head.

"So, the more mental energy you use to control your powers, the more tired you become. It's like that two p.m. feeling, except turned up to eleven," Lyla says.

"So, what do we do about that?" Hutch asks.

"Sleep it off, honestly," Lyla says. "Rest is the only way it works for me. If you're too tired, you can't use your abilities." Lyla shrugs.

"Gotcha…" Wayne says. "What do we do now?"

"We could have you try the same thing with your abilities, but you control water, so do we need some kind of source?" Lyla says.

"Yes, ma'am," Wayne replies. "Can't make it."

"So, what do you think we should do?" I ask.

"Well…" Lyla says, scanning the environment, "we could use that fire hydrant right there." She points to the fire hydrant on the sidewalk behind Wayne.

"That'd make a good source of water," Wayne says, turning around to face it.

"Sure. But how're we going to open it?" I ask, as the three of us walk up to it.

"We'll need some kind of tool. Doubt any of us can open it with our abilities," Lyla continues.

Hutch steps forward, pushing us out of the way.

"Stand back, ladies, I've got this," he says with a smirk.

"All right, give it a shot, then," Lyla says, slinging the snark back at him.

Hutch takes a breath, holding his hands out.

"All right, check this out!" he says, twisting his hands as if he's opening it himself. A large gust of wind passes by all of us, seemingly swirling around the fire hydrant. The hydrant rattles, as if Hutch's idea had some merit to it. However, as the wind subsides, the hydrant doesn't look any different compared to before.

"That was a good try." Lyla chuckles, turns around, and starts walking towards the front of the restaurant.

"I'll go see if my parents have a wrench or something," she says, her voice trailing off, leaving the three of us alone again.

"How long do you think that's going to take?" Wayne asks, still looking at the fire hydrant. "I was kinda excited for my turn."

"Hopefully not long," I reply.

Chapter 38

Lyla

Walking to the other side of the restaurant, I see my mom and Riley moving tables out into the middle of the T-junction in the road.

There's a van parked just down the road in front of the restaurant, blocking both lanes. The tables are scattered out into a U-shape around the road.

"Hey, Mom," I say, as she and Riley set down another table.

"What's up?" my mom says, turning to me.

"You see Dad around? I need something to open that fire hydrant," I ask.

"Why do you need to open the fire hydrant?" my mom asks.

"'Cause I'm teaching Wayne how to control water, and we need a lot of it," I say.

"As absurd as it sounds, I can't help but believe you," my mom says.

"Do you know where Dad is?" I say.

"No, but we can go find him together," she replies. "We need a break anyways." She turns to Riley.

"I won't complain," Riley responds.

"All right, let's go find your father," my mom says, heading towards the other side of the restaurant.

I follow my mom past the set-up tables, and we start making our way to the side of the restaurant. A car is parked, blocking the other side of the restaurant. My mom clears her throat, as if trying to get my attention.

"What's up?" I ask.

"Lyla, do you think that this is a good idea?" she asks.

"What do you mean?" I say.

"All this fighting we're planning on doing, you think it's a good idea?" she asks.

"Are you having second thoughts?" I say.

"No… Yes… I don't know," she says.

"What's the matter?" I ask.

"Honestly, you," she says. "We haven't seen you for how many years when you went to college, and when you get back, you don't want to come over, you don't want to visit, you don't want to join in on the family business. And now, all this is happening, and you're ready to just throw yourself at a bunch of people who'll drag us apart again."

"You don't want me to fight?" I say.

"No, it's not that I don't want you to fight. You and your friends, you're right. We've gotta do something more than just run away. But, as I've been setting up this whole barricade thing, I've been thinking. What happens if we… if we lose you again?"

"I won't let that happen," I say.

"You can say that, and I know I believe that you will with all your heart. But I can't help but shake the feeling that you might not be able to keep that promise." My mom sighs.

"I'm all for me and your father going in there and making a stand. But you, you're young, you've got a lot to live for. You're still the daughter I raised, and even now, with everything that's happened, you've still got a bright future ahead of you. I don't want you to risk being taken away, or worse."

"Mom… I…" I go to say, before she stops me.

"I know your dad would feel the same. And… I know that things are a lot different than they used to be. I mean, look at us. But we're still family, and you're still my little baby. I can't shake it. I don't want you to go put yourself on the line," she says.

"I know you don't," I say. "If I'm being completely honest, I don't want to either. It's a dangerous thing to do…"

I take a breath.

"But I'm not the little girl I once was. I'm older. I'm old enough to make my own decisions. I'll admit, I didn't connect with you guys. I talked to Aunt Jessie about this too. I pushed you guys away. I thought you guys just focused so much on working because you didn't want to be around me, and when I left, you guys just up and started going back to doing the things that you wanted to do if you didn't have me."

"Lyla," my mom says. But I cut her off. I have to finish what I'm going to say.

"I know I was wrong. I can admit that. I know now that you guys weren't just leaving me out to dry. You guys did what you did for me. 'Cause you cared, 'cause you loved me. I didn't see it that way, and it's my fault for not coming to that conclusion sooner."

"No, sweetie, You're right. We worked a lot to make sure you grew up in a good home. We wanted to do right not just by us but by you too. We couldn't let you live a life where you weren't cared for. Maybe we did work a little too much, maybe we didn't spend enough time with you. We didn't live lavishly. We did good. But us not connecting with you enough when it mattered is our fault too."

My mom sighs, before continuing.

"I talked with your dad once after you left to live with my sister. I told him that I felt like we might have pushed you away."

"You did?" I ask.

She nods solemnly. "After you were gone, I told him I felt like it was too late. He said that I was wrong. He said… that it was too late for the child we raised, but it wasn't too late for us to connect with you, as an adult. That's why we tried to get you to work with us. To connect again," she said.

"I know that now," I reply. "I feel like a fool for not thinking about it that way."

"I don't blame you." My mom continues, "But you did come back, despite being in that facility, despite being chased down by those RCC people, despite having the perfect reason to not come back…"

My mom puts her hands on my arms.

"You did come back, and you've changed, not on the outside, but inside. You're more mature, you're smarter, you're more resourceful than we've ever been. To see the person you've become, it makes me and your dad proud."

"Mom…" I say.

"I don't want to see that person be taken away or taken down by these people…" my mom continues. "But I'm not in control of that anymore. Am I?" she asks.

"If we want to make a difference, and be left alone…" I say. "No."

"I thought so," she says. "I'm not thrilled about it."

"I'm not either," I say.

"Just… promise me one thing?" my mom asks.

"What is it?" I say.

"Be careful. For your own sake," she says.

"I will," I respond.

My mom doesn't respond. I know something is eating her inside. I know she doesn't want me go fight against the RCC, but she knows, just as much as I do, that someone needs to do it. If I were unable to do anything, like Riley, like my mom, like my dad, like James, maybe running away would have been a good option.

But with Wayne, Kellie, Hutch, and myself, maybe there's a chance something good can come of this after all. I won't know… until I try.

"Mom," I say.

My mom looks at me. She's getting a little choked up.

"I love you," I say, wrapping my arms around her.

For a moment, my mom doesn't respond. Even though we've done this many times before, she doesn't know what to say. Maybe it's because I don't say it enough, or something as simple as a hug is just like shaking hands to her and me. I don't know. But eventually, she does respond.

"I love you too," she says.

My mom breaks off from the hug and wipes her eyes.

"Sheesh, you got me all worked up," she says with a slight chuckle.

"Well, let's go find Dad and get that hydrant open, yeah?" I say.

"'Course," my mom says with a smile.

As we start walking, I can't help but feel like something inside of me is free, something long buried in my soul. Something that was withering away was given new life. It feels good. I feel like a missing part of me has been restored.

As we round the back, I see James and my dad moving dumpsters out from the back, both of them struggling to move it.

"Why are these so damn heavy?" my dad grunts.

"You're telling me," James says.

"Having trouble?" my mom asks.

"You bet," my dad replies. "Can you help us push?"

"Sure," I say.

My mom and I get on one side of the dumpster, as my dad and James start pulling on the other side.

"All right, you girls ready?" my dad asks.

"Yep," I say.

"All righty, then push!" my dad exclaims as the four of us start pushing the dumpster. The wheels give a loud creak, as if they're being unshackled from rust for the first time in a long time.

We start moving the dumpster, inch by inch. But not as far as we'd like. We all stop in unison.

"Ohm that tears it!" my dad grumbles to himself. "We can't use these if we can't move them."

"You're right," James says.

He pauses and thinks for a moment, before snapping his fingers.

"I've got an idea," he says.

"Anything'll help," my dad says, defeated.

James turns to me. "Lyla, do you think your powers could lift this?"

"Lift the dumpster?" I say.

"Yeah!" James says. "If we could lift it with your powers, maybe we could move it."

"I don't think that's how electricity works," I say. "Besides, I'd electrocute you guys even if it did."

James thinks for a moment and then points at Kellie, Wayne, and Hutch. "What about them?"

I look over to the three of them. They're all locked in conversation, and they seem to be having fun, despite everything that's going on. James makes a good point. Hutch has been working on his abilities, and him being able to raise the dumpster could be possible.

"That's not a bad idea," I say, before cupping my hands around my mouth and shouting.

"HEY, HUTCH! COM'ERE!" I shout.

Hutch looks around for where I'm shouting from, before jogging over to us.

"Hey, what's up?" he asks.

"Got another task for you to test your abilities on," I say. "Part of your training."

"Oh yeah?" he says, lighting up. "What is it?"

"This dumpster," I respond, pointing to it. "You can move stuff around with your powers, but now, let's see if you can lift something instead."

"All right. I can give it a go!" Hutch says.

"Same thing we did earlier, visualize, and then do it," I assure him.

Hutch nods. He takes a stance again, rolls his head, and shakes his hands off. He's focused. I can tell all the extra eyes on him is giving him some kind of confidence boost.

"How high do you want it?" he asks.

"Just enough to make it easier to move," James says.

"Should be simple enough," he says, taking a breath.

Hutch holds his hands out again, and just like every other time, a gust of air brushes past all of us; this time, it's brushing past our legs and congregating under the dumpster.

Soon enough, the dumpster rises from the ground, not very high, but enough to be noticeable.

"Try… pushing it now," Hutch says in a strained voice.

"All right," James says, putting his hands to the dumpster. Just as he starts pushing it with force, the dumpster glides across the ground, like a puck on an air hockey table.

"Oh wow!" James exclaims. "This works out great!"

"Good… to know," Hutch says, still straining in his voice. "Why is this so heavy?"

"You're lifting a dumpster," I say, "Remember, it takes energy to channel your abilities."

"Let's move it before I can't do it anymore," Hutch continues.

"All right!" James says, continuing to push the dumpster.

As James and Hutch start moving, my dad starts walking to join them. But before he gets too far, I manage to get his attention.

"Dad! Wait!" I say.

"What's up?" he asks.

"I need a wrench to open the hydrant out front," I say.

"Oh, all right," he says.

James jumps into the conversation. "I can handle the dumpster from here," he says.

"Sounds good," my dad replies.

As James and Hutch walk the dumpster to the front of the restaurant, my dad approaches us, pulling a wrench from the toolbox right by the door behind us.

"Here you go, sweetie," he says. "Dunno if it's going to work, but it's the biggest one we've got."

My dad places a large adjustable wrench in my hand.

"Thanks, Dad," I say.

My mom gives my dad a look as if they're talking without saying anything. My dad nods his head as if he knows exactly what she said to him.

"You guys talked?" he asks.

"Yeah," my mom says.

"Then I don't have anything to add. Your mom's always been the one who knows just what to say. She speaks for me too." He turns to me.

"I know," I say.

My dad nods.

"You gotta do what you gotta do, right?" he asks.

"Seems like it's the only thing we can do," I say.

"I can't stop ya, you're a woman now. You make your own decisions," he says.

"I know," I respond.

"I love ya, Lyla," he says.

"I love you too, Dad," I respond.

We both share a moment of silence. It's not as flowery as the conversation with my mom, but I can tell my dad knows what we've said.

"All right, well, I'm gonna finish this up with James, and after that, we should be ready," he says. "We'll find some way to help when they come."

"Sounds good," I reply.

"Come on, Connie." My dad gestures to my mom, heading towards the back door.

My mom nods, and the two of them head back inside to make way for the front of the restaurant.

As I follow my parents around the back and into the parking lot, I see Kellie and Wayne jog up to me.

"Hey, Lyla!" Kellie says. "What took ya so long?"

"And where's Hutch?" Wayne says. "Shouldn't he be here too?"

"He's over there." I point to him and James moving the dumpster to block the road off. I can tell Hutch is struggling. While this is good training, if he keeps this up, he'll be too tired to fight.

Then, a thought appears in my head.

"Here, Wayne, take this," I say, handing him the wrench. "I gotta talk to Kellie about something."

CHAPTER 39

Kellie

WAYNE TAKES THE wrench from Lyla.

"Oh, all right, this should work," he says.

"Try opening it. We'll join you in a second," Lyla says.

Wayne walks over to the fire hydrant, leaving Lyla and me alone.

"I just had a thought," Lyla says, turning to me.

"You did?" I ask.

"Yeah, something clicked in my head. I wanted to ask you about it."

"What is it?" I ask.

"I was going to ask you about your powers." Lyla continues, "I know how to get Wayne and Hutch ready for this. But I don't know what to do about you…"

She pauses for a moment, running a hand through her hair. Clearly, the gears are turning in her head.

"But, then something came to me," she says.

"Well, spit it out then," I say.

"I'm getting to it," Lyla says. "You remember when we were talking, out back?"

Of course I remember. It's not like I haven't thought about what she said… or that I don't really want to remember what happened back there. But… now's not really the time for that, is it?

"And… you remember what happened when you looked at me before we started talking?" Lyla continues.

"Yeah, I remember," I say. "I'm sorry… Seriously, Lyla, I didn't mean for that to happen."

"No, it's fine, it's just…" Lyla says. "You think you could do it again?"

…What?

"What… what do you mean by do it again?" I ask.

"I had this thought," Lyla says. "If you can do that… and sense emotions… What else could you make others feel?"

"Are you suggesting I use this against the people?" I ask.

"Well… yeah, of course," Lyla says. "We've got to have every advantage we can get, right? You can make them feel, fear, or feel something to keep them from trying to hurt us."

"That's true," I say. "But I've never tested it out."

"Why don't you try it out?" Lyla says.

"On who?" I ask.

Lyla looks up from our conversation, The way her eyes dart from one area to another, she's looking for someone. Someone I could test my powers on.

"Him." Lyla points to the front of the restaurant.

As I look up to see where she's pointing, I can see Hutch, finishing up moving the dumpster with James. He relaxes his arms, and the dumpster stops floating in the air, setting itself down on the ground. He breathes out a sigh of relief; it's clear he's tiring himself out moving something so heavy.

"You want me to use my powers on Hutch?" I ask.

"Yeah, see if you can get him to feel something."

"Like what?" I ask.

"Maybe… try something calming, rejuvenating," Lyla adds.

"I mean, I can give it a shot," I say. "What am I supposed to do?"

"Just do what comes naturally. It worked for my powers, but I don't know anything about yours," Lyla says.

"All right. I can give it a go," I say.

I try to remember what Lyla told Hutch when he was using his powers. Take a deep breath… visualize what you're going to do, and then do it.

I try to dig into myself to find a feeling that could make Hutch feel refreshed. I think I understand what Lyla's looking for. Hutch looks tired. He's running out of energy, and he needs to be in top shape if he's going to fight alongside us…

So, find a feeling that will make him feel that way… But I'm giving emotions to someone else. I can't conjure up an emotion out of thin air…. I need to find something I can grab on to…

At least, that's the only thing that makes sense about this.

I try to remember back to a time where I felt… calm, rejuvenated… Something like… a second wind?

A second wind. That could work… I remember plenty of times I stayed up way too late, or I went to bed and woke up feeling like I could take on anything… I had that feeling when we were at Paul's, waking up and being excited for whatever the day had in store for me.

That works. That works really, really well!

As I'm concentrating on those memories, I can feel my own aura for a moment, crisp like clean linen, chilled like a spring breeze… It feels fresh.

I open my eyes, and for a moment, I can see it, the blueish green aura surrounding my own body, and around Hutch, a dark blue, it warps and controls sluggishly around him.

I know what I need to do now, just like what happened in the kitchen…

"Hey! Hutch!" I shout.

Hutch's ears perk up as he turns towards me.

"What?" he says, looking in my direction.

Gotcha.

As I connect looks with him, I can see the color around my body bleed into the color around his, as my emotions take over. The sluggish bubble starts speeding up until it's a smooth wavy shape, the colors lightening from a dark blue to the blueish green I have.

Hutch stops for a moment, entranced, until he breaks himself from eye contact. He takes a deep breath, standing up just a bit straighter.

As he breaks eye contact, I blink, and the auras… they're gone… But, as soon as they disappear, I feel it. That feeling from earlier today. Like a hand reaches through my chest, grabbing at the essence of my body, squeezing it with all of its might.

It hurts. A lot…. worse than earlier.

I can't help but grab my chest, as I take a breath.

"You okay?" Lyla asks.

No… no, I'm not okay… It feels like my soul was hit by a fire truck… It hurts…

But… it's not just that I feel. Seeing me change Hutch's emotions… I thought I'd feel good, giving him some kind of boost that he clearly needed. But there's this nagging thought in the back of my head.

I can't shake it. It feels… guilty. Like I did something wrong. I feel like I cheated on a test or stole something from a store.

It doesn't feel good. It doesn't feel good at all.

Hutch jogs over to us, a big grin on his face.

"What did you do?" Hutch says.

"What… what're you talking about?" I say, regaining myself for a moment.

"I looked at you, and now… I feel great!" Hutch punches the air like he's practicing for a boxing match.

"I thought that moving the dumpster was going to be the last thing I did today, but hot damn, I feel great!" Hutch says. "What'd you do?"

"I, uh…" I say.

Should I tell him? They don't know I can do this… and part of me doesn't want them to know… It's that guilty feeling inside of me telling me not to tell him what I did… that I shouldn't… If I do…

What will they think? Will he be okay with me toying with his emotions like that? Will he be okay with me altering how he feels? It's not his own feelings; it's me… projecting them onto him.

I open my mouth, saying the first thing that comes to my head.

"I just gave you some of my energy," I say. "I have the ability to make you guys feel better."

"Oh, that'll be a huge help!" Hutch says. "We get tired during the fight, you'll be there to keep us topped off, huh?"

Hutch gives off a big smile, giving me a tap on the shoulder before running off to Wayne, who just opened the fire hydrant.

I stand there in silence. Still thinking about what I did… Lyla taps me on the shoulder.

"Kellie… you okay?" she asks.

"I… I don't know…" I say.

"Do you want to talk about it?" Lyla says…

"I…" I attempt to tell her yes, but the sound of rushing water interrupts my thought. We both look over to see Wayne and Hutch high-fiving like a couple of teenagers at the sight of water rushing out onto the street.

"Hang on, Kellie," Lyla says. "We'll talk as soon as I'm done with Wayne."

Lyla then rushes over to the guys at the fire hydrant, leaving me alone with my own thoughts.

I'm… I'm not fine. I'm worried about what I'm feeling. I need to talk to someone… but I can't just talk to anyone. Lyla's over with Wayne and Hutch, and they don't need to know… I can't talk to Lyla's parents; they don't know anything about what's going on. I don't think Riley is going to understand, let alone believe I'm being genuine if I tell her.

Which leaves James… He's been there with us since the beginning. If anyone's going to listen… it's going to be him.

I start making my way over to the front of the restaurant. That's where I saw James last. So maybe he's there. Right?

As I pass the barricade of tables in the middle of the intersection, I wave to Riley and Connie as they finish setting up the barricade.

"You done with your training?" Connie asks.

"Yeah, for now," I say. "Have either of you seen James?"

"He should be up at the front," Riley says. "He just finished moving the dumpster." She stands up and looks to the middle of the intersection.

"He was just over there…" she says.

"I'll go look," I say. "Thank you."

"'Course!" Connie says with a bright smile.

I continue walking to the front of our little base. Two dumpsters and a car block the road that we walked down to get here. I can't help but look around at the buildings. It's weird… I could've sworn that there were people in these buildings earlier… but now, as we're setting up, it's like nobody's here anymore. It's a total ghost town now…

I make my way to the barricade, looking around for any sign of James.

"James?" I call out. "You here?"

"Yeah, I'm here. I'm on the other side!" James's voice calls out from the other end of the dumpster.

"You got a moment?" I say, peering around the corner of the dumpster.

"In a second… just wrapping this up…" James says, his voice slightly strained.

"And… done," James says, as he emerges from the other side of the dumpster. He climbs over the hood of the parked car, dusting himself off.

"So, whatcha need?" James says with a grin.

"Uh…" I try to formulate a sentence, but I can't… "I just…"

"Something wrong?" James asks.

I try to say something, but the words… they just won't come out. I nod instead.

"Is it about us having to fight these people?" James asks.

"Sort of…" I manage to squeak out.

"Well… It is kind of scary, isn't it," James says.

"Yeah, it is," I finally manage to say. "But that's not what I came here for."

"What is it then?" James asks.

Again, I know what I want to say, but I can't say it. I can't formulate the words. I can't… I need to try to think about what I'm going to say.

I breathe in and try to figure out what I'm going to say.

These emotions, these feelings, there's got to be some combination of words to explain it to him. I feel guilty. I feel awful about what I did, about altering how Hutch felt. Of course I did it for a good reason, but that feeling I got from doing it, it wasn't good. It felt wrong… it felt evil.

But how do I tell that to James? What's he going to say about it? Is he going to condemn me for doing something like that? Is he going to understand? He doesn't have powers; he doesn't know what I'm feeling.

I take another breath and blink. But as I look up to tell him…

I see it.

The auras again. A fading color of dark green dances around my hands, and as I look at James, that color overtakes the violet around his body.

No, this isn't what I was trying to do!

I turn around to mitigate what I'm doing to my friend, but as I turn around and try to blink again to make the colors go away, James's voice turns to disbelief.

"What the…." He trails off.

"James! I'm so, so sorry! I didn't mean to—" I say, but he cuts me off.

"What did you do?" He continues, "One second, I was fine, but now..." He doesn't finish his sentence.

"James, I'm sorry," I say, turning around, the colors dissipating from around us. "I was trying to talk to you about that."

"You made me feel this?" he asks.

I nod. "It's... something I do. It's part of my... abilities?"

"How many times have you done this?" he asks, his voice now more concerned.

"This is... the fourth time?" I continue. "But I've only done it once intentionally."

"You can just change the way people think?" he asks.

"Yes, it's... it's scary," I say. "I did it once, to make Hutch feel... more energetic."

"That... that explains it," James says. "He definitely looked like he felt better."

"Yeah, I know." I continue, "but the feeling I got afterwards. It didn't feel good."

"It felt wrong; it felt like you did something you shouldn't have?" James says.

"Exactly," I say.

"You're making me feel it now," he says.

James takes a breath and sighs.

"But I can shake the feeling. It's not mine," he says. "You know how bad this is."

"I know," I say. "But it scares me, having this much control over someone."

"'Course it does, it'd scare anyone," James says.

"I'm just worried I'll use it for the wrong reasons," I say.

"That's a normal feeling to have," James says, pausing, like he's trying to formulate the right words to say. "You can control it, can't you?"

"What do you mean?" I say.

"I know you, but I don't *know* you," James says. "We've been through a lot, but I can't judge your own moral compass. It's… I know it's rude, but you've tricked us before."

"You're talking about…." I say.

"When we escaped, yeah." James continues, "But you ended up doing the right thing… right?"

"… Yeah. I did," I say.

"I don't know what's going on inside your head, but if it came to it, could you do the right thing again?"

"Of course," I say.

"Seeing you do that to me, feeling what you felt, I'm sure you know what I'm going through. You mentioned you can see… emotions." He continues, "But… I have this feeling, not one you gave me, but of my own volition, that you wouldn't do something like that. It makes me feel better… but I can't help but feel like you've got something more powerful than just controlling something like Lyla and the others."

James takes a breath.

"Kellie, you have the power to change minds, definitively. That's dangerous," he says.

"What am I supposed to do?" I raise my voice. "It scares me. I don't want to do anything bad with it."

James pauses for a moment, scratching his head and staring off into the distance.

"I guess… We can keep it a secret. Between me and you, and Lyla, of course. We can try to keep you in check, we can try to make sure you're making the right decisions. But that won't always work. You can just change our minds."

"I wouldn't do that," I say. "I couldn't ever do that."

"I know, but… it's not a matter of words, Kellie. It's a matter of action," James says.

"You… don't believe me, do you?" I say.

"No, I do," James says. "We've been through enough without your powers where I know you'll do the right thing. But this… this changes a lot going forward, you know? You'll have to prove to yourself that you won't do these things. I can tell you when you've gone too far. But you'll be the one who makes that final decision."

James trails off after that. We both stand there in silence, his words seeping into me like a sponge. He's right. What I possess… it's dangerous. I can make anyone I want think anything I want. That's… that's terrifying. But I'm worried. I'm worried that my fear of myself won't be enough to stop me.

"I guess… I guess you're right," I say. "But the others, they're counting on me."

"I know they are," James says. "We all are. Do you think you can do the right thing again this time?"

"I think so, but using my powers makes me feel… like this," I say.

"That can keep you from going too far." James continues, "At least, that's how I see it. I'm not you."

I nod.

"I… I guess you're right," I say.

"I don't have to be right. It's your responsibility," James replies. "Now, I'd like to finish this up. You're more than welcome to join me." James gives a slight grin.

"I guess I can," I say.

"All right, sounds good," James says, getting ready to hop over the car hood again. But before he does, I hear something.

"James… Wait," I say.

The sound of rumbling engines in the distance… there's more than one of them…

Wait… more than one engine? More than one car.

I look to the stores again… They're empty. Of course they're empty…

Oh god. It's them.…

They're here.

Chapter 40

Lyla

"Hey, that's not bad!" I say, watching Wayne manipulate the water on the ground into projectiles.

"Try hitting the road sign with it!" Hutch exclaims, pointing to the street sign on the corner.

"Sure, I'll give it a go," Wayne says, aiming his water orb to the sign, before taking a breath.

"Just like I taught you both," I say, "Visualize and focus, right?"

"'Course, I got it all down," Wayne says with a smirk, before swinging his arm like he's throwing a ball, sending the orb flying through the air, keeping its shape, and splashing against the sign with a *SPLOOSH*.

"Good throw, not bad," Hutch says. "'Course, I'm sure I could've done that in half the time."

"Oh please, you couldn't throw a ball to save your life." Wayne chuckles.

"Hey, man, I was a star athlete! I could've!" Hutch snaps back.

"You played wide receiver. All you know how to do is run and catch." Wayne gives his friend a smirk. "Like this."

Wayne hurls another glob of water, this time at Hutch. Instinctively, Hutch holds his hands out to catch it, but instead of catching it in his hands, the ball of water splits apart in his fingers, knocking him on his behind, soaking him.

"Argh, you ass!" Hutch grumbles to himself, standing up before raising his hands in the air, as a gust of wind shoots up from the ground, drying him off.

"Why didn't you use your powers to catch it?" Wayne snickers.

"Maybe I'm saving them," Hutch snaps back. "You dunderhead, you got my clothes *and* my fur wet. Now I'm gonna be damp all freakin' day."

Hutch continues using his powers to blow dry himself.

"Should've caught it then." Wayne laughs.

"Really?" Hutch asks, before a gust of wind tosses a loose can at Wayne, who blocks it with a wall of water he raised in front of him.

"Really." Wayne smirks.

As the two of them continue their bickering, I hear someone call out for me.

"Lyla!" Kellie yells, sprinting towards me. Her voice cracks in desperation.

"What is it?" I ask, meeting her halfway.

"They're… they're here!" she exclaims.

I hear the sound of another voice calling from the front of the restaurant.

"Is this really all you could do?" the voice says. The condescending tone, the pure arrogant energy anyone could sense. It's him.

They're here.

I turn to Wayne and Hutch, who've stopped arguing to listen in on the conversation. They both give me a glance, as if asking if it's time.

"Let's go," I say, walking past Kellie, who follows me. Wayne and Hutch aren't close behind as he rounds the corner to the front of the restaurant.

As we walk towards the barricade the others set up, I see him, standing on top of the roof of the car parked in the middle of the road, the two dumpsters on one side and the food truck on the other, covering the sidewalk.

It's clear as day Thorn anticipated us fighting back. His men train their weapons on us from their side of the barricade. Their cars block the exits down the road. Thorn dons a Kevlar vest. As we get closer, he unholsters the handgun on his hip, although he doesn't raise it to any of us.

James stands at the second barricade, a group of tables in the middle of the road, not thirty feet from where he set the dumpsters up.

As we walk past him, James pipes up.

"He wants to talk," he says.

"Talk?" Hutch asks.

"I think it's clear where we stand." Wayne scoffs.

"Who knows," Kellie says.

The four of us go to step up to the barricade, but Thorn calls out to us before we walk any farther.

"Only you!" he says, pointing to me.

We stop, and I turn to my friends.

"You guys stay back," I say. "If they try anything…"

"We've got your back," Wayne says.

I give the three of them a nod and start walking closer to the car where Thorn is standing.

"So, you wanna talk?" I ask.

Thorn laughs.

"You call this a barricade?" He stomps on the hood of the car. "It's pathetic."

"Please, we'll make it work," I snap back.

"Won't do you much good, Lyla," Thorn sneers. "But you know me, I like to talk things out. Part of the job, isn't it?"

"After what you tried to do to Kellie? You really expect me to believe that?" I ask.

Thorn rolls his eyes.

"Perhaps I was a bit too brash with that one, but I did learn something from that," Thorn says, adjusting his glasses.

"What's that?" I say.

"That there's no way I'm going to let you people roam free. Not when you're as dangerous as you have been," he says as his expression changes to visible anger.

"But I'll allow you one more chance. Everyone here can surrender, and you can all be happy together in one of my facilities…" Thorn says.

"Or what? You kill us?" I reply.

"If it has to come to that, then so be it. Either way, you're under my watch, or you're six feet under." Thorn looks to his men behind the barricade, all of them ready their weapons.

"So what'll it be?" Thorn asks.

I look back to my friends, and it's clear they know my answer. James gets down behind the barricade, Hutch and Wayne ready to fight. Kellie takes a step back. Riley and my parents step inside the restaurant.

"Try us."

Kellie

Thorn chuckles, as if that's what he's expecting. He turns around, stepping down from the roof of the car.

"All right!" Thorn exclaims.

Within a second, the guns trained on us all take aim… Lyla immediately turns around and starts booking it to the barrier.

RATTA

TATTA

RATTA

TATTA

RATTA

TATTA

RATTA

Gunfire erupts from the barrels, bullets flying through the air, aiming for the barrier we're standing around. The street signs on the side of the road are reduced to warped pieces of metal. Glass shatters from the buildings where stray shots ricochet off the ground.

As I crouch behind the barrier, Lyla jumps it, joining us, not a scratch on her.

"You okay?" James shouts over the gunfire.

"I'm fine, Wayne's backing me up!" she says.

We all peer over the barrier, as we see none of the ammunition coming directly towards us has made it to where we're crouching.

Wayne stands in front of the barrier, both of his hands outstretched. A massive wall of water sits in front of us, each bullet hitting the wall, slowing down until it plinks onto the ground on the other side, barely moving.

Wayne's breathing is slow but intense. Determined to protect us.

Hutch stands behind him, awestruck at the sight. He's not moving.

"Hutch!" Lyla calls out, snapping him out of his trance.

He turns to us, running behind the barrier.

"What… what do we do?" he asks, holding his chest. His breathing is erratic.

"Hold it together, we've got this!" Lyla says. "We need to wait for an opening!"

The gunfire continues to echo through the street. Wayne calls out to us from the front.

"We need to do something! Soon!" he shouts.

"Come on, think, think!" Lyla says, closing her eyes.

James pauses for a moment before getting an idea.

"Hutch, can you do something for me?" he asks.

Hutch doesn't respond. He's fallen into his trance again, staring at the floor.

"Hutch?" James asks. No answer.

"What're you planning?" I ask.

"I know how we can get Wayne out of there and give us enough time to fight back," James says. "But we need him to be… here!"

"How do we do that?" I ask.

"I'm working on it," James says, but he's cut off by the harsh whistling of a bullet making it past Wayne's defense. As I turn to James, it's clear he's starting to crack as well.

If we don't do something, this could spell the end for us. And after… after what I've experienced, I know Thorn isn't going to stop until we're finished.

But… I can't do anything to help…

Can I?

Another whistle of a bullet goes over us.

I can do something… but… I don't know if I want to.

"Hutch, come on!" I shout, pushing him, to no avail. He's still zoned out.

I… I have to.

I take a breath and close my eyes. I take a breath and open them once more.

I can see them again, the colors.

As I turn to Hutch, I can see his aura. His colors are grey, dimmed, and weak around him. He's receding into his own mind.

But I can pull him out. I can save him. I can save everyone… Even if what I'm doing is wrong. We need him to stop the onslaught from the RCC. Whatever James's plan is, it has to work.

But what do I make him feel? What can pull him out of here?

It's got to be something he can latch on to, something to pull him out.

Confidence, of course.

I need confidence. But if I'm going to give him the confidence to fight, it's got to be something from me as well… I try to pull from myself…

Confidence.

I hear my own voice in my head.

"For once, I'm content with myself. Nothing you can say to me will destroy my own feelings about myself. I… am… happy."

Of course. That confidence. That's what I need.

I look as I see the aura around me change to a fiery red, billowing with strength and tenacity. This is what he needs. This is what we all need.

I reach out to Hutch, the aura dances off of me, and latches on to him, and like a flame to a grill, it explodes around him.

Hutch takes a breath, like he's just been pulled out of a bad dream.

The fire inside of him erupts, as his energy is added to those I gave him.

"I'm here! I'm here," he says.

"Great!" James says. "I have a plan."

"What is it?" I ask.

"Can you pull air away from places?" James asks.

"I can try. What do you want me to do?" Hutch asks.

"If you can remove any air from the wall Wayne has, you can freeze it in place," James says.

"Like ice?" he asks.

"Yeah!" James says.

Another whistle from a stray bullet flies over us.

"Do it now!" Lyla shouts.

Hutch nods, standing up from the barrier.

We all peek over the barrier, watching as Hutch pulls his hands apart, the wind coming from around the water blowing against us.

"Come on… come on…" James mutters to himself, as the water starts to slow down, becoming opaque. Wayne starts stumbling, his breathing more strained, as the water freezes. A chill of air hits all of us as the water freezes into ice. The bullets continuing to hit the ice, it cracks with each shot. James and Lyla grab Wayne as he stumbles back and pull him over the barrier.

"T-thanks, dude," Wayne says between breaths.

"'Course!" Hutch says. "You okay?"

"Yeah… just… just a bit tired," Wayne says.

"I can help with that," I say.

"You… you sure?" James says.

"We need to win," I say. "Or at least survive."

Lyla nods. "Go for it, Kellie." She stands up. "Come on, Hutch, let's show them what we're made of."

"For everyone," he says, getting up.

The two of them stand up, rounding the barrier. Hutch lets out a cry as a burst of wind blows past us.

Now's my time to shine. I close my eyes and open them to reveal the colors once more.

Wayne's aura is weak, and he needs energy… just like Hutch did before. I know what to think of.

Warm mornings. Waking up in a cozy bed. Being ready to tackle the day. The aura changes again to a light blue.

I reach out and let my aura take over Wayne's. As the colors around him change, Wayne sits up with a reinvigorated strength.

"Thank… thank you," he says with a determined grin.

He stands up now. Water runs from the fire hydrant behind us to his feet and rises up around him.

"Let's win this," he says, before sprinting off past the barrier, leaving me and James alone.

"You did the right thing," James says.

"I had to," I say.

"I believe in you, Kellie," he continues.

The sounds of crackling electricity and whooshing wind echo through the street, followed by the shouts of men, followed by gunfire.

"Now go! Help the others. I'll check on everyone back at the restaurant!" he says, standing up and making a dash to the restaurant.

All right. I guess it's my turn now.

I stand up, rounding the barricade. The bullets have stopped hitting the ice wall, which is slowly starting to melt. As I look to the side of the street, I can see the rushing water from the hydrant leading underneath the cars and into where the RCC showed up.

As I round the ice wall, I'm attacked by a man with the butt end of a rifle. As he swings the rifle at me, I duck under it. But as I duck, I'm hit in the face with the butt of the gun.

The man spins the rifle in his hands, pointing the barrel at me as I lie on the ground. He says nothing, as he goes to pull the trigger.

I blink, and the colors appear again, I raise my hand out instinctively, bringing up my fear from the alleyway into my mind. As the fear briefly flashes through my thoughts, the colors change.

My aura jumps from my body and engulfs him in a split second.

The man steps back, the gun quivering in his hands. His breathing becomes sparse as his eyes widen. As he steps back, he bumps into something. As he spins around…

CRACK.

As he crumples to the ground like a pile of bricks, I see the person who saved me.

The unmistakable white shirt and shorts. Except… that's all there is. As I blink, the form around the clothes change, and James is there, wielding a baseball bat. His actual colors change from the red brick to his natural green.

"You good?" he says, holding out a hand.

"Yeah, you saved me there," I say as he helps me up.

"You're welcome," James says.

As I dust off my clothes, we hear a shout from someone in front of the barricade. As we look over the barricade, we see Hutch, Lyla, and Wayne booking it towards us.

"They've got more!" she shouts, diving over the car.

The sound of screeching tires is heard as more men pile out of the cars, more men in SWAT uniforms, and men wielding stun sticks, electrified.

"What do we do now?" Hutch asks.

James

"We've gotta do something," Lyla says.

The sounds of rushing boots shakes the ground, as the men approach the barricade.

I try to look over the car, only to see a stun stick bash the hood in right in front of my face.

"Move back!" I shout, as we all start moving to the barricades closer to the restaurant.

As we hop over the barricades, more bullets fly through the air, narrowing missing us… until…

"AH!" Kellie lets out a cry.

"Kellie!" Lyla shouts, running towards her, as she tumbles to the ground, out in the open.

"Hutch, Wayne!" I shout. "Focus on Lyla!"

Hutch and Wayne stand up, both protecting Lyla from the hail of gunfire, Wayne raising up water, as Hutch turns it to ice.

Lyla approaches, Kellie grabbing her and carrying her back to the barricade where I'm at.

"Check on her," Lyla says before immediately turning around and rushing towards the group of guys, letting out a determined yell.

"Kellie, are you okay?" I ask.

"Y-yeah, I'm fine," she says, letting go of her side, her red hoodie stained with blood.

I raise her hoodie up enough to get a look at her side. Luckily, she's just grazed. I let out a sigh of relief.

"Okay, you're just grazed," I say. "You'll be fine."

"That's a relief," she says. "Is… is it normal I can't… I can't feel it hurting?" she asks.

"That's called shock," I say. "Come on, let's get you inside."

I peer over the barricade and see Lyla taking on the men with the stun sticks. Lyla gets knocked down by one of the men with the sticks but gets back up again, determined to win. Wayne and Hutch are fighting the men with the rifles, Hutch tearing the weapons from them, as Wayne knocks them down with a torrent of water.

However, we're still being pushed back closer and closer to the restaurant.

I pick Kellie up, before starting to carry her back inside, hoping to god that I don't get hit with a stray bullet.

As I open the door and step inside, Riley and Connie both run up to me, Connie taking Kellie out of my hands.

"Is she okay?" Connie asks.

"Yeah, just grazed," I say.

"I think it's starting to hurt," Kellie says, wincing a bit.

"You'll be fine," Connie says, carrying her to the back.

"And what about you?" Riley asks.

I pat myself down. Nothing hurts, but… nothing is on me aside from Kellie's blood.

"Yeah… Yeah, I'm fine," I say.

"Riley, I need you!" Connie shouts.

"All right, I'm coming!" she says, rushing to the back.

I turn around and start heading out. As I open the door, the assault has continued to get closer to the restaurant. We're losing ground, and fast. Something needs to be done.

As I scan the fight, I can't help but notice that Lyla isn't making any headway with the men with the stun sticks. They're locked in a stalemate, and their sheer numbers are pushing her back. Wayne and Hutch are doing okay, but they're not fighting enough at once.

Then… it all clicks in my head. I know how to contribute to this fight.

"Wayne! Hutch!" I yell.

"Kinda busy!" Hutch yells, using his wind to pull weapons away.

"Don't fight them!" I yell, pointing to the men Lyla is fighting.

"Wayne! Short them out with the water!" I yell.

Wayne glances over for a brief moment in between his attacks, making the connection.

"Oh! I got it!" Wayne says, hurling a torrent of water over to the electrified men.

Lyla sees the torrent coming, before dodging back, letting the men's gear short circuit. Hutch finally makes the connection before knocking them all down with his powers.

"I've got it!" Hutch says.

"Your turn, Lyla!" I shout, pointing to the men with the weapons. "Chain your electricity!" I say.

Lyla nods, running over to the men who are regaining their footing from Wayne and Hutch's onslaught. She holds her hands out, arcing her electricity between the guns, causing the men to seize up, collapsing onto the ground.

"Yes!" I shout, before something else gets my attention.

More cars. They're coming from the sides now… Luckily, we've got barriers up.

"More people!" I shout as the cars stop just short of the barriers.

I can't see the cars, but Lyla, Hutch, and Wayne all prepare for the next wave of enemies.

However, something else happens. A group of ten figures hop over the barrier. None of them wielding weapons…

None of them human…

Another set of cars stop at the barricade on the other side…

More altered get out, hopping the barrier, and ten turns to twenty, and then twenty turns to thirty.

The one to approach me is a coyote.

"You guys need some help?" the coyote asks.

The sound of screeching tires is heard once more; this time, however… the shouts of Thorn's men are coming from all sides. Gunfire echoes throughout the town, as some of the other changed start readying their hands, just like Lyla, Wayne, and Hutch.

"We need all the help we can get," I say.

"We're here to help. What do you need us to do?" he says, gesturing to all of the others who are ready to fight.

I nod, putting my hands to my mouth.

"If you have abilities, we need you to fight, hold the ends of the street! We're aiming for unconscious, DO NOT KILL! If you have a medical background, go inside; we'll need all the help we can get if things get too tough!"

Everyone shouts in agreement.

"WE DO THIS FOR EVERYONE!" I shout.

"EVERYONE!" the group shouts back.

"Now! GO!" I yell.

As the men in SWAT uniforms start piling towards the barricade, the new group of altered take their places. One with earth abilities like Paul's forms new barricades. Another with fire powers lines the inside of the barricades with flames.

A couple head inside into the restaurant to help with Kellie.

"How did you know to come?" I ask the coyote.

"Word spreads fast. When the SWAT guys leave facilities, you know something's up. This bar, some of us thought it was only a myth, until people who ran started talking… Hearing people were taking a stand… We knew we had to come."

"You got that right!" Lyla says, running up. "I think we can actually win this thing with your help!"

"I think we can…" I say, taking a deep sigh of relief.

THUNK.

What… what was that? I look around to see what that sound was… until…

It feels like someone punched me. Jeez. That aches.

I reach to my shoulder. As I grab it, it feels wet. I look down at my shoulder, until…

Oh… that's… that's blood.

That can't be good.

As everything around me blurs, I hear Lyla call out for me.

Lyla

"JAMES!" I scream, as he collapses to the ground, blood pooling out from his shoulder.

I turn around to see where the bullet came from, seeing the unmistakable face of Thorn turn away from the top of the building across the street.

"Take him inside," I say to the coyote.

He nods, calling over someone else to help him carry James inside. I start booking it towards the building I saw Thorn on top of. Pure unbridled rage courses through my body. As I sprint to the building, I see Hutch helping someone free themselves from a small group of RCC thugs with his powers.

"Hutch!" I shout.

He looks over in my direction as he frees the person. "What?" he asks.

"That building," I say pointing to the roof of the building Thorn is on. "Get me up there. NOW!"

Hutch nods before spinning around, raising his hands up. The ground below me disappears as Hutch manipulates the wind to push me upwards.

I rise up into the air, passing window after window as bullets fly through the air, followed by the sounds of shouting, burning, moving earth, and of course, the wind.

When I make it to the top, I feel a gust of air push me onto the roof. Landing on top, I see Thorn on the other end, wielding a rifle.

"THORN!" I shout, frothing at the mouth from rage.

"There you are," he sneers. "Ya know, I used to be a good shot back in the day."

I start sprinting at him, electricity arcing from my hands crackling as it hits the ground with every step I take towards him.

"Fine," Thorn says, readying his rifle.

As he raises the rifle, I fire a bolt to it, causing him to jolt and drop it on the ground. I reel my hand back into a fist and put my full force into it as I reach him.

I remember for a moment what I was taught by my dad. Shoulder, then arm, then fist. Like a well-oiled machine, my fist carries the weight of my whole body into his face. I connect with him, knocking him to the side, throwing his glasses off.

He falls to the ground, and for a moment, he doesn't move, before he starts coughing, hacking up some blood onto the pavement. He picks his glasses up off the ground, one lens cracked.

He flashes a grin at me as he stands up, brandishing a knife, coated in red.

I grab my side, feeling my own blood ooze out from my side.

I'm stunned for a moment, but… it doesn't hurt.

It's got to be the adrenaline…

Thorn rushes at me once more, this time holding the knife with both hands. I manage to sidestep by just enough for the blade to graze my stomach.

As Thorn passes me, I hold out a hand and arc electricity from my hand to his knife.

As we stop, Thorn gives me another grin.

"I knew... I knew you'd try that." His eyes widen as a maniacal grin crosses over his face. Holding the knife in one hand, he shows me the handle.

"Rubber," he says with a sly grin.

He starts charging me again.

"I've... had it with you! You've ruined everything."

He slashes at me again, cutting my arm as I step away.

"You and your friends. You're all beasts!"

He takes another lunge at me. I manage to sweep his leg out, narrowly missing his blade.

"Your humanity is gone, you're nothing but vermin, you don't know your place in this world!"

I charge at him, putting all my effort into a sucker punch to his gut, my fist charged with my power.

"You're the beast. You're hunting us."

Thorn stumbles back, kneeling.

"I will not stand by and let you hurt my friends. Hunt my family."

Thorn stands up, grabbing a rock and hurling it at me like a baseball.

I duck under the rock, and Thorn charges at me again.

As he lunges at me, I charge the electricity in my hands and push them into him, pushing him over me, shocking him.

Thorn tumbles onto the ground, lying motionless on the pavement. I take a breath, before composing myself once more. I'm starting to feel lethargic; I'm running out of power. But he can't know that... not now. Thorn continues to lie on the pavement motionless. I take a step towards him before... he starts moving again.

"I..." he mutters.

"I... WILL GUT YOU."

Thorn stands up once more. His expression contorts into one of pure rage, just like me.

"YOU ARE BEYOND SAVING, POSSUM," he says, sprinting at me once more.

"Try me, Thorn," I say, readying myself.

As he sprints at me, I attempt to use what little power I have left, but to no avail: the electricity sparks, but nothing happens. Thorn tackles me to the ground, pinning me down.

He grabs the blade with both hands, thrusting it towards my heart. I grab his arms, struggling to hold the knife above my flesh.

"You listen close, creature," he sputters out in between erratic breaths.

"Once I'm done here, things will change. Tighter facilities, stricter rules. You might be able to hold us off enough to win now. But this will be the only time. Nobody else will be able to accomplish what you did here today. I WILL MAKE SURE OF THAT."

It's getting tougher to hold the knife back. I can feel my muscles ache in pain, my brain finally starting to recognize the wound in my side.

"Killing you… is the first step to putting a stop to this conflict. Then, I can use you as an example to everyone else who doesn't fall in line," he says.

"No…" I say, using what's left of my strength to push the blade to the side, plunging it into the pavement. As Thorn falls on the weight of the blade, I bash my head into his, knocking him back.

Thorn drops the knife. As I get up, I toss the knife to the side. Once I'm on my feet, I kick Thorn back onto the ground. Thorn lies on the ground. It's clear we're both at the end of our ropes.

Holding my side, I drop to my knees on top of Thorn. Using what strength I have left, I punch him in the face.

"We're still us," I say, landing another punch.

"Living." Another punch.

"Surviving." Another punch.

"Having normal lives." Another punch.

"Those are all in our nature." Another punch.

"Those make us human!" I say, reeling back for another punch, but stopping. I don't… have the strength.

I get off Thorn. He's not moving, but he's still breathing. His eyes are following me as I sit down on the ground next to him.

"Call off your guys," I say. "Leave us alone. Before someone actually gets killed." I glance over to the rifle.

"This won't… stop anything," he says.

"It will," I say. "You saw all those people, the new ones, the stronger ones. You're losing now. It's over."

Thorn pauses for a moment, before speaking again.

"They still won't accept you," he says. "You'll still be seen as outsiders, as animals. This doesn't change anything."

"Never said it wouldn't," I respond. "Now are you going to call off your guys? Or am I going to have to make you do it?"

Thorn chuckles. It's like everything I've said to him has gone through one ear and out the other. For a moment, we both sit in silence, listening to the sounds of the fighting below us. People standing up for themselves, for everyone, like we wanted. And Thorn's men, shouting as they're tossed aside, blown away, sprayed down, or attacked by people who just want to go back to the way things were.

After a moment, Thorn reaches into his coat, pulling out a radio. He holds it up to his head.

"How… how're we looking?" he asks.

"We're losing people fast, there's too many of them now! We're having trouble just pulling people out!"

Thorn looks into the sky. He tries to sit up but can't. He turns his head to me. I can see the fury still burning inside of him, but… there's something else in there, something more… sorrowful, almost… jealous.

"…" He doesn't say anything.

"Sir?" the voice asks.

"…Retreat," he mutters.

"What? Are you serious? They're not killing us!" the man says.

"But they will eventually. Retreat…" He looks to me, that pained look in his eyes breaking through his scowl.

"We've lost."

"…Understood," the voice says.

Thorn drops the radio, and I watch as he takes a breath, before passing out on the roof.

I struggle to stand up and lean over the edge, watching as the men in SWAT uniforms start to drag their unconscious brethren out from the street, and cars start peeling out.

The remaining changed in the street start cheering in celebration: whoops, hollers, howls, meows, and shouts can be heard.

"Hello?" I shout.

"I need…. I need help!" I yell into the crowd.

The world starts to grow hazy. I check my side. I'm still oozing blood.

"Hello!" I shout.

"H-help," I mutter, falling backwards onto the pavement.

Then… nothing.

CHAPTER 41

Lyla

THE COLD WIND rushes against my body. As quickly as the world vanished, a new one appears around me. One I remember.

A pale light casts through the tall trees onto me, as I stand alone inside a forest…

The first thing I do is reach for my side. I remember being stabbed by Thorn… just a few minutes ago.

But as I look down at where I was stabbed, the only thing I see is my clothes, torn where I was stabbed.

The wound, however, is gone.

I hear something rustling in the brush outside. Something I can't make out. But the feeling it gives me, it's all too familiar.

As the sound approaches closer and closer to where I'm at, I can feel myself tense up. But the feeling is muted, part of me is telling me to book it, avoid whatever's coming my way. But… I know I can't do that. Whatever is coming to me, I need to face head-on.

I ready myself, as I watch a figure emerge from the brush in front of me, the pale moonlight illuminating the figure.

I know who this is… I know what's happening.

It's… myself. The human version of myself.

Same pants, same torn shirt, same hair, same sunglasses resting on my head. Except… it's clear. Her face, her slim eyebrows, her tired eyes, her slight smile.

She stares at me, the look inside her eyes giving off some kind of relief, like finding a lost pet, or reconnecting with an old friend.

"…Hey," I say.

The figure doesn't respond, as it starts approaching me. Pure silence, except for the chirping of crickets and crunching leaves.

As she steps in front of me, I prepare myself for anything. But my doppelganger reaches out, her hands touching the sides of my face, before pulling me in, resting her forehead to mine.

For a moment, everything clicks. Like a warm blanket wrapped around on a cold night, or good news after months of bad. I'm overcome with a feeling of… completion.

I close my eyes. As everything vanishes from my vision, a light forms. I go to open my eyes again and see my mother and father watching over me.

"She's up!" my mom cries out. "She's up!"

"Oh thank god," my dad says.

As I try to move, I feel my mom gently push me back down.

"Sweetie, don't move," she says.

"What… what happened?" I say in between groans. I look around to see I'm lying on a cot. "Where… where are we?"

"We did it," a voice says.

As I glance over, past my mom, I see James, sitting on another cot, his arm in a sling.

"We won," James says.

"We're in the restaurant still," my mother says. "Some of the people are doctors and first responders. They brought in equipment for us."

"What about… what about Thorn?" I say.

"Gone," my dad says. "As soon as the men started retreating… your mother and I ran out looking for you. It was that Hutch kid who told us where you were. When we made it to you, he was gone."

"They're gone?" I ask.

"Yeah," my mom says. "We drove them off, like we planned."

"What about the others? What about Kellie?" I ask.

"She's fine," James says, gesturing to the other side of the building.

As I focus to the other side of the building, I can see Kellie standing on a table, her hoodie tied around her waist, her shirt still stained with blood. A bandage contrasts the stained tear where she was shot. She's waving her arms around to a group of changed. All of them are engrossed in whatever story she's telling. Whatever it is, it must be funny, as she dances atop the table between lines, making sure everyone is able to hear what she's saying. She stops for a moment to grab her side, as some people reach out to make sure she's okay.

"How bad are we?" I ask.

"A lot of people are hurting bad," my dad says. "Beat up, bruised, shot… It's tough."

"But nobody's died yet." He continues, "We're doing all we can, and hopefully it's enough."

"But we've gotta help," my mom says. "Remember, we said we'd make sure no one's hurt."

My mom stands up from the cot and turns to me once more before moving.

"Don't try to move too much. You'll tear your stitches," she says.

"Your mom's right, sweetie," my dad says. "I'm not losing you to some infection." He offers a slight smile.

Both of them walk away, as some others get their attention.

I turn my head to James, who's still sitting on the cot next to me.

"How long was I out?" I ask.

"About a day maybe," James says.

"Really?" I say.

"You lost a lot of blood," James says. "You can't just put that back in. You needed a transfusion. Luckily, all of our blood functions as when we were human. Turns out, you and Riley have the same blood type."

"That's… that's good," I say. "How're you feeling?"

"I'll be okay, got a real sore shoulder, though." He winces. "But I'll be fine in enough time."

"I was worried," I say. "Seeing you get knocked down like that."

"I bet. I took a pretty nasty fall," James says with a slight grin. "But you fought Thorn. You beat him."

"Only because you told everyone what to do," I say.

"Maybe." He chuckles. "We all did something."

"That's called teamwork." I chuckle, before the pain in my side reminds me to stop.

"Just… relax," James says. "You're hurt bad."

"I know," I say.

"But be happy, Lyla, we did it. This is the first step, remember?" he says.

"I know."

As I start to relax in the cot, I see Riley approaching us.

"Hey, Lyla, how're you feeling?" she asks.

"Better, not dying. Thanks to you," I say. "Seriously, thank you, Riley. You saved my life."

"It's nothing," she says. "I'd do it for anyone here."

"I appreciate that," I say, leaning back to my resting position, removing myself from the conversation, yet still listening.

Riley turns to James. "So… you're looking a lot better."

"Yeah, the doc says I'll be out of the sling in a week."

"That's good," she says. "I told you not to get hurt."

"I know, I know." He chuckles. "I've never been a good listener, though."

"You don't even listen." She laughs.

"How're you holding up?" James asks. "Helping everyone…"

"It's going good. I don't know much, but I'm doing what I can," she says. "There's more people coming in the next day or so with some proper beds for everyone. Apparently, there's a vet near where we live who's been secretly helping altered this whole time. Connie and I are going to drive down there and help him move some of his stuff here."

"That's great news," James says. "I can ride with you guys tomorrow."

"No, you need to stay here," she says.

"Why's that?" he asks.

"You're not in good enough shape, James. You're still in pain." She pauses for a moment, like she knows I'm listening in. "Plus, your friends are here."

"You're telling me to stay behind, to be with my friends?" he asks.

"Kinda. Mostly, it's 'cause you're in pain. But…" She pauses again. "I spent a lot of time kind of resenting everything that's happened, because you vanished. Now… I understand, and now that I've helped you… I realize now I could be helping other people."

"So… what're you saying?" he asks.

"I learned something," she says. "You leaving, it taught me something. It taught me how to be self-reliant… But you coming back taught me that what we were doing, it wasn't going to be like that forever. Even if everyone didn't become altered, you would have left one day. I should've come to terms with that sooner."

She pauses again.

"Your place is with your friends. Not just me. I can't hog you forever. You're my brother, and I'll always love you. I'll always welcome you back home with open arms, but we both know I can't keep you to myself," she finishes.

"Riley, I…" James starts to say.

"You don't need to say anything, bro." Her tone changes to a warm one. "I'll always be around."

"Quite the bedside manner." James smiles.

"Maybe I'll make a career out of it. I've got time, and I've got plenty of patience." I watch from the corner of my eye as Riley gives James a light hug, mindful of his shoulder.

"You rest up… both of you," she says.

"We will," James replies.

I give a silent nod.

"Love you, bro." Riley smiles to her brother.

"Love you too," James says.

As Riley walks away, I turn my attention to the rest of the room. Watching the many cha… altered walk around the bar. People patched up, anywhere from their head to their tails. People sitting at tables, telling stories of better times before, and better times to come…

People enjoying the company of others. The steady stream of drinks from whatever's left of the bar's tap, to water from the tap, served by Wayne and Hutch, bandaged, and wearing Hagen's Hot Spot aprons. As they pass every passerby a glass, the conversation mixes together to form a kind of song, a cheery one, its words incomprehensible, but its feeling, the song, it's one of gratefulness.

It's like something out of a story my mom told me when I was a kid, stories of knights, of battles, of happy warm taverns filled with merriment after a well-fought battle.

A battle that we won.

That thought lingers in my mind, as I watch from the cot, people passing by after being helped, people heading to tables, Kellie continuing to tell her stories to others. I see her mimic our escape from the RCC. The people around her lean in to hear what happens next.

It all finally hits me: we won, we did it. For now, we're free to live normal lives.

That feeling, it's heavy. It's like a warm hug after a bad day, like a bowl of soup when you're sick…

It's like someone pressing their head against yours.

I can't help but feel myself well up inside. Tears stream down my cheeks. I don't mind it, though. I'm not sad.

I'm happy…

It's over, and I'm happy.

One Week Later…

"Still hurts to walk?" my mom asks me, as I open the door to the front.

"Not as bad as the first day," I say. "It's just good to move again."

My mom holds my arm as I step outside for the first time since our fight. The roads are still sparse with cars, but now people have started making their way back onto the road. Whatever damage was done to the windows on the street have been boarded up.

Some of the signs have "Under New Management" written on them.

"You sure you're okay to travel?" my dad asks.

"I'm fine," I say. "We've got a long drive ahead of us."

"She's right," James says, rounding the corner, approaching us. "Massachusetts is a bit of a trip, and we won't be making many stops along the way."

"You guys better make sure that we're notified." My dad continues, "Any trouble you guys run into, we'll be running that way."

"I'm sure we'll be fine, Dad," I say.

"Can't ever be too sure," my mom says, walking me down the sidewalk to the parking lot.

As we round the corner, Riley is helping Kellie put some bags into the trunk.

"That everything?" Kellie asks.

"Yep!" Riley says. "Clothes for all of you, some nonperishables if you guys need it. And of course, medical supplies the doc gave us. Now, there's not a lot, so don't waste it."

"Do you have no faith in us?" James laughs.

"You were the one that got shot." Riley chuckles, approaching us. "The doc's friend you're going to see has been helping a lot of people… But the RCC has been breathing down his neck. So this is a whole other ball game."

"I know. I promise we'll be careful," James says.

"We'll have to do the protecting." Kellie chuckles. "James is the one without abilities."

"Which means he needs to be *extra careful*," Riley says.

"Sheesh, I get it." James rolls his eyes.

"I'm calling shotgun," I say, interjecting.

"Aw! Come on!" Kellie yelps. "I packed the car."

"Tough shit." I laugh.

"Fine," Kellie scoffs. "But only 'cause I pity you," she says, climbing into the back of the car.

"Now, you better take good care of the car," my dad says. "It's a beater, but it's the only one you've got."

"I'm a safe driver," James says. "We'll get there in one piece."

"Still can't believe you guys are leaving so soon," my mom says.

"They need us," I say. "If we can prevent what happened here, we have to take that chance."

"You should've still stayed longer," Riley says. "But I get it."

"Well…" my dad says. "I couldn't be more proud. We love you."

"Yes, we do," my mom says with a big grin on her face.

"I love you too," I say, wrapping my arms around both of them.

"You promise you'll call, right?" my mom asks, choking back tears.

"'Course!" I say. "You better make sure Aunt Jessie knows too!"

"We will!" my dad says. "Now go, before I start crying too."

I let go of both of my parents, before heading towards the car on my own.

"Good luck, you guys," Riley says with a smile. "I'll keep in touch. I'm heading back with the doc in a few days. So, I'll be around."

"Good to know," James says. "Love ya, sis."

"Love you too, bro," she says, giving him a hug.

As I continue making my way to the car, James lets go of his sister and jogs to catch up.

"You need help?" he asks.

"Don't patronize me." I chuckle.

"All right, suit yourself, but if you don't make it there, I'll leave without you," he says with a snicker.

We both make it to the car, opening our respective doors and getting in.

"Took you guys long enough," Kellie says. "We leaving?"

James turns the key, and the engine fires into a deep rumble.

"Yessir. You guys ready?" James says.

"Ready as I'll ever be," I say.

"Me too," Kellie says.

"All right, then let's go," James says, putting the car into reverse.

As the car backs out into the road, we start to pass the restaurant, my parents, and Riley standing on the sidewalk, waving at us as we pass them.

For a few moments, it's silence. I think the gravity of the situation has finally dawned on us. A few months ago, we were strangers, in a strange place, in strange bodies. Now... we're friends... we're family... And despite everything...

We're still human.

THE END.